D0960825

THE SHARP END OF LIFE

THE SHARP END OF LIFE

A Mother's Story

Dierdre Wolownick

**MOUNTAINEERS
BOOKS**

MOUNTAINEERS BOOKS is dedicated to the exploration, preservation, and enjoyment of outdoor and wilderness areas.

1001 SW Klickitat Way, Suite 201, Seattle, WA 98134
800-553-4453, www.mountaineersbooks.org

Printed in the United States of America
Distributed in the United Kingdom by Cordee, www.cordee.co.uk
22 21 20 19   1 2 3 4 5

Copyeditor: Laura Lancaster
Design and layout: Melissa McFeeters
Cover photograph: *Dierdre Wolownick gearing up to ascend El Capitan in Yosemite National Park* (Photo by Karissa Frye, www.karissafryemultimedia.com)
All photos Wolownick family collection unless credited otherwise.

Library of Congress Cataloging-in-Publication Data
Names: Wolownick, Dierdre, author.
Title: The sharp end of life : a mother's story / by Dierdre Wolownick.
Description: Seattle, Washington : Mountaineers Books, [2019].
Identifiers: LCCN 2018044364 (print) | LCCN 2018056954 (ebook) | ISBN 9781680512434 (ebook) | ISBN 9781680512427 | ISBN 9781680512427(hardcover) | ISBN 9781680512434(ebook)
Subjects: LCSH: Wolownick, Dierdre. | Women mountaineers—United States—Biography. | Mountaineers—United States—Biography. | Women runners—United States—Biography. | Marathon running—United States—Biography. | Musicians—United States—Biography. | Honnold, Alex.
Classification: LCC GV199.92 (ebook) | LCC GV199.92 .W65 2019 (print) | DDC 796.522092 [B] —dc23
LC record available at https://lccn.loc.gov/2018044364

Mountaineers Books titles may be purchased for corporate, educational, or other promotional sales, and our authors are available for a wide range of events. For information on special discounts or booking an author, contact our customer service at 800-553-4453 or mbooks@mountaineersbooks.org.

 Printed on recycled paper

ISBN (hardcover): 978-1-68051-242-7
ISBN (ebook): 978-1-68051-243-4

An independent nonprofit publisher since 1960

*For Charlie, who made my life better in so many ways,
and who gave me the greatest gift of all.*

*And for Stasia and Alex, with all my love, gratitude, and
admiration—for being my guides through this adventure
of life and life of adventure; for bringing balance,
amazement, and so much love to my life; and for always
encouraging me to be more than I thought possible.*

Author's Note:

This is my story and my perspective on the events of my life. While I have made every effort to provide an accurate account of the people, places, and events included in these pages, I have relied on my personal memories and journals. Any errors or misrepresentations are unintentional.

one

AN OCEAN OF ROCK. That's what my son calls this monster wall of smooth granite that stretches toward the sky for three thousand feet, so high I can't see the top from the base of the route we're about to climb. I lean back so far my neck creaks.

"It's an ocean of rock, and you're just a speck," Alex has said in many media interviews. He's climbed El Capitan, in Yosemite National Park, many times, with and without rope. Standing in its shadow, I can't force my mind to comprehend what those words mean. I know he's done it. I've seen pictures. But now, as I cower at the foot of this monster, the thought of someone up there without a rope, clinging to the wall without any protection, makes my innards clench and my heart race. To go up there *with* rope is still unimaginable to me. And yet, here we are.

To be fair, I'm not actually going to climb the granite. I will climb the wall, but mostly with my feet, not my hands; they'll be pushing the jumars up the rope. Alex will lead, putting in protection as he goes, the way he always does when we climb together. But this time, I'll ascend the rope he carries up.

I'll use jumars, daisy chains, a Grigri, specialized gear I've been learning about all year, to keep me safely attached to the rope as I battle my way up it. And it *will* be a battle. I'll push one set of hand gear up the rope, stand on its attached foot strap, and then thrust the other hand and foot gear up to meet it, essentially pushing and stepping my way up the rope. At sixty-six, I won't exactly be climbing rock. A fine distinction, as I stand here debating whether to run out into the woods one more time before we start and throw up.

Something deep inside me insists on that distinction, needs it. Climbing the rock of El Cap—there are over a hundred routes—is what the young studs do. Alex and his friends, they run up routes that are impossibly hard the way I run to the store: a few hours or so, and they're on their way back down.

Most climbers take a few days to inch their way up El Capitan, the most impressive, iconic rock wall in Yosemite. I can almost make out some of the climbers on the routes near ours. They'll sleep on a portaledge hanging from a few pieces of gear stuck in the rock. They'll eat and make coffee hanging on the wall, raving about the incredible vistas with their legs dangling over Yosemite Valley a thousand or so feet below. They'll take a dump up there, into a little plastic poop tube. They'll probably talk to their girlfriend or boyfriend, or maybe their grandmother, because the higher you get on the walls here in Yosemite, the better the cell reception is. Maybe they don't know they're just a tiny speck that we can't quite see. Or maybe that's comforting to them.

To me, not so much. Alex and I plan to do it all, up and down, in one day. That means we have to work harder, or at least faster, than the portaledge folks. We'll probably come down in the dark. Here on the ground, my breathing comes in short spurts, although I draw it in as calmly and evenly as I can. I try to swallow, but whatever it is that's stuck in my throat feels like it could easily come back up.

I wonder if those specks up there ever throw up. Do they do that in the poop tube?

He did try to warn me. And months ago I'd heard him muttering to his friends at other crags where I'd tagged along to practice: "I don't think she'll do it." Climb El Cap, he meant. At my age. For Alex, it's an advanced age he can't even imagine. He probably didn't think my old ears could hear him. He doubted I'd be strong enough. Capable enough. Brave enough. Whatever it was he thought I'd need enough of, he didn't think I'd have it by now.

I hope he's wrong. No, he *has* to be wrong. Because once we launch, once we're off the ground and become two tiny specks on the wall, we can't change our minds. Once we've gone up a few pitches, or rope lengths, the only way back down is to top out three thousand feet up.

Or by helicopter.

Breathe.

I've trained for this for seven months. Longer than I'd trained for my first marathon, back in my fifties. Almost as long as I'd carried each of my babies.

By the time I finish this ascent, the past will have been sloughed off against the rock, left in a valley that I will have put behind me, forever. It's been a monumentally long struggle that could have had many different endings.

But this isn't an ending. It's a beginning.

two

POLISH WAS THE SECRET language of grown-ups in my extended family as I grew up in Jackson Heights, Queens, in the 1950s. They could talk about us kids even when we were right in front of them, confident we wouldn't understand. The mumblings in the kitchen, the overheard pillow talk in bed, the whisperings in the front seat of the car—all the important, not-for-kid conversations were in Polish.

Which, of course, just made me eavesdrop even more intently. If I really listened closely to the grown-ups around me, whether I was playing or drawing or reading, I could pick out verbs, action words. Descriptions. I could tell if they were talking about a girl or a boy, if it was present or past, good or bad. By four or five, I could usually pick out the gist of what they were saying about us.

I never let on to anyone that I understood them. That part was easy, since none of the adults talked to me, or to any of us kids. They talked *about* us. Conversation was something that happened between adults; kids just played, preferably out of sight or quietly. Those were the rules.

But the rules in our house were different than at other kids' houses. My mother needed me to be her legs, and sometimes her arms. The great polio epidemic of the twentieth century had claimed her as a baby. She couldn't run, couldn't walk on an uneven surface, couldn't carry anything heavy that might throw her off balance. She'd beaten all the odds just by having my brother and me—that was her conquest. When she called, we came running, even as very small children, knowing she couldn't run after us. Carrying us or lifting us was a task left to my father, at least when he wasn't away at work.

I was the girl, so chores were my domain (boys did only minimal chores; boys were king). As soon as I was old enough to understand her directions—four years old? five?—I did all the dusting, the vacuuming, reaching things in the cupboard, running up or down the cellar stairs for whatever she needed. I rarely spent time at anyone else's house. Instead I read, or played the piano, or painted where I could hear her call, and listened.

Listening became what I did best, whether for a melody, a chord, my mother's call, or a new verb I'd never heard. So I became more and more privy to the secret language of adults as I grew, and no one knew. My brother never got to the point of understanding Polish. But then, I couldn't memorize baseball scores like he did. Everyone had their particular skill. I knew that even then.

When I was five, two burly men carried the most beautiful thing I'd ever seen up our front stoop and into our living room. My mother said it was a Baldwin piano. The rich brown wood gleamed golden in the sun as they labored to get it up the twelve cement and slate steps. I'd never seen anything quite so large, or beautiful. As they placed it in the front corner of our living room, I touched some of the keys. They looked the same as the keys on my mother's little accordion, but the sound that came from them was much more impressive. That day began the love affair that would save my life so many times over the next few decades.

Soon after we got the piano, my mother started showing me how to play the same old Polish melodies she played on her accordion, teaching me to listen and figure out how it should go. I used the same skills I used as a language learner: listen, discern some of the sounds, make sense of them, use them.

From my mother, I learned to play by ear, and from the nuns at school, I learned to read notes—a magic, secret code—and follow the instructions written by people long dead in places far from New York. After a few years, though, the nuns had no more to teach me: I was on my own. It would turn out that I was a far more demanding teacher than they had been.

. . . .

IN HIGH SCHOOL, AT least at the beginning, I'd bring a new friend home now and then. The kids in my classes came from all over New York City, even as far away as Staten Island. What an adventure, taking a ferryboat to school every day! When I started high school, at thirteen, it was challenging enough just to take the subway from Queens into Manhattan, to the High School of Art & Design on Fifty-Seventh Street.

Even walking to and from school was an education. I saw people doing jobs I'd never heard of behind plate glass windows, or holding meetings as they walked or bought breakfast out on the sidewalk. I watched how they built skyscrapers through holes in the wooden walls that separated Manhattan's sidewalks from construction zones. I crossed paths with actors and singers I recognized. It was a different world from Jackson Heights, and I relished every difference and every opportunity to learn about the larger world.

My mother loved meeting the friends I brought home. To someone housebound like her, they must have seemed fascinating—from different parts of the city or the world, different cultures, backgrounds, languages. She'd ask question after question about them and their life, and get them to talk about the places she would never see. What kid wouldn't love that? And I would listen. And serve more cookies. And wait to have my friends to myself.

Sometimes she wanted to sketch them, do a charcoal or pastel portrait. What kid could resist being the star of a portrait? It was flattering, and different, and none of them ever said no.

And I waited.

My mother's parties were like that, too. Everyone loved to party at our house. My mother knew how to draw other people out, to make sure they had fun. So my friends loved my mother, were flattered by her interest in them, and never seemed to notice that they had very little time to spend with me when they came to my house.

Having friends never became part of my life.

three

I BURNED ALL MY bridges when, at twenty-six, I moved west from New York City to southern California. There weren't many to burn, and I wasn't aware of doing it. Being aware of what was going on with the people in my life wasn't my strong suit. I could talk for hours with anyone about music, art, languages, literature, geography—but people? Not part of my life experience.

It would take a few painful, wrenching decades to reach the conclusion that I had never had a normal human relationship. I had filled the emptiness at home with other endeavors—music, painting, languages— and so hadn't noticed the lack.

Our parents wanted only obedience. Their philosophy of child-rearing was simple: a child who caused no problems for their parents was "good." One who caused problems was "bad." Simple as that. The corollary to this obedience-centered philosophy was that adults didn't talk to children. Children couldn't reason like adults, so their input simply wasn't necessary during adult conversations.

The saddest part was that they really believed this. My father summed it all up for me once, when I asked why they never considered our opinions— my brother's or mine—when making decisions that affected all of us.

"Why would I? You'll never be my equal," he said.

My mouth probably dropped open when he said this. I was in my early twenties.

"You can't be," he explained further. "I've had so many more years' experience than you."

That philosophy justified my parents' making all family decisions. My mother, in particular, carried it to extremes. She told us all when to get up—she had the only alarm clock in the house—and when to go to bed. She told us when to eat, where, how to prepare the food, and in which pot or pan. She told us what to wear and when to brush our teeth. She always told my father when it was time to go dress or shave. And he did. Everyone did what she ordered. No one in our house had any decisions to make on their own, all day long. She made them all, for all of us.

But their biggest job, my parents often told me when they thought I was adult enough to understand, was to criticize. To my mother, especially, this was completely clear: "It's a parent's job to criticize their children. To make them better. How else will they learn?" This philosophy also meant, as both of our parents stated many times, that children became full-fledged adults only when their own parents died.

I was twenty-five when my parents decided to retire to my mother's hometown in Pennsylvania. They planned everything out for all four of us. John, the boy, would get the family house where we'd grown up, in New York, because he would have a wife and family to support someday. I, the girl, would move with them. In their eastern European mindset, the girl stayed at home until she married, wherever that home was. Then someone else took care of her.

But I was a high school teacher by then, as was John. My choice to stay in my job in New York made no sense to them and was probably the first time I'd ever completely refused to go along with their decisions.

So our parents moved to Pennsylvania, John stayed in the family house, and I got the street. I was on my own.

· · · · · · · · · ·

A YEAR LATER, I met the man I would marry, while visiting my aunt and uncle in California. When I first met Charles Honnold, I still hadn't had much experience making decisions about my life. I had no one to talk to and no basis for understanding anything about this man, so different from any man I'd ever known.

Charlie's powerful shoulders and sheer physical presence filled a room in a way that I'd never seen in any of the small, slight European men I'd dated. Huge, kind doe eyes and a thick, black mustache fought a hero/villain battle, but his voice was deep, resonant music. Basso profundo, I called it right from the start. He thought that was silly and called me cute. No one ever had.

But it was just a summer vacation. He was a friend of a friend, recommended as a travel guide for my trip west. We camped and hiked in the Sierra Nevada, waded in its icy lakes and streams, held down our tent against wild desert winds, walked across the Golden Gate Bridge. My adventure there, with him, bore no resemblance whatsoever to my life in New York. And then I went back to Queens, to the house I shared with a roommate. To real life.

What an empty life it was! All winter, as the metal garbage pails clattered down the street in the unrelenting wind and I shivered in the snow and slid on the thick ice that coated the sidewalks, I thought about California. And Charlie.

That winter, we wrote. Often. Postcards filled with run-on paragraphs in tiny script, long letters, Hallmark cards with writing on every available side and in every direction, notes scribbled on the back of class handouts. I told him about the wet, whirling snow that made chaos out of the bridge traffic, the biting, subzero wind that rattled windows and made my eyes water if I ventured out, and about lighting a match to heat the key so I could put it into the frozen keyhole of my car door. He told me about his last basketball game out in the warm sun and his drive to the beach to read on the warm sand. And how hot it was out on the tennis court.

In the spring, he helped me apply for jobs all over southern California, where he worked. The fact that I could teach French, Spanish, and Italian and direct school musicals gave me an edge, and I ended up with several offers to choose from.

I had wanted to live in California since I was five, when a new family moved to our block. The father was a professor who had taught in Kenya for a while, and they were all on their way home to California after a few months in New York.

They could have been Martians, for the stir they created. They were all blond. I had seen blond hair in real life a few times, but only on women, and my mother always said it was applied from a bottle. These people really *had* blond hair, all seven of them!

The kids played out on the street with us for the few months they lived in New York. But they weren't like us. Even their names set them apart. The boys were called Bryce, Curt, Brad, and Judd. One short, punchy syllable each. I'd never heard anything like it. The girl, a little older than me, was Janelle. They didn't sound like *real* names to us. In our world, kids were called John, Paul, Giovanni, Kazimir, Angela, Peter, Mary, Joseph, Athena, Wanda, Helen, Agnieszka ... even Dierdre. Names with thousands of years of history. Names that had evolved over millennia, from all over the European world. These kids' names came from the movies. From California.

In high school, I had wanted to go to college at UCLA. California. The land of exotica. Palm trees. Earthquakes. People with blond hair and strange names. I didn't know what to expect from a place that bizarre, and I didn't care. It was as far as I could get from New York, from my parents, and still be on the same continent. That was my goal.

But it wasn't allowed. I was told it was too far. Too dangerous for a girl. Too heathen. And the kicker: too expensive. Whatever their reason, my parents wanted me nearby. Decades later I learned that their plan had always been for my brother to go to college—so he could better support his future wife—and for me to marry after high school and have children. In my parents' world, girls lived at home until that goal was achieved.

Fortunately for them, I didn't know about their plan. Had they explained it to me then, it might have driven me to go to UCLA even without their consent. As it was, I settled on commuting from home to Queens College, with the proviso that I could spend my junior year in France with the study abroad program. An equitable compromise since they were, after all, footing the entire bill except for the bit of scholarship money I'd won.

By my midtwenties, I was teaching in New York and paying my own bills. I'd met Charlie while on vacation, and our nonstop barrage of letters and cards had worked their magic. I had no trouble finding a job in southern California, and I shared my decision to move with my parents the way they'd always shared their decisions with me. I announced that I was moving and began getting ready. I simply had no idea that it could be done any other way. My parents never said anything, positive or negative, about my *fait accompli*. In my family, no one ever said a word about anything that mattered.

In a few short weeks, I packed or gave away everything I owned and drove west to my new home. To compensate for the large cut in pay I had to take, the school I ultimately chose had offered me free lodging. I would live in a Mediterranean villa nestled in the foothills of the San Gabriel Mountains in the town of Sierra Madre, near Pasadena.

After the kids went home for the day, I shared the villa and park-like grounds with Joyce, another teacher. We could run on trails under exotic trees I couldn't yet name or play tennis on one of two courts or pick avocados and oranges off the trees. I had seen orange trees only twice, on vacation in Florida and in Rome during my one Christmas abroad. There were even olive trees, which I had never seen growing before. An alleyway of carob trees filled the whole park with the rich, chocolatey, homey scent of fresh-baked brownies. My new life was a delicious, idyllic fantasy.

And the central focal point of this idyll was Charlie. We spent all our weekends and free time together that year, and under the potent spell of the magic of this new life, we decided to share our lives forever.

· · · · · · · · · ·

GETTING MARRIED IN PENNSYLVANIA the following summer was my gift to my mother. She'd been planning and dreaming about it for years and loved telling me all the details. How Lobitz would do the catering—he'd gone to school in Hazleton with my mother—and how he'd catered my cousin's wedding and it was so beautiful. There had been all the Polish food and a band from Philadelphia at the reception. Mine would have one, too, someday. It didn't matter to me. I would have happily eloped. And Charlie's whole family was against organized religion. A big church wedding was anathema to him.

Fortunately, my mother approved of the gown I'd bought in California. The rest, though, brought out *tsk-tsks* and pursed lips.

"No, no, you can't wear a veil like that. It's old-fashioned! And look, look how skimpy it is, here." She poked so hard that she pushed her finger right through the veil. "See? See how skimpy it is?!"

So now it was useless—I couldn't wear a ripped veil to my wedding.

And sandals! Beautiful, patent-leather, shiny sandals from California.

"No, no, no—no one wears sandals to a wedding!" More pursed lips and head-shaking. "Have you ever seen a bride in sandals?"

I had to admit I hadn't. I'd seen very few brides in my life. But my mother knew clothes; she had made my clothes for me for over twenty years. Every Sunday she carefully perused the *New York Times* fashion section for ideas. Her biggest delight was to greet me after school with a new blouse, dress, or pants that she'd made that day. Sometimes they fit and I loved what she'd made, sometimes they looked awful and I hated them. But she'd worked all day on it, so to her my lack of enthusiasm made me "an ungrateful brat." I was her doll, to dress and show off.

Nothing had changed. She was still the adult. I was still the child.

During that week, not a word was exchanged about people pledging to love each other for life. Or love, devotion. The future. Not a word. They were still the adults, who had nothing of import to say to a child.

As always, my mother and I spoke only of the details, the chores, the doing. Never the thinking or the feeling. Life, for my parents, was in the details. I was a kid again, and I longed, ached for someone to talk to me, to care about my opinion, my feelings. Adult to adult. About something that mattered.

I could have initiated it. But I'd never learned how, and I didn't want to start something that my mother or father might not be able to finish. I didn't want to mar this perfect time that she'd dreamt about and planned for so long. So I let my parents be. I followed their rules. I kept the peace.

. . . .

MY MOTHER COULDN'T DANCE, so I had seen my father dance at only a few family weddings or parties. But it was important to me, even if I didn't quite understand why, to dance with him at my wedding. We had rarely done anything together, and I thought a dance after my first dance with my new husband would be something meaningful we could share.

When the emcee announced the first dance of Mr. and Mrs. Charles Honnold, I didn't recognize a single note of the waltz I had requested. The band was winging it, having clearly never heard of the piece I'd chosen. My father took over from Charlie after a few minutes. I was surprised at how smoothly he moved, guiding me easily across the floor. I had rarely seen him smile so much. Through his warm fingers, I seemed to feel all the things that he never dared say. All those years of remote silence melted away as we shared our first, and likely last, significant moment together.

Only the love came through. I knew they both loved me as much as they could. Either of our parents would have died for my brother or me; they loved us that much. I had never doubted that. They just didn't know what to do about it.

Charlie and I left in a rush after the reception, to drive to New York. From there, we set off for our honeymoon in the Caribbean Islands. We quickly changed our clothes in the large room where we had stored our suitcases and dashed out to a waiting car, driven by friends from out west who were on the same flight.

I didn't understand what had just happened. I knew it was the end, but of what, I wasn't sure. I was just beginning to comprehend the devastating absence of connection that my parents had taught me to live by. But I still didn't understand how that would affect the rest of my life.

In the car, glimpses of what I had lost, and what that loss might mean, began to crash over me, wave after wave. It felt as if I'd just left a funeral, not a wedding. A monumental sadness gripped me, wracked my body. I cried, as softly as I could in the back of the car, for all the things no one had said when I was young. I cried for the father and mother I'd never had. For the emptiness that had been my life. I cried all the way to New York.

Charlie just held me and let me cry. He never asked why.

four

IF YOU'RE GOING TO conquer a monster wall like El Capitan, you have to have a damn good reason. My friends in Sacramento were too polite to ask me outright. *"Why? You retired from teaching; you can rest now. Read the books you always said you had no time to read. Write some books. Why this? At your age?"* But it still came through in all the things they didn't say. I recognize it, because I've asked all those questions myself.

Eight years before I stood at the base of El Cap, when I was fifty-eight, I asked my son to take me to the indoor climbing gym where he trains. A bout of tendinitis was keeping him from climbing for a while, so it seemed like the right time to start on my modest goal: to see what he was up to. To learn the language of climbing so that when he came home from one of his adventures and told me excitedly about what he'd done, I could: a) understand what he was talking about, and b) wisely choose my reaction. The vocabulary of climbing is so specialized that often I didn't quite get whether the adventure he was relating was a triumph, a mishap, a day well spent, or a disaster. And I wanted to know. I wanted to be part of his life, to share his triumphs as well as his disasters.

People had begun writing about him. An occasional ad for climbing shoes or gear, or a feature article, would be accompanied by a photo of Alex on a granite wall, or having breakfast in the van he lives in as he travels to his next climb, or just looking over a cliff into the void. Small articles featuring him or one of his climbs trickled into our house. *He must be pretty good*, I thought as I placed copies on the coffee table and on a shelf in my office. After the first few, it seemed important to save them for him. The term "archive" didn't occur to me until years later. At the beginning, it was just an unusual collection that embarrassed him and made his Grammie proud.

So that day, at the gym with my son, my goal was to learn as much about his life as I could, and maybe make my lumpy, uncoordinated way up half a wall so I could understand what was involved. Although Alex couldn't climb that day, he could belay me.

Dealing with my fear of heights is definitely going to be a big part of this, I thought as I struggled into the unfamiliar harness. I'd been up many skyscrapers in New York City and remembered viscerally the twisting in my gut any time I approached an edge, a railing, whatever I perceived as the end of safety. Even thick glass didn't deter the feeling.

So I began the first climb with trepidation and a frank acknowledgment of limits. I was thirty-four years older than my son, who was already an adult; he was babysitting me. My chicken arms were weak, my body was flabby, and I knew I must look silly and awkward to him as I struggled up the artificial wall. But those thoughts fell away in a few seconds. Then all that existed was the wall, the handholds, and the tiny chips I could push against with my toes to get taller and reach higher. Only the next move.

I tried to remember to use only the same colored holds for hands and feet, as Alex had instructed me. When I reached the top of my first route and exultantly slapped the metal bobbin, it took several seconds for the thought to occur to me: I was forty or so feet above the floor, hanging on a skinny, little rope—and having the time of my life!

I looked down (I shouldn't have been able to do that) and smiled at Alex. That fraction-of-a-second glance linked us, bonded us in a way I'd never expected. This was what he'd been up to all these months and years. This exhilaration, this thrill that coursed through me was just a tiny bit of what must drive him, what he must feel when he ventured out onto real rock. It reminded me of how much I'd always loved climbing on things when I was little. Trees. Lampposts. Fences. Buildings.

I climbed twelve routes that day, each one all the way to the top. I didn't know, then, how unusual that was. Now, years later, I'm happy if I get in seven or eight climbs in a gym session. The routes I do now are harder, of course, but back then they were all hard. All new.

· · · · · · · · · ·

THAT FIRST DAY ALEX took me to the climbing gym, it was just the two of us. And then he left. Off on another adventure that would probably wind up in a magazine somewhere. For weeks, that afternoon replayed in my mind. Each time, I felt the same rush of excitement, of rediscovery. I'd loved climbing as a kid—now I knew I still did. How had I let myself forget?

For the next month, my mental replays were a mixture of longing and fear. How could I go back to the climbing gym without Alex? I didn't know what I was doing or what anything was called. He'd explained it all that day, but the intervening time had erased a lot of that knowledge. I knew, though, that I could learn the gear, the knots, and the vocabulary while seated at my computer.

That wasn't what kept me away.

Each time I walked back to my office after a day of teaching, I saw the photos and posters of Alex on a wall outside my door. I had been on a wall, too—a small, artificial wall, but a wall nonetheless—and the intervening month had left me feeling bereft. Fifty-eight, lumpy, out of shape despite the running I'd started a few years back. My roles—as mom, teacher, freelance writer, musician, and property manager—defined my life. I spent my days seated at a computer, in class, on the phone, or doing chores. I had no time for yet another life, especially one that demanded youth and fitness.

But then I remembered my afternoon with Alex . . . and it got harder and harder to remain the responsible adult. The mom and the teacher both wanted to go climbing! So one day, I wore pants that I could climb in to work, tossed a T-shirt in the car, and, after my last class, I headed downtown instead of home. Before I could chicken out.

At the counter, I rented a harness and special climbing shoes. They were stiff and hard to put on, but the rubber coating would help my feet stick to the tiny holds I'd need to use to push myself upward. I carried my gear into the main climbing room and sat down on a small set of metal bleachers. All over the sculpted plaster walls, people hung on colorful handholds in various contortions, creeping upward. Some shouted as they moved. Some stopped for a while and seemed to be thinking. One young man fell off the roof section suddenly and swung. I gasped. He dangled on the rope while his partner lowered him slowly to the blue foam surface at the base of the climbs.

They were all young. They all had perfect, thin bodies and back and shoulder muscles that rippled as they moved. All of them.

I looked down at my pudgy legs. Moved my shoulders and knew full well that nothing was rippling behind me. Jiggling, maybe, but definitely not rippling.

But I had driven all this way. Shame to waste the gas.

It took several tries to remember how to put the harness on. The waist was simple enough, and I managed to buckle that. I knew how a harness looked when someone was wearing it—but there were more straps than I seemed to need, and they hung in all the wrong places. The loops I thought should be circling each thigh . . . didn't. It resisted all logic, a humbling reminder that even a simple thing like a harness wasn't intuitive yet. I finally figured it out, just before deciding to go ask for help.

Once I'd conquered the harness and put on my shoes, I fiddled with the belay device I'd rented, trying to trigger some memory of what Alex had showed me. I hadn't belayed that first time, only climbed, so I'd never used one. The young man from behind the counter came out to the practice ropes to watch me to prove to him that I could tie in as a climber and knew, at least in theory, how to belay. He gave me a temporary card to certify that, and I stepped a bit closer to the climbing area.

Then arithmetic stopped me.

It takes two people to climb, one on the wall and one on the ground, belaying. The climber's rope is looped over a bobbin at the top of the wall, and the other end is threaded through a device on the belayer's harness. If the climber falls, the belayer locks off the rope, stopping gravity from taking over. After that, the climber can dangle until he's ready to either get back on the wall and try again, or lower off. Then they switch roles. It's a symbiotic relationship.

So if I wanted to climb, I needed a belayer. But as the old saying goes, to have a friend, be one. To find myself a belayer, I'd offer to belay for someone. So I walked around the perimeter of the climbing area, looking for groups of an odd number.

"Would you like a belay?" I said timidly to the first person I saw who was waiting for his two friends to finish a route. He did, and I explained how new I was. His name was Mark. He helped get everything rigged properly, and started to climb.

I gripped the rope as hard as I could, suddenly smitten by the awesome responsibility of the belayer. Everything else was pushed out of my mind. I couldn't even think of my climber's name. If he fell, his life was in my hands. Literally. I pulled the rope back around my hip, the way he'd shown me, then eased up my grip and tried to feel his weight, tried to anticipate his moves. With each stretch of his arms upward to the next holds, I took up some more slack in the rope.

When he topped out and leaned back to be lowered, I was startled by how much a person weighs on a rope. It lifted me off my feet a bit. I regained control and got him safely to the ground. Then I remembered to breathe.

Now it was his turn to belay for me.

As I stepped up and grabbed the starting handholds, I was overwhelmed trying to recall everything Alex had told me, showed me, explained to me. So instead I just took a deep breath and started to climb. One hold at a time. No thoughts at all except for the next hold. And the next. And then I was at the top.

Until that moment, the only time I had ever entered the zone, where no thoughts are allowed in, was when I was playing the piano, painting, or running. Normally my mind is a constant whirl, focused on many things all at once. But sitting on a piano bench or in front of my easel, I'm often surprised by how much time has passed, unnoticed, when I get up again. Running was the same—I'd lose track of how far I'd gone or how long I'd been out.

Climbing—even on a small, introductory-level artificial wall like this—made me dig so deep that nothing else could penetrate my mind. This was problem-solving, figuring out how to get from one point to another, using length, body weight, and angle of throw for dynamic moves, where you throw your body at a handhold. And then there was the sheer physicality of it.

For the rest of the evening I focused, dug deep, and climbed with Mark. We're still friends, eight years later.

I tried other things at the gym that evening, including a yoga class for climbers. Things I never did in my normal, ordinary life. At the end of the first class, I talked with a young woman—they were all young—I'd noticed because of her beautiful, perfect body and smooth yoga moves, and her climbing harness lying on the floor next to her. I needed a partner to climb, and she was in the same predicament. It was her first day climbing.

Eight years later, Michelle and I are still friends, and each January we celebrate our "climberversary," our annual observance of the day that changed both our lives.

All of a sudden, I had friends. Lots of them. But like everything else in climbing, these new relationships made me dig deep. And remember.

five

OUR FIRST YEAR TOGETHER as a married couple was a whirlwind of exploration and travel as Charlie introduced me to his California. Every Friday, we would load camping gear into his little red Volkswagen Beetle and head somewhere wild. I was content to let him choose our destination, to share the places he loved. I was his eager student, along for the adventure.

The language Charlie used as we traveled around California intrigued me as no European language ever had. Alluvial fans. Adiabatic lapse rate. Rain shadow. Dry river. (If it's dry, what makes it a river?) Teddy-bear cholla and Indian paintbrush and ocotillo and Joshua trees... I absorbed this new language eagerly, piecing together my new world, California, during our explorations.

Oleanders formed a soft, endless row of pastel colors down the middle of the road. Obsidian chunks lay on the pale ground like hardened drops of India ink at the base of gigantic columns of black basalt. The air was so dry that my water-based paints dried on the brush. Cute and fuzzy plants lodged barbs deep inside my foot. I learned fast why cowboys always wore boots.

In this world you could die if you didn't prepare carefully.

Even the words I thought I already knew eluded me. We drove past signs that proclaimed "National Forest," when there wasn't a tree for miles. We camped in what he called a desert, surrounded by a solid, impossibly vivid carpet of multicolored wildflowers. Years later, I learned from the internet it was called a "super bloom" and that tourists drive for days to see it. We were just lucky.

But the first time I heard coyotes howling, I knew exactly what it was. I'd watched enough westerns as a kid. The chilling sound made me snuggle closer against Charlie, my rock in this crazy new world. As their song traveled across the hills that surrounded our campground, I understood for the first time the stories from my childhood about wolves in Poland, the old world. These weren't wolves—I imagined a sound even more frightening—but the chill they raised in my gut made me need Charlie's warmth.

In the high Sierra, weekend after weekend, we hiked and explored and scrambled, camping in a tent surrounded by ponderosa pines or Joshua trees or just sleeping out on a tarp in a clearing under a billion stars. Nestled in our double sleeping bag, we counted shooting stars or coyotes' voices before we slept.

The eastern wall of the Sierra Nevada rises, suddenly, thousands of feet of granite towering above the already-high desert floor, its jagged spine snagging clouds and draining them. That wall of granite looms over Highway 395 for hundreds of miles as it snakes between mountains and desert. On one drive, Charlie pointed out a peak, barely visible between the others.

"There," he pointed. "See it?"

"What?" I craned my neck to see where he was pointing.

"Whitney." He told me it was the highest point in the Lower 48. A staggering 14,505 feet high.

How amazing it would be, I remember thinking, to stand at the top of that. The top of the world.

. . . .

SUDAN. GUATEMALA. THE SAHARA. Charlie had traveled to places I'd read about, dreamed of all my life. I listened to his tales for hours. And exploring was such an integral part of our life together that it seemed normal to always be talking about travel—at the beach, in the car, in the supermarket, on campus. Where we would go next, or had gone, or wanted to go. It was our life. I never noticed that nothing else ever entered his conversations. I was too happy. I'd found the love of my life.

After that first whirlwind year of marriage, cracks began to appear in the veneer of our new life. Just tiny cracks at first, like the hairline webs that cover the bottom of your great-grandmother's soup tureen or sugar bowl, but that don't stop you from using it. Small, inappropriate remarks on his part that I found odd, but not odd enough to question out loud. I would never do that. He was my husband, we were a unit. But there were moments when I wished he would answer me, or answer the person who had spoken to him, that he would be civil, say *something* . . .

But what did I know about men, anyway, or love? Like so many other emotions, love had not been part of my childhood. It was unexplored territory. I had no map, no guideposts, nothing and no one to point to and say, "that's how I want my life to be" or "that's the kind of relationship, or the kind of man, I'm looking for." So I overlooked those moments, those tiny striations in the fine china of our union. They wouldn't stop us from using the bowl, the plate, the tureen into which we would ladle all the experiences of our life together. Our fine china was intact.

I would see that it remained that way.

six

AT UCLA, CHARLIE WAS working on a master's degree in teaching English as a second language, so I expanded my teaching credentials to include TESOL as well. We both taught classes there while we finished and had no trouble finding good jobs together at a university in Japan. The Japanese school year begins in the spring, so after our last fall teaching semester, we vacated our apartment in southern California, left our things with family and friends, and moved in with his parents, in Sacramento, for a couple of winter months.

But while we lived in their house, the house Charlie had grown up in, things changed. Or maybe they just changed back. I'll never know.

"Charlie," his mother asked in her sweet, innocent voice, as we all finished lunch in the kitchen, "where's the cover to the peanut butter?"

"How would I know?"

His nasty tone made me look up quickly, from son to mother. I cringed, fearing a reaction. If I'd lashed out like that at home, in that tone of voice, my mother would have hit me. And I would have deserved it. But my mother-in-law didn't react, and so neither did I.

The first time Charlie refused to acknowledge one of his father's questions, I held my breath. If my brother had done that at home, some parent or aunt or uncle would have yelled at or slapped him, a reminder to answer your elders when they ask you a question. Charlie's father repeated his question, something about the yard or the car. Charlie remained silent, reading something at the table where they both sat.

I had never seen anyone act so disrespectfully, especially to older people. Parents. I was dumbfounded. Sometimes, instead of refusing to answer, he would mumble his reply. When his parents asked him to repeat it, he got even nastier.

We lived there for two months. No one ever mentioned his frequent atrocious behavior toward them, or toward me. I said nothing, neither to them nor to him. This was their house, their rules, their family. Meanwhile, new cracks were spreading across our fine china.

I was sure that once we were alone together, once we had settled into our new life in Japan, things would get back to normal. I wasn't sure yet what "normal" was, exactly, but this clearly wasn't it.

Finally, in March, we squeezed into two airplane seats, wearing our hiking boots, heavy socks, and the many layers of clothes that were too bulky to fit in our two suitcases, and flew off to our new life on the other side of the world.

· · · · · · · · · ·

CHARLIE AND I HAD each lived abroad, so we expected the transition to be easy. But as soon I headed for the restroom after we deplaned at Tokyo Narita Airport, that sense of comfort started to fray. I might have been fluent in four languages—but I couldn't tell which restroom to use. I had to wait for someone to come out, like a child who can't read.

Two men from the university where we'd be teaching met us at the airport. They wore trench coats and bowed a lot, almost obsequiously. It seemed an uncomfortable exaggeration of our new prestige as foreign professors. As we stepped out of the terminal into the dark evening to walk to the bus, a sticky blanket of humid air wrapped itself around us, oozing inside our too-heavy clothes and making it hard to breathe. I was accustomed to humidity in New York, but Charlie, used to the aridity of the Central Valley, hated it.

All the dark gray concrete buildings around us were streaked even darker by rain. Once inside the bus, our welcoming party led us all the way to the back. The farther we walked, the lower the ceiling became, until Charlie and I were hunched deep into the collars of our coats. We all sat against the back window. Sweat trickled down my neck. It was going to be a long ride. Once the bus started rolling, people began lighting cigarettes. A *really* long ride. As the bus veered sharply onto the two-lane highway, I hoped I wouldn't throw up and embarrass us both.

I hoped Charlie wouldn't, either. He hated smoke.

As it turned out, he hated lots of things. The rain. Twenty-eight days out of thirty, our first month there. Even for me, that was a lot of rain. For him, it was an emotional hardship. As were all the rules. Whenever I'd mentioned politics or philosophy in California, he'd say he was a nihilist or an anarchist. I usually laughed it off, assuming he was being outrageous for effect. But now I began to wonder . . . the rigors of the strictly hierarchical Japanese society seemed to gnaw at his sense of individualism. He made fun of the gestures people used as they talked. Of everything. When we learned that there were no street names and that addresses were meaningless, merely chronological, he was irate: "How could anybody run a country without knowing where anything is?!"

From the beginning, I attributed a lot of that malaise to the physical aspect of our life there. We were just too big for Japan. We couldn't see out of the low windows in the subway to know which station we were at unless we bent over. We also had to bend way over to use the tiny washing machine in our apartment or even to do the dishes. Our backs always hurt. And Charlie was taller than me.

That had to weigh on his psyche as well as on his body, I told myself. Why else would he be so unhappy? This was our first big adventure together. We had chosen this. I was having a grand time, learning fascinating things every day. But he didn't seem to like what he was learning.

At the beginning, we both signed up for the Japanese lessons offered by the university for all foreign experts, as they called us. I went at the beginning, but it was too basic for me. I acquire languages easily, and was learning fast just by living there and talking with people. Charlie went for a while. He never talked about what they did in class, but after a month or so, he stopped going. Eventually, if anyone asked how his Japanese was coming along, he would pat my arm and say with a wry smile, "She can do my talking for me."

Trouble was, in Japan, the man speaks for the family. Mr. Honnold's presence and voice were required when dealing with any issues or questions about our apartment, parking space, or insurance—all of which came up that year. Not Mrs. Honnold's.

The unfairness of that requirement just made him angrier.

seven

PEOPLE ARE REALLY PACKED together in Japan. Dense doesn't begin to describe it. Charlie grew up in California accustomed to wide-open spaces, empty sidewalks, sprawling highways, and vast, empty stretches of nothingness. So during our first summer vacation from teaching in Japan, we went to Australia for two months. He needed it, he said. I understood.

On our camping tours through the outback, the thousands of miles of desert in Australia's center, we were known as "the newlyweds." When the others all went to visit the pub, usually the only sign of life in the tiny crossroads where we stopped, Charlie and I chose instead to savor the landscape around us. Amazing bird life. Silence. Stars. The Southern Cross. The "real" Australia, he called it. Together we feasted on the natural beauty of the country. Only that.

The unending, stark beauty of Australia's outback distracted me so that I didn't notice until years later how much I had missed. The people. The culture. The unique lifestyle of the outback. The cuisine, the drinks, stories, camaraderie. The human Australia. I believed Charlie when he explained how depressing pubs were, smoke-filled and uninviting, how much more serene and lovely it was where we strolled, or hiked, or sat and watched the sunset or the thousands of birds nesting for the night. I had no other point of reference. This new world of mine was so different, so strange, so full of new wonders. Charlie was my guide, and I followed, unquestioning.

Living in Japan was a bit easier for him after Australia initially. The cherry blossom festivals captivated both of us, from a distance—we never joined in, just observed and took pictures. But little by little, he slipped back into bouts of long, disgruntled complaining. Traffic was ridiculous. Streets were too narrow. The buildings were shoddy. Our apartment was too small and designed all wrong. The country needed less of this, more of that. Eventually, I just had to accept that everything outside of the natural world frustrated him.

So we went exploring every chance we had—castles, cherry blossoms, beaches, mountains, whatever the season offered. And some of the magic worked, for him and for us: soon, I was pregnant.

At the beginning of our relationship, Charlie didn't want kids. "They're too much work," he had insisted. But I wanted four. So we compromised on two.

Growing up, I was the baby in my family. I had never held a baby before, never even seen one close up. Stasia, born at the end of our first two-year contract at the Japanese university, taught me everything I knew. The learning curve was intense.

The loneliness was equally intense. I was fired from my job when I had my baby—apparently common practice in Japan at the time—so I was often alone with Stasia. I learned from her constantly. While she clung to my leg, I sat at my typewriter and sold my first article—about having a baby in Japan. Then a second. And on and on, to magazines, newspapers, and journals in several countries. I made friends with other mothers. Almost every day, Stasia and I walked across our small street, carefully navigating the deep, open storm drain culverts, to the house of one of these friends, Mochizuki-san.

One of the few pieces of furniture in Mochizuki-san's tatami room was a *kotatsu*, a low table where three of us mom-friends knelt or sat during our visit. Stay-chan, as they called Stasia ("-san" for adults, "-chan" for children), sat with us moms at the kotatsu, while the four little boys did what little boys do with cushions, toys, games, and each other. Stasia had her little juice cup on the table in front of her, and a few tiny dolls or toys, which she lined up and played with calmly. Occasionally a little body would come hurtling by and she would grab the cup to keep it safe. My friends, amazed, called her *reetoru redi*, my "little lady." Even during our twelve-hour flights between Japan and California, her sweet smile never flagged, and she charmed passengers all around us.

A crying child would instantly get her attention. Any time there was a child in distress, she would toddle up, pat or stroke the other toddler's arm—big, dark eyes fixed on the tear-filled ones—and say softly, "*Daijobu.*" (It's okay.) Or she'd hand them a toy, something that would comfort.

My little lady also loved adventure. Charlie and I would take her on long walks in a baby backpack or for rides on the back of my bike. She loved riding in her fast-moving seat behind me. The joy she brought to the world filled some of the void that was forming in my own.

During my pregnancy and the first two years of Stasia's life, Charlie traveled. It was the only thing that lifted his spirits. The only thing he talked about. Sex was fun, but to him, travel was life. He hiked up Mount Fuji when I was too pregnant to go with him. He flew to Taiwan when he had several days off for a holiday. As I settled into my new role as a mother, he explored South Korea. And when he was home, his constant negative comments colored my perception of life in Japan. He wore me down into believing some of his scathing assessments. He was, after all, my husband; I wanted to be like him, to share his life, his thoughts. So I listened, and commiserated, and if I didn't share his opinions, I kept that to myself.

But even as the rift between Charlie and me continued to grow, I was having the time of my life. My freelance writing was published with some regularity. I was learning more about my new daughter and language acquisition every day.

Three years before Stasia, Charlie and I had agreed that if we ever had children, I should give them the gift of being bilingual. He left it up to me to choose which language I would use. So Stasia heard only French from me, only English from Charlie, and Japanese from the rest of the world around her. Seeing her put all that together made each day, each moment, fascinating.

When I learned I was pregnant again, I looked around our tiny apartment and tried to imagine where the second baby would sleep. I walked the whole apartment several times but couldn't escape my first, obvious conclusion: in order to find room for another baby futon, we were going to have to get rid of one of our few pieces of furniture. There just wasn't any space.

When Charlie came home that evening, he was grumbling about a new regulation that had been handed down at work. He was miserable, and our new baby would be squished into a tiny spot on the living room floor. That night, we decided it was time to go home.

. . . .

"HOME" TURNED OUT TO be his parents' house in Sacramento again, at least until we could find jobs and a place of our own to live. So the neighbors who came to see our baby the day he was born were Charlie's neighbors, but not mine. I didn't know any of them.

Without insurance, eleven hours at the hospital was all we could afford. People started coming to visit only a couple of hours after we were back at the house, when Alex was about twelve hours old. I was in a postpartum fog and too exhausted to care what they said. One comment, though, got through the fog, because I heard it over and over: "What big hands he has!"

Not how beautiful he was, not which parent he resembled. Big hands.

When they saw the twelve-hour-old baby on my lap grab my pinkies and stand up, excited comments flew.

"That's impossible!"

"Are you helping him?"

"Babies can't do that!"

I had only had one baby before, and that one had been so roly-poly that my Japanese friends had all called her "little Buddha." This one was scrawny, tiny, and seemed to weigh practically nothing. With big hands.

And, apparently, powerful thighs.

Everyone wanted to try it. Each time, the little comma curled up on their lap would reach up, grab their pinkies, launch himself upward, and stand up. Only for a few seconds, and it was a very wobbly stance. But my newborn was definitely getting vertical.

His big sister, at almost two, was unimpressed. Stasia had taken to heart everything I'd told her about the baby joining our family and her new duties as a big sister: to help me and her brother. She was eager to start her new job.

Stasia assumed those duties from that very first day Alex appeared, rushing to bring me a diaper, gently patting his tiny head or arm if he cried, and dutifully relaying messages to Grammie or Grampie. Big sister was a job she took seriously.

Over and over that first week, as people came by to meet our new son, she heard us all say, "His name is Alexander, but we'll call him Alex for short." We didn't realize how many times we'd said it, until one day she proudly informed a visitor, "His name is Alexander, but we call him Alex because he's short."

She delighted our visitors as much as her new baby brother did.

· · · · · · · · ·

I HOPED THAT THE house I finally found for us, with its huge backyard, would relieve some of Charlie's dark angst. It hadn't lessened since we left Japan, but he was also commuting every day to several different community colleges to teach. As much as he loved to travel, such a regimen had to be stressful.

I could only guess about that, though; at home, he rarely spoke. He read.

He often spent the entire day absorbed in a book, sometimes several books in one day, stretched out across the living room carpet in our new house. The entire day we all stepped over him, doing chores and housework and yard work and homework and just living around him. He seldom spoke. He read.

When my new friend, Maureen, came over for tea one afternoon, Charlie was on the floor, reading. He did manage to get up to shake her hand, but went right back to his book, several feet away from us on the floor. Now and then, as we chatted over tea, Maureen glanced in his direction, clearly uneasy. Our visit was brief, and she rarely came back.

Eventually, I caught on: even though the two children and I had grown accustomed to Charlie's odd behavior, others didn't know how to react to being snubbed so completely. Even when lots of people came to our house for a party, it wasn't unusual for Charlie to sit in his recliner alone, reading, while everyone partied around him. Despite my efforts, friends coming over to our house never became part of my life in Sacramento.

If I mentioned it later, he would usually shrug and leave it at that. I never did figure out the best answer to a wordless shrug.

If I needed information—like who was driving which child where or when—I often had to physically push whatever he was reading aside and insist on a reply. Which made him even angrier. He was always angry. I didn't know why.

But he was my husband. My partner. Partners were supposed to talk to each other, share things. Even in my bizarre home life in Jackson Heights, that function of marriage had always shone through. My parents talked to each other all the time. They discussed everything. There were arguments, bouts of yelling, but they talked. That was what partners did.

So each time Charlie snapped at me over a magazine or book, I didn't know how to react. He would just go back to reading, as if nothing had happened. The silence that followed these outbursts echoed heavily with unanswered questions. I was left standing in front of him, wounded, reeling, with no clue why he'd flared up like that.

And no one to talk to about it.

As I coped with my non-marriage, my little lady from Japan became the person I often turned to for inspiration. She was a touch of sanity in an insane situation. With her happy, little face and her radiant, infectious smile, Stasia became a symbol of how beautiful life could be as I wallowed in an abyss of frustration and silent shrugs.

She also helped her brother survive his childhood, acting as a buffer between him and me. As a toddler, Alex would push all of my buttons; in those moments, I understood viscerally how some parents can be driven to violence. Inconsolable as an infant, incredibly stubborn as a toddler, obstinate without limit, he put all of my parenting skills, patience, and self-control to the test. Daily. Stasia the Diplomat was always able to tell when he'd pushed me too far. Right before I would start to consider tossing him through a window, she would come take his hand and gently lead him away from the scene. Somehow, she always knew.

After I'd calmed down, or cleaned up his mess, or both, reminding myself that I really *did* love him and he would grow up someday, they would come back from their little walk. And each time they came strolling back into range, hand in hand, his dimples and her sweet, knowing smile would remind me again of the big picture. I have no idea what she told him on those walks, and she doesn't remember, but all would be well again.

I rarely saw other adults in our new neighborhood in West Sacramento. The parents worked and left their children in daycare or school. Even on weekends I saw only garage doors going up and down as they rushed in and out doing all their errands. My experience of suburbia was desolation. Emptiness. It was just me and the kids. And a surly, uncommunicative spouse.

It made no sense to me. Nothing had happened between us, that I was aware of, that could have made him dislike me so much. But I'd seen him treat his family the same way, and it didn't seem to bother them. Was I just too sensitive? Was this what marriage was really like?

I was sure it wasn't . . . but that left me with only questions.

When Charlie was a child, no one had heard of some of the disorders or syndromes we now know people can suffer from, like autism, obsessive-compulsive disorder (OCD), or attention deficit hyperactivity disorder (ADHD). I wouldn't learn about them myself until years later, when some of my friends had little boys whose behavior seemed to mirror my husband's. But back then, as we whirled through each day, my main job, besides caring for my children and our home, was to do whatever was necessary to avoid an outburst. To appease.

Old habits die distressingly hard.

eight

YEARS LATER, AS I watched others at the climbing gym, I often found myself moved in ways I would have never expected. Seeing a good climber glide up the wall is like watching ballet; the grace, agility, unexpected movement, the sheer beauty of it often captivated my gaze as I shrugged into my harness, pulled on my shoes, or just waited my turn. To a lumpy, nearly sixty woman who had just begun to climb, the sight of someone *older* than me, like my friend Mark, making his way skillfully up the wall was thrilling.

Mark was inspiring. All of the climbers I'd met and befriended so far were young. Supple. Strong. Their muscles rippled. Besides just climbing, they ran or skied, flew on hang gliders or climbed ice. They did pull-ups and push-ups and all kinds of contortions that I knew I'd never be able to do.

Mark had shoulder issues. A hearing problem. A foot thing he mentioned now and then. He was retired, and he climbed—hard. At least from the point of view of a beginner who only climbed indoors, it looked hard.

A climber I could relate to!

He loved to teach, and I wanted to learn it all. His climber friends—and there were lots of them—became my climber friends. It was the best kind of therapy.

With a sport where one mistake can kill you or your partner, it's good to have a mentor who can show you what to do and what *not* to do. How to thread the rope through the belay device. How to pull it back so you have control over your partner's descent without burning your hand as the rope slides through your fist. What to clip to your harness in case you fall off your climb. Even something as simple as tying your shoes—I had no idea that the laces on some climbing shoes could affect their fit and their grip on the wall. I watched Mark and all my new friends at the climbing gym, studied them and their moves, their choices. And tried it all.

I knew I could do this. If I could learn to play the piano, master several languages, and travel the world by myself—then I could surely learn to climb a rock. That thought flashed through my mind over and over as I worked hard to follow the others. Especially after we started climbing outdoors.

. . . .

AFTER A FEW MONTHS of climbing in the gym together, eating pizza and drinking ciders and beers together downtown after our sessions, my climbing tribe decided it was time for me to climb outdoors. Laura, Mark, Bob, and some others I didn't know yet were going to climb at Cosumnes River Gorge, about an hour from Sacramento, and they invited me to go with them.

I woke several times the night before. As my daughter often puts it, adventures are exciting! She gets so psyched about starting her thousand-mile bike rides that she rarely sleeps well the night before, either.

We took Highway 50 as it snaked up into the Sierra, before turning onto a smaller road, and then an even smaller one. The others chatted during the ride, but I just listened. They had been climbing for years and the more they talked, the more ignorant I felt. I didn't know any of the Sierra climbing areas they spoke of. I marveled at how Mark and Bob, both older climbers, could recount how they'd made their way up a particular route. I doubted that I would ever remember every move of a climb like that.

It was March, and I shivered from the cold as I shouldered my pack, stepped over the metal guardrail, and followed them onto the trail. Everyone but me wore special, rugged shoes they called approach shoes, all the color of dirt and the outdoors. I was wearing light, white running shoes.

We hiked single file into the gorge. The others pointed out sticks growing on both sides of the sandy, narrow trail.

"Poison oak. Don't touch it. Don't even get it on your clothes." They each had a poison oak story to share.

I looked intently each time they pointed one out, but all the sticks rising from the sand looked exactly the same to me. I'd never learned to recognize poison ivy in the east, and it looked like I was going to be equally unsuccessful identifying poison oak in the west.

The trail became rockier and steeper, and soon we were scrambling between trees and boulders, down into a narrow gorge. The Cosumnes River rushed past, thirty or forty feet below. It was swollen with spring snowmelt and, at times, we had to shout to be heard over the roar.

When we reached the base of our climb, everyone put their packs down and started pulling out gear, some of which I had never seen before. I knew I'd learn what it was used for soon enough, but for now, I focused on my harness and staying warm. The layers I'd worn, a turtleneck and flannel shirt topped with a thick fleece jacket, were clearly not going to be enough. I jammed my gloved hands into my pockets and stamped my feet.

I knew how to belay in the gym, but this was real rock, and the consequences of a fall were much more serious. I watched Laura climb a short route that followed a crack twenty-five feet up a sloping, curving face of granite. She pushed her hands into the crack and pulled on them. I winced. That had to hurt.

In just a few minutes, she was at the top. Confused, I stepped back and tilted my head to examine the top of the wall. Mark explained that while I'd been getting my harness on, Bob had walked back up to the top of the small formation we'd walked across on our way in, and set up the top-rope. I craned my neck more to get a better look.

The anchor bolts looked like they were right on the edge of the wall. Those metal rings, permanently attached to the rock, would hold the anchor that would in turn hold the climbers' rope as they took turns climbing up and lowering off. The image of someone setting up an anchor at that exposed point, while leaning over the top to work on the knots, left my stomach in knots. Probably not a good sign for a climber.

Whenever someone started getting ready to climb, I offered to belay, but each time someone else stepped up to the chore. They were friendly and jovial about turning me down, but after several offers, and watching several people climb, I realized they were right: I didn't know enough yet. I was the novice. A raw beginner.

It was like being the toddler who asks to help with the dishes or any other chore. It usually leads to "no, dear, you go play now." Then an adult takes over. It was humbling, refreshing, and an insight into child-raising—a little late, but it's never too late to understand something better.

After everyone else had climbed the wall, each one a bit differently, Mark asked if I wanted to try. I was eager to get on my first real Sierra Nevada rock wall. It started on a series of big blocks and then flowed upward on the sloping face. They'd all taken just a few minutes to climb it. I figured double that for me. Triple, maybe, if I got stuck somewhere.

I tied the rope in a figure eight to my harness, the way I always did at the gym. Mark checked it.

"Doubled back. Check. Attached at two points. Check. My 'biner's locked. Check. Belay is on. Climb when ready."

"Climbing," I replied, using the standard formula.

"Climb on."

The rock was icy cold as I pressed my bare hands against it. I couldn't feel my fingers. Leaning in, I stepped up onto the first block. So far, so good. Another step, another block. Easy. A few more chunks of rock, some tipped forward, some cracked apart, all different sizes. I got about ten or twelve feet up, breathing fast, excited as a little kid. I was rock climbing! On real rock!

And then the blocks ended.

I stopped. Looked around. Nothing. No holds to grab, no blocks or cracks or fissures or anything else for my feet. Nothing.

"What did you hold, here?" I shouted down to Mark.

Everyone shouted up advice, none of which made any sense to me. I looked all around me, sliding my hands over the cold rock, but couldn't find anything to hold or pull on.

How can you climb if there's nothing to hold? It made no sense. And yet, I'd just watched all of them climb this stupid wall. That had no handholds on it.

I'm not sure how long I stood there, trying and thinking. I slapped or slid my hands all around me to find any little nub I could hold. Caressed the rock. My numb fingers searched above me, to both sides, reached behind me to explore the wall that stuck out next to this route. Everywhere. I tried to step up a little higher, leaned against the cold, hard granite, prayed for weightlessness. My foot slid back down. Tried again, slid again. Over and over. Finally, I settled back down onto the last block where I'd stopped.

More advice floated up from the ground, all of it equally meaningless to me. I couldn't do anything they were telling me to do. I was a failure. A miserable, abject failure.

Frustration started to pool in my eyes.

I wasn't prepared for this. I'd had no experience with major failure—except in my marriage. Even when I was smaller than everybody, all my cousins, my brother, everybody—even then, I'd always kept up. How could I not be able to get to the top of this puny, little curving rock? As a scrawny five-year-old girl, I'd climbed, no problem, to the very top of the Mile Rocks in Hazleton, Pennsylvania—*huge* compared with this! Enormous! Several stories high.

What was going on here?

Mark lowered me, slowly, and as I untied I tried to think it through objectively. The Mile Rocks were rough conglomerate. This little wall was smooth, featureless granite. The Mile Rocks had tons of features—bulges and ledges and gullies, striations to push your toes into, big knobs to hold onto—that made climbing just plain fun. This miserable, empty wall had nothing—but I couldn't wait to try it again.

"Nice try, D!"

"Good effort."

"Well done."

Well done? Their cheers and comments made me think they understood how far outside of my comfort zone this day had pushed me. I knew I'd try this route again. Maybe not today. Today was about learning, about getting ready. They knew that I had learned what real rock is like, and some of the frustration of not being able to conquer it. I'd have to learn to cope with that.

Even more, though, than figuring out the wall, I'd learned I needed these people in my life. Unaware and ignorant, I'd hungered for friendship all my life, only realizing it after more than a decade with Charlie. That hunger was relentless. None of my new climbing friends had any idea how important they were.

In northern California, in my life as wife and mother, tour guide, teacher, musician—I had longed to make connections with people. Lasting connections. But I lived with someone who acknowledged no one. Needed no one. Not even me.

Battling that became my life. Instead of connecting with other people, I had spent my days trying to figure out what was going wrong at home, and whether I could do anything about it.

Home, with Charlie, had been a desert. I'd survived it, like the desert flowers survive from year to year, buried, dormant, waiting for lifesaving rain. And when it finally comes, the resulting super bloom is breathtaking. These new friends were my long-awaited rain.

Wounds needed to heal before I could begin using that part of me again, the emotional part. It still lay buried in that desert, waiting for the life-giving rain of friendship.

Most of my climbing friends were married and young—I was usually the odd one out, the oldest in any group, except for Mark—but still, little by little, they brought water to the desert of my life and began to patch the monumental hole in my existence with the cement of joviality, the warmth of common desires and goals, the love of friendship freely given.

I would learn this climbing stuff. That, I knew. The skills I'd need to get up this wall, and all the others I wanted to climb, were within my reach.

And now, with my new climbing tribe, friendship was, too. I'd work as hard as I needed to, on both.

nine

ONE OF CHARLIE'S MOST frequent complaints at home was that we never had enough money. Each time I put a date on the calendar for us, in the hope that we might reconnect for an evening, I would later find it erased, with another teaching job or convention or some other professional activity written over it. He *had* to work, he said. We had no money.

I had to believe him. He handled all the finances for our little family and never talked to me about any part of it. I had no idea how much we spent on what—I knew only that Charlie worked full-time, more than full-time, and that I was working part-time, but that we still had no money.

Childcare required money. His parents would occasionally watch our children, but only so we could go to work. Babysitting was costly and out of the question, so we were never alone together.

Professional help also required money. My suggestions that we talk to someone about how to manage our life a little better were met with derision. Charlie's view of anyone in the mental health professions was simple: they had gone into that discipline to figure out their own problems, so they were more screwed up than the people they were trying to help. Clearly, we couldn't give someone like that our hard-earned, scarce money.

So instead of trying to discover why Charlie was so angry, so distant, I worked. I wrote, for whoever would pay me. I taught part-time, a class here and there, like him, but near home so I'd be there for the kids. I guided multilingual tours of the Sacramento region for groups from other countries, as I had done in southern California. Work dulled some of the pain.

We both ran from job to job. Charlie taught, at one college or at several. Or read essays for international English as a Second Language (ESL) testing. He became an integral part of the administration at the college district and traveled to conventions all over California, and later, the country.

So he wasn't home when I discovered that our new baby had learned to walk.

By ten months, Alex had already decided that sleeping was a waste of time that he could spend instead on his favorite activity, climbing. He fought as hard as he could against going to bed, every night. I'd always read that babies needed lots of sleep. Our first one had. Our second just couldn't bring himself to shut down for the night. Life was too interesting.

Often, his body decided for him. Alex would fall asleep standing, leaning against the wall and clutching Blue Blankie, at ten, eleven, or even later. Charlie and I were ready for bed by seven or eight at night.

But every day, no matter when he had fallen asleep the night before, he was up at four thirty or five, his large, dark eyes brimming with adventure. Time to get active and vertical.

Every day.

In an effort to survive such a regimen, we would leave a tiny plastic bowl of dry cereal on the kitchen table before going to sleep ourselves. Maybe, if we were lucky, he'd feed himself breakfast in the morning and play by himself for a few minutes before pouncing on one of us to "go play."

He couldn't walk yet and never slowed down enough to bother talking. But he could travel. Months prior, I'd given up hope of finding him where I'd put him down. Books call it "cruising," when babies who can't walk get around by holding onto objects within reach.

But "within reach" refers to a normal, earthbound baby. For Alex, cruising was a cinch, whether it was horizontal (what most babies do) or vertical (garage shelves, closet partitions, towel racks, open drawers, etc.).

The morning I learned our baby could walk, I stumbled out of bed at five thirty. Unusually late. No one had woken me. It was already getting light. I dashed into Alex's room. Gone. He wasn't in the kitchen, and neither was his bowl, which meant he was already fueled up and doing some high-octane cruising.

Ten months old. Where could he go? I checked the top of the refrigerator and of all the furniture. Inside every cabinet, low or high. The shelves above the washing machine and the garage door that led to the backyard outside. All the places I'd found him before. The patio sliding glass door was out of the question—it had a heavy steel frame and an uneven, rusted track filled with debris, making it difficult for even adults to open.

My breathing got faster and shallower. He wasn't inside, climbing any shower curtains or rods, or hanging from any towel bars. Or closet poles. It was warm enough for him to go outside. The neighborhood was still asleep, so if he cried, or knocked over the garbage pails or anything else, I'd hear it.

Dead silence.

My palms were sweating now, my heart pounding. Ten months old. Not walking. Where could he be?

The front door was heavy wood with a regular doorknob, and it was pretty high for a baby. I unlocked it—a pretty good clue that he hadn't gone out that way—but, desperate and not thinking clearly, I ran out front into the quiet court. No traffic, no baby. I ran to the corner. No tiny body anywhere.

Ten months old! Could someone have come in and abducted him? (That's how frantic mothers think.) Charlie was away at a conference, the neighbors were all still asleep—it was just the kids and me. I was alone.

Before calling the police, I convinced myself to calm down and check everywhere one more time. Just in case. I ran everywhere I could think of, checked everything again. Wore out my last reserves. He wasn't there. I was shaking by now. Someone had taken my baby!

As I picked up the phone, there was one last nagging thought: the patio door. It was ridiculous, really. I had trouble with the old, rusted door myself and needed both hands to drag it open.

I put down the phone and looked out into the big backyard. At the far end sat the brand-new swing set that Charlie had just put together. And there, on top of the six-foot-high slide, stood Alex.

All mothers have those memories that stand out, the ones we can't forget no matter how hard we try. This is one of mine: my ten-month-old baby in his fleece sleeper, standing six feet high in the air, clutching Blue Blankie and looking calmly over the fences into all the other yards. Surveying the neighborhood. No doubt checking to see if there was anything worth climbing.

I ignored my pounding heart and raced out the patio door, which opened with just a flick of my adrenalin-enhanced wrist. I didn't stop to think about what it all meant—not only had Alex gotten the monster door open, he'd closed it behind himself. Then, while I was running out, he climbed back down and began walking (*he was walking now!*) back toward the house.

I knew then that life with Alex was going to put me to the test.

This, on top of the other bewildering test I faced every day. I wondered whether I could stay sane long enough to raise my children. Alone.

• • • • • • • • • •

BRINGING UP MY CHILDREN in West Sacramento was like bringing them up in a ghost town. I worked many jobs when they were little, but while Charlie was at work, or away, I was a stay-at-home, work-at-home mom. My kids and I often walked or biked the mile to the playground, usually without seeing another person. We passed many stray dogs and cats, an occasional duck or two near the pond, but seldom another human being.

All the other kids in the neighborhood went to daycare, so most days Stasia and Alex had only each other to play with. Despite his non-stop physicality and her quiet, thoughtful demeanor, they spent hours together exploring their world. Stasia continued to take her job as big sister very seriously. When they went off on an adventure in our large backyard, she usually held her baby brother's hand. If they were whirling or swinging or twirling, or if Alex was climbing atop the swing set or on some other structure, she was always nearby, alert, giving him space but always there to protect him. In almost all of our photos from that time, Alex is on the go and Stasia is either watching him carefully from a safe distance or holding his hand.

She also served as his interpreter. For the first few years of his life, Alex never bothered to slow down enough to put words together. The three of us often sang songs—in a variety of languages—and I spoke only French with them. Humming these melodies was easier for him than forming a sentence so, when he wanted to communicate something, he would hum the melody of whichever song fit the need. If he wanted his little fleece lamb, he would hum "Mary Had a Little Lamb." If it wasn't forthcoming, he would hum louder. If he saw the moon and wanted to show someone, he would point and hum "Au Clair de la Lune" (*lune* is moon in French). For his stuffed kitten, he would hum "Ah, Ah, Kotky Dwa" ("Two Little Kittens" in Polish). And so on. Only the three of us knew all of our songs—and languages—so when he hummed a need to Grammie, Grampie, Aunt Carol, or anyone else, Stasia was always ready to interpret for him. They were an inseparable unit.

So we shared a special language at home, in between bouts of non-stop motion, but having another adult to talk to was still the highlight of any day. I regularly took the kids to the playground, weather permitting, and looked forward to it as much as they did. Riding our bikes there—with Stasia on her little red bike and Alex in his seat behind me, or later, all three of us on bikes of varying sizes—was a big adventure. And usually, after we'd been at the playground a while, another mother with a child or two would show up and my kids would have playmates.

That is, until my son became a playground pariah.

The first time it happened, I heard the cries while playing with Stasia in the sandbox. I looked up fast, knowing what Alex was capable of. But he was fine. The other little boy was standing under the monkey bars, pointing up at Alex and wailing.

Had Alex done something terrible? Thrown sand at him? Pushed him off the bars? I took an inventory as I ran over: Alex was high up and climbing, as always, already swinging from the top bar. The other little boy was not holding an injured limb, not rubbing sand out of his eyes, just standing there, looking up, pouring out a heartbroken wail. His mother had come running, too. As I arrived, I heard her trying to soothe her baby's frustrated feelings.

"I know you want to follow him up there," she crooned in a soothing mommy-voice, "but you can't. See? He's a big boy, he's much too high for you."

Trouble was, anybody could see that Alex wasn't "a big boy." In fact, he was smaller than most boys his age. Which, of course, only made the little guy angrier. And louder.

No one takes well to having their deficiencies pointed out. And Alex did just that, unknowingly and unintentionally, everywhere we went.

Any wall, any tree, any apparently featureless vertical structure was home to Alex. In a few seconds, he'd be on top—the professional in him already making the dangerous and difficult look simple and attainable—as, over and over, the other boys or girls would attempt to follow. He would gladly have shared the fun with someone else, but the effect of his effortless athleticism was just as devastating as an intentional put-down.

The other kids fell. They got hurt. Frustrated. They cried. Some called Alex names. And I suspect the mothers wanted to as well. Eventually, the mothers at the playground began to recognize us. When we arrived, they'd call their little boys for snack time, or it would suddenly be time to go feed the ducks. Anything but follow that crazy little boy with the even crazier mother who let him climb places where no little boy should go.

"That's so dangerous!" one mother hissed at me as she ran to rescue her son from Alex's bad influence. "Can't you control your son?"

Control him? Her words stopped me in my tracks. Was I a bad mother? What Alex was up to did seem dangerous. From the other mother's perspective—a person with a normal fear of high places or of falling— he *was* a bad influence. Kids that small shouldn't be on the top of the monkey bars, hanging by one hand. Or up on the highest branch of the biggest tree. Or standing on the top edge of the eight-foot-high brick wall surrounding the water-control machinery at the local creekside park.

But he wasn't reckless, or a daredevil, as that mother assumed. He was training himself to recognize fear for what it was: a warning. For her, for the other kids, that warning kicked in sooner than it did for Alex. He was training himself to evaluate the warning, and if he considered himself safe, up he'd go. The other kids probably never did that. Their own fears, and lack of physical skill, stopped them from following him.

It reminded me of my summers at the beach. Before I got in the ocean, I would stand and watch the waves for a while. If they were crashing, breaking hard, I would gauge my fear level. Could I get in without getting hurt? Would I be able to get back out without being upended or scraped along the rough bottom? If everyone else seemed to be having fun, why did I hesitate?

Everyone's fear threshold is different. And, of course, as Alex's mother, I tried—constantly—to rein him in. But it was always clear that he was different. By two and a half years old, wearing a helmet way too big for his little body, he could already ride his tiny yellow two-wheeler around the quiet court we lived on. He never needed training wheels. On our big swing set in the backyard, he would stand on a swing, launch himself through the air—what climbers call a "dyno," I now know—grab a cross bar, and then climb up the thick metal pillars, or feet, of the whole swing set. His sister would calmly swing, giving him lots of space as she watched.

The activities changed as he grew, but the goal always seemed the same: to get higher. A tree, a wall, a building, everything in his world was a means to get higher. As the three of us walked through the big park in our neighborhood, a constant litany went something like this:

"Alex, don't go up there!"

"Why, Mom? It's really easy."

Or:

"Alex, get down from there!"

"Why?" Or just, "I'm fine, Mom."

And he was. But that never stopped him from negotiating with me. By the time he was five, we had moved into a one-story ranch-style house. Alex started asking me if he could go on top of the roof. But he was little, and I still thought like a mom, so I always said no. This went on for several years. One day, when Alex was about eight or nine, I heard crunching sounds overhead from inside my kitchen. I ran outside and looked up. Caught in the act, Alex smiled his irresistible smile and chatted with me as though we did this every day. He told me all about his adventure, how easy it was to get up there, what he'd found, how he could see the whole neighborhood . . . I couldn't recall the last time I'd seen him this animated, this enthusiastic—this happy. I complained, of course, and demanded he come down. But while we negotiated, he was walking back and forth, pulling debris out of the gutters that ran the length of the whole roof. He pulled out a tennis ball, other toys and leaves and gunk. He looked completely at ease, more than I knew I would ever feel, up there. He was at home.

I had lost this round. I knew that if I forbade him from climbing on the roof, he would just go up there whenever I wasn't home. So I did the only logical thing: I asked him to clean out all the gutters anytime he climbed up on the roof. A win-win finale.

I always talked with my children as adult to adult. With respect. The way I'd always wished grown-ups had talked with me when I was little. I had learned a lot about parenting—especially what *not* to do—from observing my parents, and my own children benefited from this. This scene would have ended differently if my parents had been in charge. They would have yelled until Alex came down, probably smacked him, punished him, and forbidden any more ascents.

But I'd lived with this child enough years to know that nothing would stop him from getting higher, any way he could. Beyond that, I knew that he could argue longer than most adults could stand: about chores, clothes, food, homework, or any other life obligation. He often out-argued his father, who would just give up in disgust and walk away. Alex and I, however, were well-matched in stubbornness. When I thought it really mattered, I could out-explain, out-argue, out-detail my son until he very grudgingly complied with whatever stupid rule we were talking about.

But I picked my battles carefully. I'd seen how comfortable he was up on the roof. Nothing good would come of trying to forbid it.

But I did forbid—absolutely, completely, unequivocally—another request a year or so later. There was a pool a few feet behind our ranch-style house, and just beyond the pool, in the corner of the property, sat a wooden play structure, like a frontier fort. Both kids thought it would be great fun to string a rope from the chimney of the house, over the pool, to the wooden structure. Once that was in place, they could slide down the rope from the roof and jump off into the pool. That one was a simple "no." They both brought it up often, with Alex the most intent on it, but it was always a firm "no." They never did go up the chimney or string the rope across the pool.

. . . .

"CAN'T YOU CONTROL YOUR son?"

That mother's question, that day in the playground, was off target. It wasn't about control, at least not mine. The force that drove Alex upward controlled him—I suspect it always will—and he knew how to control the fear that came with it. It never entered his mind that other kids might be too afraid to go where he went, or wouldn't be physically able to. He knew where he was going, and he knew he could get there—and back.

I didn't have most of this figured out at first. Back then, my stomach lived in a constant state of tension. I was always poised, ready to jump, to catch, to intervene. But I rarely had to.

I learned that first from Sit 'n Spin, a toy the kids had when they were small. It seemed simple and safe—kids sit on a plastic bobbin-shaped thing, wrapping their little legs around the center. Turning the top ring spins the toy around, like on the teacups at Disneyland, until they get dizzy or fall off onto the floor, laughing.

That was not nearly adventurous enough for Alex. He would place it near a wall or a piece of furniture and stand on the top circle—sending visiting adults into a tizzy. Then he'd push against the wall, making the toy, and him, spin around. Faster and faster he'd spin, until he reached escape velocity. Then he'd launch.

The top of the recliner, side of the piano, countertop—it was all fair game for a leap and a try at a handhold. If he missed, he'd fall on the floor, laugh, ignore the adults desperately lunging to catch him—and pick himself up and try again.

That was his cycle: launch, laugh, repeat. Fortunately, his impish smile was irresistible to the adults around him. And his laughter soothed the most terrified scream whenever the closest adults leapt to their feet.

That wasn't me, though. Experience had taught me what he was capable of, and I knew that unless there was blood instead of laughter, or he lay writhing on the floor, things were as they should be and I could keep cleaning the kitchen or making coffee for my guests. And his big sister, his partner in adventure, took it all in stride; he was the only baby brother she'd ever known, so it was all normal, to her.

My father used to talk about a similar experience he'd had during World War II, when he was stationed in North Africa. He was terrified when he shipped out of New Jersey for a place he'd never heard of on the other side of the world—a place where a lot of people were getting killed. People he knew. But he used to tell me that it was impossible to keep up a fear like that. Eventually, it dulled into a vague ache in the back of the mind, fading behind the wear and tear of daily life, lying dormant until it was needed for survival.

Thanks, Daddy. Lesson learned. Over time, my fear for Alex's safety had faded into something that could come screaming to life if needed. But for my own sanity, I had to train myself to put that aside as life chugged along.

The more parents I met like the woman at the playground, the more I realized that none of them would have been able to live with—let alone encourage—the skills my son worked so hard on every day. They, like my own mother, would have tried to shut him down. From their viewpoint, what he loved to do was far too dangerous for a little boy.

On weekends, I'd often see kids, usually with their dad, practicing with a bat or kicking balls across the cul-de-sac. And I knew that some of them went to dance or acrobatics or swimming classes. It seemed their parents had their own list of acceptable endeavors that they would encourage. Alex just wasn't interested in any of those.

Some parents I talked with even suggested that I take him to a professional for evaluation, so he could be put on a drug that would slow him down—make him more "normal." A drug? I didn't even like taking aspirin. To give a perfectly healthy child a drug just to make him conform to someone else's concept of normal seemed filled with hubris. What made their version of normal more valid than my son's?

Other people advised trying gymnastics when I talked with them about the difficulties of raising Alex. "That'll harness all that energy," they promised.

For a year or two, we tried it with both kids. Alex hated it. The teacher controlled what his students were allowed to do during the class. To Alex, this was intolerable. His little body yearned to do so much more— to do what he knew he could do on those bars, rings, and ropes. He was probably more in control of his body than the gymnastics teacher was of his own. Instead of harnessing excess energy, gymnastics made Alex more pent-up and frustrated.

Can't you control your son?

I could only ever think of one sensible reply to this: Why would I want to? Don't you want your child to know what he's capable of? How much she can accomplish? I wanted both my children to know that about themselves.

That was why I gave them the gift of bilingualism. I knew from experience that children can grow up using multiple languages—each one helps expand their brain, helps them view and interact with the world in ways incomprehensible to a monolingual person.

In the same way, they needed the freedom to choose the activities they loved, the ones that kept them up at night with anticipation. Stasia sampled many activities as she grew—soccer, dance, piano, flute—before finally settling on the few that would become the foundation of her adult explorations: running, cycling (often with camping involved), and anything that took her outdoors (with the written word and music as secondary passions). In Japan, one of her first words was "outside," pronounced without consonants. "Ow—eye" she would exclaim any time we sat her down to put on her shoes for an excursion.

If I hadn't given my children the freedom to discover the things they loved, their lives would probably have been much safer, and my life would have been much calmer. Easier. Should that be our goal?

I was sorry that Alex had no one to share his adventures with. I could relate to that from my own childhood, and now from my marriage. I knew from experience that loneliness can be survived, even surmounted. But I wished for better for my son.

I was married for life. For better or for worse. When I made a vow, I kept it. And we had been married in my parents' Catholic church, in Pennsylvania, where the rules about that were very clear: "What God has joined, let no man put asunder." And I had never known any divorced people. Back then, that word was always whispered, never said out loud, especially not in front of the children. It wasn't a polite word, at least not in my world, not allowed by church or social milieu or family.

There would be no sundering, for us. I would *make* it work.

ten

IT TOOK ME DECADES to absorb the fact that I had never been a part of my husband's life. Little hints were thrown in my path over the years, but no normal person could have understood what they were. Even simple things like saying hello or goodbye were complicated, or even frightening.

By the time Stasia and Alex were about seven and five, I was regularly writing articles for the local newspapers and for magazines, and short stories for whoever would pay me. I worked every school day in my quiet little office, the fourth bedroom of our house, accompanied by occasional distant barking that only highlighted the peace and made it easy to concentrate.

One day, around midafternoon, I was working hard on an article, hoping to finish it that day. I knew I was alone until the kids got out of school.

Suddenly, no warning, I heard a basso profundo at my elbow.

"Any mail?"

My pen flew across the desk as my other hand reached for my heart, which whipped wildly into arrhythmia.

"Charlie! Please don't do that! You know I'm here alone—you scared the shit out of me!"

"Any mail today? I'm expecting a check."

"No! God, could you please not do that again?"

He shrugged as he walked away.

The second time was a repeat of the first. And over, and over. For years. He would never let me know when he came into the house. Or left it.

In my European childhood, back in New York, everyone hugged and kissed each time they left or came home. It was a ritual that solidified family, made friends feel welcome. Everyone we knew did it. I'd never given it a thought until it disappeared from my life.

I never learned why Charlie did the things he did, but it wasn't for lack of trying. I lost track of how many times I stood in front of him, repeating a question over and over. There was nothing wrong with his hearing. So I'd repeat it again. How stupid is hope? How blind? I'd repeat my question until he got angry enough to lash out at me for bothering him. But I'd still have no answer to my simple questions about day-to-day life.

"When are you leaving for your conference?"

"When did they say we can pick up the car?"

Simple things I needed to know to run a household of four people.

Charlie's silence made me a single parent. But I kept trying. That tenacity would serve me well later, but then it was the kind of blind, mindless repetition with the same predictable, empty result that can lead to insanity.

"Charlie, who's picking up the kids today?" I tossed over my shoulder as I ran down the hall to help someone dress for preschool.

"Charlie, are you picking up the kids?" I asked again as I raced through the kitchen, throwing together everyone's food in little bags or boxes. I picked up the crushed cereal bits off the floor. Closed the drawers Alex had used as steps to climb up on the counter. Wiped the juice off the table. Wiped the footprints off the counter. Brushed Stasia's hair. Straightened the blinds that Alex had left askew on one of his breakneck passes through the kitchen.

"Charlie," I said as I saw him walk past our blur of activity, "are you picking them up today, or am I?"

Only one sock is fine for some kids, including mine. But not for mom. Down the hall again. I threw some clothes on me, too. My hair could wait.

I couldn't see Charlie anywhere. He wasn't in any of the many places that I needed to be to get both kids out the door on time.

"Charlie?"

No answer.

"No, you can't wear those heavy pants today," I told Alex when he appeared in his favorite corduroy pants. It was already over ninety degrees, common for September in Sacramento. Off to find another pair.

"Charlie, can you hear me? Are you picking up the kids, or am I?"

Finally, it was time to take them to their respective schools.

I searched the house quickly, one last time.

His car was gone. He had already left for the day. Without a word to anyone.

Each time this happened, a tiny chip of my self was scraped away, like exfoliating granite. Confusion became my permanent state of mind. *Why won't he answer me?!* I'd scream inside my head. *If only I knew why . . .*

Each time this happened, the hardest part was forcing myself to still be mom. To see that he had left without a word, again, and then turn around and be someone else—someone whose heart had not just been ripped out and trampled on. Who didn't want to scream in frustration and anger. Who loved the two kids waiting for me to take them to school, but who needed the love of someone else even more.

Silence.

I canceled all my appointments and interviews and drove to pick them up at school at the end of the day. When I got there, his car was parked in front of the schoolyard. He was reading.

. . . .

THE FIRST TIME I considered that Charlie might be suffering from something diagnosable was when my friend Laurie came to our house with her little boy, who was around Alex's age. I began to notice his odd behavior. He played by himself, not with the other kids. He wouldn't look directly at anyone, and hardly talked at all.

No matter how many times I tried to engage him, he never replied to me. He spoke to no one but his mother, usually only when he wanted something. It was as if we were all cardboard cutouts in the background of his world. My friend told me how bright and intelligent he was, and about autism and Asperger's.

Could it be that? A simple illness? Not so simple, though.

In those days, doing research meant a trip to the library with both children in tow. But when we went there, one of our favorite places, I spent my time in the children's section, reading with them or just keeping an eye on Alex.

I probably could have slipped away and asked the research desk librarian for information. But something always stopped me from going through with it. The possibility that my husband might suffer from something diagnosable, something pathological with a real name, something that was ruining our lives, filled me with even more dread than his sullen silences. I wasn't ready to accept that.

As long as I didn't *know*, there was hope. I had never heard of autism, or any of the other similar disorders, until I'd met my friend's son. I was sure that Charlie's parents hadn't heard of it when he was a child. Even if it was autism, from the little I'd learned from Laurie, there was no cure.

It didn't matter whether his behavior had a name, really. I still had to live with it.

And both children looked up to their dad, for which I was grateful. Kids should. To them, Charlie was a fun guy, always ready to leave on a trip or adventure. He never insisted on any rules or responsibilities, never made them clean up or do their homework. He was always ready to go play.

But each time I saw my friend's son—who was on medication, who couldn't function in mainstream classes, who still would never reply to any of my questions—he reminded me more and more of Charlie.

I tried not to think about what it would mean to live like this the rest of my life.

eleven

EVERY TUESDAY AND THURSDAY afternoon, completely spent after teaching a full day of classes at the college, I threw material for the next day's classes into several briefcases, cleaned up my office after another day of whizzing in and out, and dashed into the restroom to change into my climbing clothes.

I didn't dare give myself time to think. Too dangerous. That would have allowed me to think about how tired I was. Two solid class hours in the morning, an office hour, and four nonstop class hours in the afternoon is enough to max out any teacher's exhaustion level.

Once I'd changed my clothes, I'd rush back to my office so no one would see me in my climbing pants or T-shirt. The more formal attitudes in Japan and New York City, where I'd taught in Brooklyn and the Bronx, had made me wary of letting my students see my nonprofessional side. When I'd started teaching, in the '70s, women teachers at our high school weren't even allowed to wear pants to work. Things were different now, and I knew those old rules didn't apply in California. But habits tend to linger, even after forty years.

After I was out of the office, I'd put my brain on autopilot as I drove a half hour across Sacramento to the climbing gym in the heart of down-town. Walking into the gym was like flipping a switch. Once I met my partner, or partners, we often started by catching up about our work day. But that would quickly fade into chatter about our project—the route we were working on climbing, clean, without falling. Or our climbing shoes. Or our gear. Ropes. Whether our cracked fingers had healed. Our elbow issue. Nothing existed inside the climbing gym but climbing.

"Did you see the new 10b they put up? It's really fun!"

"Yeah. I sent it last time. Too easy for a 10b. Can you give me a catch on my proj?"

"You didn't send your project yet?"

"Came off right before the last clip Tuesday. It's really thin. You have to drop your knee and reach high behind you for this little sloper. Put all your weight on it. I flew right off."

"Bummer."

Teaching was another world. No matter how demanding or exhausting the day had been, no matter what condition I was in, mentally or physically, when I got to the gym, it was instantly gone. There was simply no room for both; climbing demanded all my concentration. Each time I got on the wall, I stepped up into my zone, where all of life was completely focused, distilled down to the next hold.

At the beginning, I was reminded of Alex as a toddler. Each time he flew off the little Sit 'n Spin, landing on the floor or against a piece of furniture, he'd bounce back up with a big grin. He knew he'd succeeded at another bit of training. He knew his balance was getting better with each fall, that his tenacity was improving, as well as his capabilities in general. When I started climbing, Alex told me that if I wasn't falling, I wasn't trying hard enough.

I'd been going to the climbing gym for a few months and occasionally climbing outdoors, when my climber buddies decided to teach me to rappel.

If you climb outdoors, at some point you're going to have to rappel. Sometimes you can walk off the back of a mountain or wall, but often you have to lower yourself back down the way you went up. Mark had already showed me, at the gym, everything I'd need to know: how to thread the rope through my belay device to rappel, attach the backup, and tie a Prusik knot. Easy—while standing on the ground.

So back we went to Cosumnes River Gorge one weekend. Mark was going to show two of us newbies how to rappel on real rock. We'd been here many times over the last few months, and each time I had a little more success as a climber, eventually finishing that sloping wall that had stymied me the very first day. Since then, I'd followed my gang up several of the short, but more vertical, walls that rose up from the river canyon. I'd heard them talk about rappelling off this or that piece of rock, but I'd never tried it. This would be a new skill to add to my ever-expanding set.

It was late spring, and the river had transformed from a raging bully into a well-behaved, gray ribbon, adorned here and there with nearly black pools that shone like mirrors. On the far side of the water rose Gutenberger Wall, a slab of granite several stories tall, sprinkled with shrubs, several climbing routes, and an occasional goat straying down from the houses at the top. On the side we walked in on, the rocks were only one pitch, or rope-length, tall.

The half-hour hike down to the gorge flew by. My stomach was jittery as I thought about how I was going to try rappelling. I'd heard my son and other real climbers talk about rapping down off some wall—it always sounded dramatic and impressive. I was about to join that club. I could already see myself easily gliding down a big wall, one hand controlling my rope, the other waving to the camera.

We picked our way carefully between boulders and slippery grades covered in grit, holding saplings or rocks for balance. At a flat, rocky outcropping, we stopped and put our packs on the ground. Mark selected a small pile of gear from his bag and quickly carried it down the slab toward the edge of the cliff.

The overhang. The abyss. Those were some of the words that battered my mind as I watched him disappear. He was walking casually, so I knew he was safe and secure. That didn't stop my stomach from twisting.

When I talked about climbing at the college, my colleagues often said they could never climb because they were afraid of heights. But whenever I went up anything really high, like a skyscraper, and looked over the edge, I felt it too. Right in the pit of my stomach. Now, the intensity of this moment grabbed me out of nowhere, anchoring me to that spot high on the granite.

My fellow newbie climber, Betty, followed Mark down the slab, all the way to a sort of rock railing right before the drop-off. They both leaned over the edge to attach gear to the anchor bolts that were almost at the top of the wall we would be rappelling down.

It was no higher than the walls at the gym. I could see the bottom, even from way back where I stood, motionless. Frozen.

My feet refused to move me any closer to them. I was rooted to the spot by a wave of fear unlike anything I'd ever felt. I tried to force myself to breathe deeply, slowly. It didn't help.

Mark was showing Betty how to attach slings to the bolts as they peered over the wall. I tried to slither forward a few inches, following a small, shallow crack filled with spindly grass that wound its way down to where they were crouched. I wedged one foot into the crack. The other. Then I stopped.

I can't do this! I shouldn't do this! my mind screamed. I'd parented two kids. I knew when something looked dangerous.

But the others were hopping around, carrying ropes and gear back and forth as if they were on a sidewalk. What was wrong with me?

I pushed a foot forward a few more inches. Then I made the mistake of looking down toward the edge, where they were setting up. Nope. That was it. I was done. I'd just have to go home un-rappelled.

But that was unacceptable.

I sat down, pretending to nonchalantly take in the beautiful vistas we had from so high up over the gorge. What a coward! It was all a mistake. I was a fraud. I didn't belong out here. How could I be a climber, if I couldn't even get close to the climb?

I stood up, moved one foot forward. Felt the dampness on my cheeks. This was real fear—and I wasn't even doing anything dangerous! At least not by the standards of the real climbers working all around me.

Clearly, "dangerous" was a relative term.

Mark shouted for me to get closer so I could see what they were doing. I forced a smile, shouted back something noncommittal, and moved one foot forward again.

No! my little protective angel, or devil, screamed at me. *You don't belong here! Go back!* I shut him up again and moved the other foot. My stomach was clenched so tightly I could hardly breathe.

Why am I doing this? That question whirled around violently in my brain. I didn't *need* to be here, perched atop this abyss. (Does forty feet count as an abyss?) What the heck *was* I doing here? I was clearly not cut out for this.

But even more frightening than all those thoughts was this one: that I might not be able to get beyond this fear. That it might control me, forever. That scared me more than anything else.

So I pushed a foot forward, focused on the smooth rock, the weeds growing out of the crack, the crisp, cool air that filled my nose—when I could force myself to breathe.

I stubbornly beat back all the images my mind was tormenting me with: me tripping and falling over the edge and bouncing off the rocks and into the river, me scraping and bouncing down the low-angled wall. One misstep, that's all it would take . . . I forced myself to concentrate only on my feet. One at a time. Wedge a foot firmly into the crack, balance with the other one on the slab. Then change sides.

I looked up. I was closer!

I forced a deep, slow breath through my rigid body. My partners were close now. I could almost see what they were doing.

The edge was closer, too. I tried fiercely to ignore that. I came here for this. *I came here for this* . . . A climber has to be able to rappel.

After an eternity, I planted one foot down in the gully behind the natural rock railing at the top of the cliff. Both hands grabbed the edge in a death grip. I was here! I looked again, because I couldn't believe it.

I'd made it!

Mark was explaining to Betty the physics of how to build the anchor. The calm murmur of their voices had been my anchor, all the way down. The sky was still blue. The river still rushed past, forty feet below. Not so far, anymore. Only forty feet. I'd made it.

This time, my smile wasn't forced, and the tears were happy tears. I swiped them away, moved closer to where they were working, and began to learn how to rappel.

No one here knew how close I'd come to giving up. They assumed— don't we all?—that everyone was in the same head space.

I would never assume that again. This climbing stuff was clearly going to take more stick-to-it-iveness, more determination than I'd imagined. I thought I'd already been pushed to the edge of my limits years ago. Being forced to live in silence, alongside someone who lived alone, while raising my children to be thoughtful, caring people, had used up my reserves of tenacity. I thought.

twelve

WHEN THE CHILDREN WERE young, traveling was the only thing that brought Charlie to life. When he talked about going somewhere, anywhere, for any reason, his face and his voice grew animated, and he would remind me of the man I fell in love with in southern California. He could go on about travel plans, about a mountain or a waterfall or a road, for as long as anyone seemed interested. And I was—I loved it, too. But it had little to do with our day-to-day life with children in Sacramento.

When we were all home together, he would often lie on the floor and read novels for twelve hours or more, without a word to anyone. He'd get up, step silently past the three of us, make his own lunch, and eat it without a word, all while reading. Then he'd read some more, or watch football, alone. Silent, for the whole day, as we lived around him.

It seemed as if he were actively trying to make my life as dark and empty as his. I had no idea why, but I wasn't going to let him. Since I couldn't fight him verbally, I insisted on light and music and friends, activity and openness.

And love, even if it was all one-sided. It just wasn't in me to give up hope completely, no matter how angry or frustrated he made me. If he did suffer from a condition that made it impossible to have human relationships, then he needed my love more than anyone else did.

In southern California, we had both promised to love each other. I couldn't remember hearing those oh-so-important words while we lived in Japan. And I hadn't heard anything except snappish, angry retorts or practical logistics since we'd returned to California. Yet, I knew those words were still in him, even if only faintly, unconvincingly mumbled.

Physical surroundings have a great impact on a person's emotional state, so I tried to keep our home beautiful, warm, and welcoming. But every week, every day, insidiously, Charlie would fill every open space with unmanageable piles of debris.

"Don't let him do that!" my mother had once exclaimed during one of my parents' rare visits.

We had just watched him come in from work and drop his shoes, jacket, keys, and all the books and bags he was carrying, all over the floor as he headed toward the bedroom. Not a pile, exactly, just a trail of debris that he left everywhere he went in the house. And it would remain that way until I dealt with it. I had to—the rest of us couldn't live that way.

I wondered what she meant by "let him."

I'd tried asking him why he kept all his clothes on the floor of the bedroom, in front of his empty side of the closet. He'd shrug. In the garage, there was no room for his car; instead, he was constantly adding to a monstrous six- or seven-foot-high pile of things—bike parts, metal pipes, an old fan that didn't work, papers, old briefcases, cups, hats, tools, pieces of plastic, toys, old T-shirts, old electronics that had died, a boot, hundreds of pens, pencils, binders, an ever-growing, dense pile of random junk that tore at my soul each time I opened the garage door.

I'd tried lightheartedly explaining why it was a bad idea to have similar stacks of debris—a smaller version of the pile in the garage—on the floor next to his desk in the living room. I'd tried to get him to use various systems to organize his things. I'd tried . . . everything I knew how to try. I was worn down from trying.

When I taught an evening class, Charlie stayed home with the children. I loved teaching and looked forward to the adult interaction. But the price was high. As I drove home, I could feel the toll of a full day with two busy kids, a house, yards and chores, followed by four hours of being in a classroom. But I knew the hardest part was waiting for me.

The first time was a shock. It shouldn't have been; I'd seen the signs, all along. Nonetheless, it stopped me midstride as I came through the door.

"Charlie!"

He looked up from his magazine. "What?"

"What happened?!"

He looked around blankly. "What?"

The small table in front of the couch where he lay reading had disappeared under the debris. Every inch of the carpet was covered. The whole room. Toys, Legos, books, little clothes, big clothes, papers, magazines, crayons, and even tips and bits of crayons. It looked as though someone had taken everything we owned and dumped it there.

In front of where he lay reading.

That clinched it. I knew then that it was all up to me. He really didn't care. Or didn't see it. Or maybe somewhere a short circuit, a loose wire, something simple I knew nothing about, was responsible for some of his behaviors and the growing, bizarre rift between us.

I glanced across the room. Maybe the three-foot-high piles on both sides of his desk were not a fluke. Maybe the fact that I couldn't really tell there was a desk there, under all the debris, wasn't because he was always so busy earning money. Maybe it had nothing to do with that at all.

I wasn't sure which scenario scared me more. Especially when it became clear that it was affecting the kids.

Alex had already made numerous visits to the emergency room—always while under Charlie's care. A broken wrist from falling off climbing equipment. A pierced toe from gardening with Dad. Little-boy stuff, but none of it ever happened while I was around. And then there was the day Charlie had called to tell me while I was working that he'd lost Alex in West Sacramento—that still had the power to induce cascading shivers of imagination and fear. When he was in sole charge of the children, Charlie seemed to exhibit the sense of a child himself.

Whatever the reason, it was all up to me now. If he wasn't pretending, and truly didn't understand what was wrong with the chaos I'd walked in on, that made fixing it, or dealing with it, entirely my responsibility.

· · · · · · · · · ·

I DIDN'T UNDERSTAND WHAT was happening at home and never had time to myself to think about it. But I did know myself, and my children. Every day, the three of us spent hours talking, examining life together, learning from each other and from other people. We talked all the time, about everything.

Stasia had always delighted in books and letters. At sixteen months old, she tossed her jump rope onto the tatami mat floor of our Japanese living room. It fell in a big coil. She shrieked with glee and jumped into the coil.

"O!" she exclaimed, pointing down at the circle around her.

Later, as she hopped onto her tiny pink tricycle, her fingers found two little round metal rings near the saddle. "O!" she said, pointing excitedly. After that, there was no stopping her discovery of letters, everywhere we went.

All day long, for years, I learned from them how children see the world. I read to them both every evening.

By the time Alex was approaching five, he had turned into an accomplished raconteur. His Grampie loved hearing Alex's complex stories about knights and battles and castles, punctuated with live action to demonstrate the scenes. After our first trip to France together, where Alex saw real castles and armor, lances and swords, his imagination knew no bounds. Stories could go on and on, with plot twists and ironies and reversals, with laughter tossed in now and then when he was pleased with a particular action scene.

But his fine motor skills never kept up with the rest of his body. Each time he sat down to illustrate one of his exquisitely detailed stories, I knew how it was going to end. I'd brace for the sounds of paper ripping or being crumpled and tossed aside, or of pencils or crayons bouncing off the wall or the floor—followed by angry sobs.

Each time, he'd run to me in tears and demand that I render his imagination on paper (both kids knew I'd done the paintings hanging on our walls). And I always let myself be suckered in. Alex knew exactly how his characters looked, what their horses looked like, how their lances sat, how many crenellations decorated their castle tower. But I brought my own imagination to the task. He would describe, I would draw, and I would invariably get it all wrong.

"No, not like that!" he would wail in despair. Over and over, through reams of paper. What I drew was never quite the scene in his mind. It was the first time I'd encountered true perfectionism. Years later, when Alex would recount how he'd perfectly executed one of his free-solo climbs, I would think back to our drawing sessions, where it first became apparent how important it was to him to get something just right.

His sister was his counterbalance. Alex called life as he saw it; Stasia was born a diplomat. He zipped through life at breakneck speed; she was thoughtful in everything she did. Complete opposites, they complemented each other's life outlook, and never fought. Are there other sibling pairs on the planet that have never had a fight?

Even if I hadn't had a full night of sleep since before Alex was born, I loved my time with both my children. They were fascinating, each so different in every way. They taught me so much and helped take my mind off the miserable failure my marriage had become.

. . . .

AT LEAST TRAVEL WAS still a topic we could always talk about, especially as the children got older. It was one of the reasons Charlie and I decided to raise our kids to be bilingual.

So I saw a trip to France as a requirement, to reinforce linguistic habits before they became unnatural for Stasia and Alex, living in an English-only environment in California. But to accomplish that, we would have to take the trip without their father, who would have spoken English with them the whole time.

I'd been to France with Charlie before, when he was doing research for his master's thesis on language acquisition. His goal was to learn to speak French and document the process. But he didn't actually use it with anyone. I talked for both of us, that whole summer.

Back then, I'd assumed his reticence sprang from the awkwardness of putting thoughts together in a foreign language. Now, I was rethinking that.

So Charlie worked the summer that Alex and Stasia, almost four and six, my little travelers, and I flew from San Francisco to Paris. After a few days sampling all the playgrounds and other beautiful spots in Paris, the three of us took the TGV, the high-speed train, to Brittany, the northwestern arm of France that juts out into the Atlantic.

With our Breton friends, we visited six-thousand-year-old burial mounds, the standing stones of Carnac (like Stonehenge), the pink granite coast, millennia-old towns. And the tiny island of Ouessant, dotted with house-sized hydrangea bushes covered in masses of flowers of deepest blue—a feast for the eyes and the soul.

This piece of French soil ends in a jumbled rock promontory that defines its wild westernmost point. The screech of gulls is the only sound heard over the roar of the incessant winds off the Atlantic and the crashing waves that pound relentlessly against a jumble of reddish-gray rocks, sending spray in every direction,

When Alex disappeared, no one in our group of two moms and three kids even thought to look for him out there. No one expected a scrawny, not-yet-four-year-old boy to be able to scramble across such forbidding terrain. When I finally spotted him, silhouetted against the raging ocean on a small ledge near the top of the promontory, it was the backyard swing set, when Alex was ten months old, all over again. My breathing stopped. I couldn't speak. All I could do was point and wait for my heart to start again. And pray.

It would have been irresponsible of me to go out there myself. One misstep, and I'd be dashed to pieces amid the jumble of rocks and crashing waves. I didn't want my daughter to go home from France brotherless *and* motherless. My friend's son, Flavien, was almost ten years older than Alex, so we both looked to him to scurry out as far as he could and try to talk Alex back down or grab him. He wasn't thrilled at the prospect, but our stricken faces convinced him.

He headed out hesitantly, one carefully placed step at a time, amid the wheeling gulls and gray mist. He shouted, but Alex didn't react. He was absorbed by the view and the climb.

Finally, Alex turned and noticed Flavien. We could see him shout something back but none of us could hear. And then, to the collective gasps of everyone watching—there was a small group of bystanders now—Alex disappeared around a corner and out of sight.

Flavien turned toward us and shrugged, obviously unable to follow.

None of us knew what to do. We could only wait.

After a few moments that felt like an eternity, Alex reappeared, and both boys began clambering back to safety. By the time they both had jumped off the rocks, landed on the sand, and were running back to us, I had recovered enough control of my emotions to think through what had happened, from Alex's viewpoint.

We had come out here to sightsee, and that's what he'd been doing. He'd gone out there, unaware that no one else could follow or that it might be dangerous, like at the playgrounds at home. He'd looked around, appreciated the view we'd talked so much about, and come back.

No big deal.

thirteen

MUSIC IS LANGUAGE. For me, it had always been the language of emotion and salvation. Back in New York, I'd spent hours each week pounding out my angst, my frustrations. Any passion I had was vented at the piano, since other expressions were forbidden in my life at home. Now, again faced with a life of silence and solitude, I turned to music for a way out.

There was no music in West Sacramento back in the '80s—it was not yet even a city. In fact, there was not much of anything at all—one store, only a couple of small restaurants, no cultural life that I could discern. For all of that, one had to cross the river into the city of Sacramento. It was in this void that I saw my big chance to make my dream happen.

For as long as I could remember, I'd dreamed of conducting an orchestra. Whenever I watched Leonard Bernstein conduct, in person or on TV, I'd studied carefully how he did things. Where the musicians all sat. How the instruments sounded, solo and blended together. Free concerts in the parks of New York were another favorite place to train. In high school, where I played clarinet, I watched closely as Mr. Shine worked to make us all passable musicians. When we'd played on stage at Carnegie Hall, for graduation, I was sure that would be the highlight of my musical career.

I'd directed small music groups in the high schools where I taught, but always figured that to conduct a real symphony orchestra I'd have to be invited to guest conduct somewhere. After all, I had no formal training, only the musicianship I'd acquired during my life of playing, studying, and enjoying music.

West Sacramento, and its fledgling cultural scene when we lived there in the late 1980s, offered me my chance. But before I approached the chamber of commerce with my idea, I had to run it past Charlie. This was going to affect our home life. I'd be gone more evenings, and he had to be willing to take up the extra childcare hours.

So I shared my lifelong dream with him and asked what he thought of my becoming founder and conductor of the brand-new West Sacramento Community Orchestra. After a long pause, he had only one comment.

"Don't you have enough to do?"

Then he walked away.

. . . .

WHILE THE ORCHESTRA WAS taking shape, a publisher from Tennessee contacted me and asked if I would consider writing a book for them. They'd put out guidebooks on traveling with children and wanted to publish one for the Sacramento region.

The serendipity was mind-blowing. I'd dreamed about publishing a book, planned for it, hoped for it, written several manuscripts, joined groups that I thought might help. And when I wasn't even working on it, the offer just fell onto my desk. Not unlike moving to a place that needed an orchestra.

Both of my children, five and seven now, tested everything that I included in *Sacramento with Kids*. But the one place that would have a lasting impact on all of us was the one I agonized over the most.

The Rocknasium in Davis, just west of Sacramento, was the first climbing gym I'd ever heard of. It was the only one in the region back then. I didn't even know that climbing was an organized sport. My son climbed all the time, but no one—not me nor anyone in my family, nor anyone we knew—climbed or knew anyone who climbed.

I thought I'd learned everything I wanted to know about climbing from Alex. It wrecked things in the house and gave me no peace. It made us unpopular everywhere I took the kids. For five years, I'd tried—with no success at all—to keep Alex, if not earthbound, at least safe. I was still learning about the powerful force that drove him, and my aim was to, if not harness, at least guide his boundless energy away from danger whenever I could.

So there was no way I was going to take him to a place filled with nothing but things to climb. Forty-foot walls covered in handholds and footholds, in a warehouse-sized building! Back then, I'd only seen him climb playground equipment and trees. It made me queasy to imagine what he could attempt in a place made for the vertical assault.

And yet . . . there was the book. My first soon-to-be-published book. I wanted it to be as complete as possible. After weeks of agonizing, I decided I needed to know what my little test experts thought of the place. For publication. And I couldn't take his sister and not Alex.

Overpreparation was the key. Get us in and out fast, before anything really dangerous could happen. To ensure we'd spend as little time there as possible, I made a list of interview questions before driving off to Davis with both kids in the back seat. I knew in my heart that this was a stupid, irresponsible thing for a mother to do.

My grip on Alex's hand was firm as we walked in. I looked up and groaned. Nothing but walls covered with handholds, footholds, ropes . . . and people hanging from them.

To Alex, it must have looked like heaven.

One of the young men in charge welcomed us and offered small body harnesses so the kids could experience the place. That was, after all, why we'd arranged to come—the kids would have fun, I would talk with the owner and get the information I needed, and afterward I would talk with the kids about the experience and write it into the chapter on regional sports.

Another young man, co-owner with the man who'd welcomed us, took charge of the kids. He anticipated my questions and reassured me that, with strong climbing ropes, harnesses made specially for little kids, expert guidance, and (maybe most importantly!) a two-foot-thick floor made of rubber, the climbing gym was completely safe. My children would be fine.

Ha. What did this *very young* stranger know about controlling a compulsive climber like Alex? He hadn't sat through all those sessions at the emergency room. Hadn't scrubbed a trail of blood out of the beige living-room carpet, from when the digging fork went through his toe. Heck, he probably didn't even *have* kids—he was a kid himself! What did he know about "safe"?

But I gave him my babies anyway, and turned to talk with the first young man.

It had been five minutes, tops, when I realized the whole gym had gone silent. The place had been buzzing when we'd come in, people talking, shouting things I didn't understand. Now, not a sound.

It had something to do with Alex. I knew it.

I turned. I only had to follow the gaze of everyone else in the gym. Everyone, climbers, belayers, *everyone* was watching my son. My five-year-old baby was poised a few feet from the ceiling, about three stories high. He was about to top out.

Both young men near me wore broad smiles and were nodding, as if they'd just been introduced to a beautiful work of art. The one to whom I had entrusted my children was smiling knowingly as he looked up at Alex.

"He's really good."

. . . .

THIRTY-SIX EYES WERE FIXED on me. Unwavering, waiting. Eager. Each one of the eighteen musicians of the West Sacramento Community Orchestra sat erect, instruments ready. The brass rims of the two huge tympani, the growling kettle drums lugged here by friends, brothers, and cousins, gleamed in the harsh lights. Black metal music stands and musicians dressed in concert black set a professional tone.

We were performing our inaugural concert at the Senior Center of West Sacramento. It wasn't Carnegie Hall. The cold linoleum floor and a wall of windows didn't promise good acoustics. But the one-room building was packed with people. All those bodies and clothes would help absorb the sound before it bounced around the hard surfaces.

I had no podium and no risers, so some of the musicians disappeared behind their stands. But no podium also meant I could move around as I led them, so they could all see me.

The piano had been tuned, but it sounded like what it was: an old, cheap piano in a meeting hall. But it was *our* piano that day. It would sing clearly and fill in some of the voices that were missing in our orchestra. That was all I expected from it.

As I rushed around overseeing every detail of our first performance, I thought about all I'd learned from Mr. Shine when he led our school orchestra at Carnegie Hall. I'd dreamed of this moment all my life. Now that it was here, I didn't have time to dwell. Too much to do.

I glanced at the clock on the wall. Showtime!

I raised both arms, baton in hand, and the crowd behind me went silent. The sudden hush momentarily turned off the detail focus in my brain, but at the first chord, my emotions washed over me in a flash flood, and the million details I needed to keep in mind were back.

The four violins and one viola, all the small strings we had, began a Strauss waltz, tentatively, hesitantly. I knew from rehearsals that they knew it, almost by heart, and as more instruments added to the mix of sounds, I could tell they were beginning to listen to each other and adjust accordingly. Exactly what I'd been trying to get them to do for weeks. They gained power and assuredness as they played.

They were making real music!

As we raced through our last piece, Hérault's driving, rhythmic "Zampa Overture," I saw in my peripheral vision fingers and hands all over the room waving in time. Through the floor I felt feet tapping and heard humming behind me. The audience was engaged and having a great time.

My lifelong dream—and the reality was far sweeter than the dream.

Charlie's whole family sat across the first row. Alex sat next to Charlie, and Stasia sat in between Grammie and Grampie. These were the musicians I wanted in my children's lives forever—Grampie had played flute in the Sacramento Symphony and Grammie taught piano, as did Aunt Carol. They all loved it, and whenever we got together as a family, there was always music.

Each time I imagined living without Charlie, putting an end to the frustration and confusion and daily struggle, the thought of losing this family always shut down any consideration. Both of my kids had a special bond with their grandparents. Charlie's parents and siblings had always been part of my kids' lives, and I didn't want to rip them away from that. And if I left Charlie, he would have partial custody. I couldn't leave Alex's safety in his hands—not after so many emergency room visits.

So each time, the same conclusion was forced on me: I couldn't do anything that might come between my kids and the family that sat in the first row of my first concert. I would continue to be a conductor and a writer. A teacher. But most importantly, a full-time mom, or rather, both parents. At least until the kids were old enough to be left alone—since that is what leaving them with Charlie amounted to.

Charlie had only one comment that day of our first performance.

"They weren't as bad as I expected."

In the four years that I conducted my orchestra, that was the only thing he ever said about it.

fourteen

I REACHED OVER AND turned up the car radio.

"Mommy, don't forget we get out early today," Stasia reminded me. The teachers were getting a half day to do some of the behind-the-scenes work they normally did on their own time. In my teacher head, I cheered for them.

"Oui, chérie, je le sais. Je te vois ici à midi." (Yes, love, I know. See you here at noon.)

The three of us talked all the time in the car as I chauffeured them to school and everywhere else they needed to go. In that little bubble of forced togetherness, I learned about their lives, their friends, and their music. They both loved to educate me about "their" music. When I was on my own, the radio was set to the classical station, but as soon as they got in the car, they changed it.

I didn't usually listen to the stations the kids picked. But that morning, when the announcer named the next song, I turned the music up one more click, blocked out the conversation from the back seat, and focused on it. "Never There." It sounded like a song about my husband. Could it be that someone had written a song about us? That someone else had also lived this purgatory?

Stasia jumped out of the car and ran across the field to school as the song played. I drove to Alex's school on autopilot, responding only vaguely to my son's chatter. The words of the song, by the band Cake, could have been written by my doppelgänger, about our life—*never there.* Alex was out of the car and running to class before the dam burst.

How did they know that when I'd needed him, he was never there?

Need? I had no needs. It wasn't allowed, and hadn't been for a long time. Only other people had needs. My kids. My students. Everyone else. Not me. I no longer knew what that word meant. I had needed Charlie, so much, needed someone to talk to, to hold, to be with. But, one silent shrug at a time, he'd killed that longing, and my needs had dried up and blown away, like so many weeds in the wind.

Memories of his touch suddenly swept over me, made me double over with pain so intense that my moans filled the empty car. The lyrics came through over my sobs—all the words I'd forbidden to be spoken, forbidden to be even thought, for so long! How could I live alongside someone who lived morosely, stubbornly alone, if I needed love?

Tears obscured everything; driving home would have to wait. *Everything* had waited, for years, and would continue to have to wait, probably for even more years. I would continue to patch the dam for as long as necessary. My kids needed love, and care. They would not get either if I left them half-time with Charlie, as was commonly required in California.

The dam would hold, as long as I needed it to. That was the only need I could allow.

• • • • • • • • • •

WHOEVER HAD WRITTEN THAT song had survived. I clung to that thought as I would to a buoy in a roiling sea. If they could survive that experience, write about it and sing about it, then there was hope for me.

On good days, I could convince myself that I didn't have it so bad. We had a nice home. I could take the kids to France now and then, so they could maintain a certain level of fluency. My kids had terrific grandparents. Wanting more would be greedy.

Charlie didn't drink or gamble or sleep with other women. I knew things could be a lot worse. But if he had done any of those things, I would have known what to do about it. And if he had lifted his hand to me, just once, it would have been over immediately.

He did seem able to speak the kids' language. He was like a kid himself, but smarter and bigger. Almost everything related to travel, they learned from him. State capitals, rivers, countries, borders—he endlessly taught and quizzed them about geography. He bought them games about the world, which we all enjoyed. And anywhere we went as a family, he always preferred to play with the kids, leaving me to talk with the adults.

This was often difficult to explain to the adults we'd come to visit.

Up and down the East Coast, he "let" me visit with family or friends I rarely got to see, while he took the children outside to play. The kids had great fun with him—but never got to know any of my family. And he never had to talk to other adults.

When we were both staying at one of my relative's homes and he had nowhere to escape to, he would sit in a corner while we all talked, or in another room, and write postcards about the beautiful places we'd seen. To his family.

"Doesn't Charlie feel good?" Aunt Helen asked me several times during visits to her home on Long Island, concerned about someone who would drive three thousand miles to sit in silence and ignore everyone.

"Does Charlie need some aspirin? Something else?" My father's friend in New Hampshire was also concerned. Everyone was. Surely after coming all this way, my husband must have a bona fide health reason for not interacting with anyone.

Being snubbed doesn't sit well with most people. They need a reason. I didn't have one. For them, or for me.

For Charlie, these trips were about the battlefields we visited between coasts, the historic sites, waterfalls, mountains, deserts, wildlife— and it was fascinating, for all of us. The children learned a lot on those cross-country trips to see my family, but they learned nothing about my relatives, their own family. And my family learned little about my husband besides how quiet and odd he was.

fifteen

POP BOTTLE. WITH A name like that, how hard could the climb be?

While the others flaked the ropes and organized their gear, I stood looking up at the climb from the base of Lovers Leap, 6,944 feet above sea level in the Sierra Nevada, an hour and a half from home in Sacramento. Lots of blocks, a big crack, a corner to stick your feet in. Of course I could climb it. My tribe wouldn't have brought me out here if they didn't think so. But this one would be different from the other climbs I'd done on Sierra granite. This one made me miss several hours of sleep last night. This would be my first multipitch climb.

Until today, we'd always worked our way seventy or eighty feet up a climb, then lowered off, back down to the base where we'd started. Like at the gym, but outdoors and a little higher, a little harder. Far more interesting.

Today we were going up several rope lengths, or pitches. My tribe thought that after almost a half year of climbing, I was ready. When the leader of the climb reached the first ledge, he'd make an anchor and belay us all up. Then we would keep going. Up.

Gary would be leading us—climbing on the sharp end of the rope—up Pop Bottle. He could lead anything. Climbing this route would be a mental challenge for me, but it would be easy for Gary. Having learned to climb on the sea cliffs of his native Ireland a decade earlier, he seemed equally at home in the Sierra, leading us all up a wall.

The leader wasn't protected against a fall until he placed a piece of gear in the rock and attached the rope to it. And then another, and another, all the way to the top of the pitch, where he'd make an anchor out of several pieces of gear, manage the rope, and pull up the slack for each climber who followed. If he did come off the wall anywhere, the gear he was placing would arrest his fall—*if* he'd placed it right and *if* it held. Sometimes gear popped. Sometimes leaders hit the ground, or a ledge, or a block . . . I tried not to think about that.

As he led the first pitch, I watched closely to see where he found hand-holds, where he put his feet, which direction he leaned at certain points. I knew from my meager experience that I wouldn't remember it all, but if a difficult section stopped me, I might recognize some of what I'd seen and know what to do to get past it.

Slowly upward he went, placing pieces of gear here and there to hold the rope, as I tried to imprint his techniques in my memory. His steady, comfortable pace and sure movements made it look easy, but I knew it wouldn't be. It never was.

Another climber went up. I was going to drag a rope as I climbed, some-thing else I had never done. In this sort of multipitch climbing, pairs of climbers are connected by a rope, one tied in at each end. After the leader makes an anchor, each following climber attaches a second rope to the back of their harness, trailing it behind them as they go higher. Once they reach the top of the pitch, the next climber ties into the end of that one, and trails another rope, all except the last person up. Today there were five of us, so four ropes.

My turn. As the climber before me neared the belay ledge, I pulled on my supertight, sticky-rubber-soled climbing shoes and stashed my hik-ing shoes and socks for the walk back down in my summit bag, the small backpack I would wear going up. I checked that my harness buckle was doubled back and tied a figure eight knot, carefully attaching it through both weight-bearing loops of the harness. Check. Double-check. Look up the wall. Triple-check everything.

Until today, knowing that I'd be back on the ground in a few minutes had given me a feeling of . . . not safety, exactly, but limits. I knew I could stand any fear, any pain for a few minutes, and then I would be back down safely. Today would be different.

Today, I didn't know where we were going. Except up.

At fifty-nine, I thought I should know where I was going. But these guys were going to lead me up, and up again, and then up again. Somewhere really high. The photos I'd seen of Pop Bottle online bore no resemblance whatsoever to the cold rock now under my fingers, with the sun glinting off the dikes and striations and sharp edges all around me.

We were going up. For as long as it took.

We were adventuring.

As I finished my preparations, the climber before me pulled up all the slack in the rope connecting us, until I felt the tug on my harness.

"That's me!" I shouted up, and heard the answering "belay is on" from the ledge high overhead. Gary was ready to belay me up, pulling in the slack in the rope as I got higher. I was on a rope. If I fell off the wall, I would dangle, but wouldn't fall. Probably bang into stuff, hit whatever was sticking out from the wall. Blocks. Chips. Little prickly shrubs. Edges of slabs. I could get banged up, scraped or scratched, but I wouldn't fall.

A fellow climber checked my knot, and up I went to a new adventure.

Moving on rock is completely different from moving on the walls of a gym. The motions are the same, the body movements similar, but on real rock, nothing is color coded. Nothing is given. You have to look all around you and make decisions about what you can hold, what might support your body weight, where your foot might stick to propel you upward. What might crack or come off if you pull on it.

It isn't always obvious. There was a bulge in the middle of this first pitch that stopped me for a few minutes. Not a roof, exactly, but an area where the rock stuck out just far enough overhead that I couldn't see what was above it, or what to hold. Where I was going next. Just enough to remove any last feeling of safety or sureness.

I felt out to the right and left. Nothing. The bulge itself was smooth and lacked anything to grab. I tried just walking my feet up the wall to get a bit higher as I experimented, but they slid right off.

After a few frustrating moments, I found it—the perfect handhold! I let out the breath I'd been holding and pulled myself over the bulge and upward. Soon I was right beneath the ledge where Gary's anchor held the ropes that kept everybody safe. It was a flat space about two feet deep, and wide enough across the wall for several people. With my feet as high as I could place them on the wall below it, I reached up to the edge and pushed downward with my arms and upward with my core in a move called manteling. I twisted and plopped my rear end solidly on the ledge.

"Way to go, Dierdre!"

"Good job!"

The encouraging voices of two friends on the ledge were lost on me. My legs dangled about a hundred feet or so off the deck. I didn't see anything but emptiness. Void. The ground—safety—was long gone.

I quickly looked up, outward, searching for something to anchor my gaze. Peaks glistened in the sun, gray-green against a cloudless, deep blue sky. Tiny patches of snow outlined the tallest peaks. As far as I could see.

What was I doing up here?

I scooted myself back toward the wall. Away from the edge. As fast as my shaking fingers would allow, I unclipped one end of my personal tether from my harness, looked around desperately, and clipped it in to the anchor. Then I pulled a sling, a loop of Dyneema nylon made for this purpose, off my shoulder. There were still two carabiners on my harness, and after several shaky stabs I managed to grab another. It took all my concentration to remember how to tie it to my harness with a girth hitch. I attached this second tether to the anchor on the other side of me.

I couldn't move. That was the way I wanted it. Safe. Secured from both sides. Shaking.

Someone stepped over me and leaned down to hand me one end of a rope.

"Hold this for a second, D," Bob said. I knew his voice, but I couldn't look up at him. My gaze was frozen somewhere between the vastness in front of me and the fear inside me.

I shook my head. "I can't."

I was glad it was Bob. One of the more senior members of our group, Bob had been climbing with me since I'd started. He understood how inexperienced I was and had helped me gain the little confidence I had so far. If I had to refuse to help someone up here, I was glad it was him.

Climbing partners, whether on single or multipitch climbs, have a lot of jobs to do together. Ropes need to be flaked. Gear has to be transferred and arranged carefully for ease of use. I knew that. And I wanted to help. But couldn't.

The suddenness of this fear held me under, like a monstrous ocean wave that pinned me to the knee-skinning sand at the bottom. My entire psyche felt skinned, abraded. I couldn't breathe.

Looking down or up was out of the question. Instead I looked at the knot that attached my climbing rope to the front of my harness. That was the securest thing around, and my mind seized on it. Instead of taking the rope Bob held out, I measured out a short section of the rope attached to my harness, made a bight in it, tied a clove hitch, and found the last carabiner on my harness. I attached my rope to the 'biner, which I attached to yet another part of the anchor behind me.

I was safe. Supersafe. Ultrasafe. Three-ways safe.

But it didn't feel safe. It felt exposed, and dangerous, and crazy. They could probably all tell from my pallor and my blank, inward stare. No one asked me to do anything else. There was a lot to do, but I knew they were all accustomed to handling it. I just sat there, trying to steady my breathing, as they hopped over me and back, doing all the chores that needed to be done before we could keep going up.

Up. I didn't dare think about that. We were going even higher than where I sat. Higher. More dangerous. More exposed.

This, I thought, is where the real climbers hang out. Where people like me are winnowed out.

But I didn't want to be winnowed out. I didn't want to be people like me. I longed to be people like *them*. My friends, who were so comfortable, so at ease up here. Up. Here.

It was decision time. Which group did I truly want to belong to? I wouldn't get another chance. I wouldn't expect that of them.

Did I trust the gear? Not yet, not really. I knew all the numbers, how much weight a climbing rope could hold, how many falls one rope could sustain without damage. I'd read all about that. Didn't matter one bit.

Gary was an expert climber. He had a lifetime of experience and knew how to make a bomber anchor that wouldn't fail. In my heart, I knew that. I trusted him. But in my head . . .

Maybe if I sat here long enough . . . ?

No. I made my decision. My transition would start today. Here. Now. I looked down toward the trail that winds along the base of the Lovers

Leap wall. A handful of ant-like people dotted the wandering gray line. If Bob had handed them a rope, any one of them, they would have grabbed it and known what to do with it. Where to attach it, with what knot, and for what purpose.

I could learn all that.

I *would* learn all that. Slowly, I detached one of my 'biners from the anchor, the one that was pulling me the most tightly in toward the wall behind me. Still safe on the other two.

The rest of our group had joined us on the ledge. Everyone was doing something necessary, or just enjoying the view. Everyone but me. It was time.

I removed the second sling from the anchor and reattached it to my harness. Then I adjusted my clove hitch to create enough slack in the rope so I could stand while still attached to the anchor.

Slowly, carefully, gripping knobs on the wall behind me, I unfurled and, still shaky, stood up, turning as I did to face the wall. The rock-solid wall. Right in front of me.

The others weren't attached. They should have been! *Good thing their mothers can't see them,* I thought. I fought to not say anything about it. They were moving all around me, as if they were on a sidewalk. Gary was flaking his rope so he could start leading the next pitch. His cheerful, understanding smile gave me the strength to move a bit closer to the edge as I watched what he was doing. I needed to learn this stuff. I hoped the learning process would quash my overactive imagination.

"How ya doin', D?"

"Fine." Almost true. Getting truer with each minute.

Two of our group were moving right, to another, harder route. The ledge was the point of divergence for the two climbs. The rest of us would continue up Pop Bottle. Now that I could actually see it, I noticed that the ledge was big enough to have a party on.

Maybe someday I would.

sixteen

CHARLIE FOUND HIS PLACE at the college where we both taught. His students loved him. When he walked through his classroom door, he took on a new persona. His ESL students fascinated him, and he talked a lot with them about other parts of the world. They brought the world to him, in his prison of responsibility. They were his vicarious travel life.

But being with people all the time wore on him. His solution was simple: teach ESL from afar. Alone. From a mountain somewhere. From Yosemite.

His timing was perfect.

The college district, like the whole region, was growing faster than they could keep up with. District-wide, the biggest problem was space—not enough classrooms and seats for the students.

When he proposed his innovative idea of teaching ESL online, what they now call distance education, it was received like rain in the midst of a drought. He was encouraged to explore the idea, to expand it across the district, the state, the nation, to lobby for it—all of which demanded travel.

Travel—the thing he lived for—had been handed to him as part of his job. He embraced it, traveled all over the country, made distance education a mantra for the district. When he wasn't on the road, he worked at the college, days, nights, evenings, weekends. Years later, the night janitor would tell me how startled he often was when he'd open a door to clean at two or three in the morning, only to see Charlie's huge, dark eyes peering over the several-foot-high piles of paper debris that obscured his desk from view.

He became an important, appreciated person in the district—all because he wanted to get away from people and teach, alone, from Yosemite.

· · · · · · · · ·

TWO ARTICLES DUE FRIDAY. Chapter exams this Thursday in all my classes, so I'd be correcting them Friday, too, and all weekend. Yesterday, Saturday, I'd spent too much time on heavy yard work, and it wasn't clear whether I'd be able to type today. But the articles had to get done, whether I typed one-fingered or scribbled them with a pen until I could use all my fingers again. During the school week, writing time was rare; I'd have to try to get both articles at least sketched out today, with a list of ideas I would use for each, ready for any moments I might find to sit down and work before Friday. The novel I was sketching out would have to wait until next weekend.

I used to love Sundays.

I finished cleaning the counter next to the refrigerator and pushed all of Charlie's odds and ends to the side. I'd need to deal with it later, before it avalanched all over the floor again. He wouldn't. The three-foot-high piles on the floor around his desk, on the desk, and everywhere he lived in the house made that clear: if I wanted order amid his chaos, I had to do it myself.

Charlie was watching football in our bedroom. I didn't want my kids to consider TV a social activity, so it wasn't out in the living room. And neither of them was interested in football, or most other televised sports. He watched alone.

Besides the drone of the mechanical voice shouting about the plays in the football game, the house was quiet. Down the hall, Alex was probably working on his Legos in his room. Those had always been his favorite, often only indoor pastime, the only thing he ever requested for a gift. As he got older, the constructions became more and more elaborate and evolved into multilayered cities and adventures that filled all the shelves on his walls, the floor, several boxes in his closet—every horizontal surface in his room. When he wasn't biking to the climbing gym, which he did most days after school, he was usually in his room.

Ten miles to the gym, where he climbed hard, no doubt, and then ten miles back—in time for supper. A grueling day, physically, for most of us. Back then, I never had time to wonder about it. He was gone, and then he was back. While I worked.

Stasia often disappeared for many quiet hours, too, as she had at the age of two when she trotted off down the hall at Grammie's house with an armload of books to "go study." Many pastimes had captured her creative eye as she grew—origami, painting, embroidery, writing, calligraphy—they came in phases as she explored what the world had to offer. And through it all, always, reading. They both had library cards and used them often.

This was my chance. While everyone was doing something quiet, I hurried to my home office to make some progress on the articles that were due in less than a week. The pay was dismal compared to the hours spent on it, but it was a trickle of money and I could work at home, around the kids' schedules. So I walked past their closed doors and into my office. Mentally, I tried to justify using my Sunday afternoon as a workday, instead of playing with them or taking them somewhere, but the irony of that thought lasted only a few seconds: every day was a workday, in my life. I didn't have time to think about it.

But once in a while, probably more often than I realized, this dark, endless tunnel of mine would glow, faintly, with distant hope. Today was one of those times. As I stepped into the office and my eyes adjusted to the gloom of the northeast end of the house, which received no sun, ever, something sunny and yellow gleamed. A sticky note, stuck to the screen of my computer.

My smile was immediate. Stasia's work, again. Just as she'd known, as a toddler, when Alex had used up the last of my patience, taking his hand and whisking him away for a walk, now she always seemed to know when I was at low ebb. And what to do about it.

Warmth flooded all the little pockets of despair inside me, filling me with gratitude. I would finish the articles, I'd correct my tests, and there would be more articles and tests. But my biggest, most overwhelming job had nothing to do with earning money. My success was down the hall.

My hardest, most Sisyphean struggle, every day, was to combat the negativity, the pall that their father cast over the household, to see that my children would turn out to be kind, thoughtful people who could see the good, the warmth, and the caring in others. I knew from experience that a young mind can learn just as much from a negative example as from a positive one, maybe even more. My main job was to try to tilt their daily learning curve toward the positive. In moments like this, I could believe it was working.

"Have a sunny writing day!" her note said, embellished by a little smiley face.

Now, I would.

. . . .

A LETTER FROM the IRS is never good news. Even I knew that.

Charlie was at a conference somewhere that weekend, learning more about distance education. He wouldn't be home until Monday. He never talked about our finances with me, but the letter was addressed to both of us, since we filed our taxes jointly. I ripped it open and began reading.

The groceries I'd been putting away were instantly forgotten. My eyes stopped at the words "attach a lien on the property." I knew what that meant.

I went back and read it again. According to their records, we hadn't filed income tax returns for the last three years. Had I really not signed a tax return for three years? Did the IRS make mistakes like that?

Stunned, I sat down heavily at the kitchen table, feeling cold and empty, and read it again, trying to digest every word.

It had to be a mistake. Not filed taxes at all? Nobody does that—it would be stupid. Reckless. I tried to think of possible explanations. Lost in the mail? Not filed correctly by our old computer? An extension that had gone awry? My mind ran through every possibility I could think of. None satisfied.

We had no cell phones, so I couldn't call Charlie since I wasn't sure which hotel he was at this time. The college probably had a record of where he'd gone, but he hadn't left that information with me.

It had to be an error, so it could wait. I made a copy of the letter—it seemed important enough to warrant that—and put it aside until Monday.

When he got home on Monday evening, I gave him the letter.

"Is this a mistake?" I asked him as he looked at it.

Shrug.

"Charlie, did you file our taxes, or not?"

He shook his head as he looked at all the rest of his mail from the weekend.

"You didn't file taxes? For both of us? For three years?"

"Uhn-uh." He kept shuffling through envelopes.

"What did you think was going to happen?"

Shrug. More envelopes shuffled. Magazines.

"Charlie?"

"It's stupid!" he shouted. As usual, when pushed for a reply, he resorted to lashing out in anger.

"What's stupid?" It seemed to me that "stupid" was getting the attention of the IRS by not filing.

"I can fix it," he mumbled as he disappeared down the hall. I followed him. His reply showed his disdain for the whole process. I knew he procrastinated every year, often requesting an extension, because he hated dealing with taxes. I would have helped, if he'd shared any information with me about our finances. But he'd always cut me out of that, so all I could do was ask.

"Fix it how?" I persisted. I was genuinely afraid now. The IRS was right, and they had the power to take our house.

"It's no problem." He was clearly irritated, as he always was when I pressed for an answer to anything. But this was too important for me to just slink away confused.

"Not a problem? They're threatening to take our house!"

Another mumble as he changed his clothes. He shook his head at my obtuseness. "They're not going to take the house." His derisive tone said clearly that I was making way too big a deal out of it.

"How do you know?"

And then I remembered his stories. The only stories he told about his childhood all illustrated how much smarter he was than the adults around him. Knew more history in a contest than his history teacher. Caught his English teacher in an English error on a paper. Got a higher score on a science test than his science teacher. I'd always laughed it off as silly. But those were the only stories he ever recounted from his childhood.

It was beginning to make horrible sense. He believed it. His logic told him he knew better than the IRS. Their rules didn't apply to him.

But they did apply to me, the co-signer on the taxes. This time, I would not back off. No matter how stupid he thought we all were.

Several weeks later, I knew he'd fixed the problem when he had to get my signature on the new tax returns. There would be no lien; it was still *our* house. But it was clear that he was only doing it because I'd insisted. To him, the whole process was just too stupid for words.

. . . .

ONCE IN A WHILE, usually when I had an article due, somehow Charlie would find the money for a babysitter so I could work. I'd found a young woman, Beth, a college freshman, who lived at home one block from us. It was perfect. She could walk to our house, or keep the kids at her house, and they could walk home when I got back.

On the day that neither she nor I would ever forget, I had several interviews scheduled that I knew would last longer than the school day. I would go to work, Beth would pick up the kids at school, and Charlie would pick them up at her house once his district meetings were over. Everyone had a clearly defined role.

I got home well after their school day had ended. The phone was ringing as I walked in.

"Oh, thank God you're there!" A frantic woman's voice. I took a few seconds to recognize our babysitter's mother. "Do you have the kids?!"

My stomach clenched so tightly I could hardly answer her. "No—"

"Beth was there, early, and waited and waited, but they never came out!" She sounded as frantic as I was beginning to feel. "She went to their classrooms. Looked all over! She talked to the principal, and they paged them. Over and over. I went, too. We all looked and looked, all over the school—"

I looked at the clock. A little less than two hours. My children had been missing for two hours. What did one do? My mind was whirling through possible scenarios, possible actions I could take.

"Okay, if they turn up, I'll call you, or you call me, whoever sees them first. I'm going to try some things."

"I'm so sorry!" She didn't know what to say. Nor did I.

Charlie was probably still in his last district meeting. I called his parents, who lived two miles from us, closer to the school than we lived. Maybe they had walked to Grammie and Grampie's? A desperate guess.

Grammie answered. "Yes, they're here. Charlie brought them over after school. So nice of him! They're playing cards with Grampie."

I didn't hear much of what she said after "they're here." Charlie had picked them up and taken them there. Knowing the babysitter was arranged. Knowing he was paying her to do just that.

Maybe the school had called him out of his meeting? Some emergency? An accident? A broken bone? But Grammie would have mentioned that. But I didn't ask. I didn't want to know before I called Beth's mother.

Deep down, I knew what had happened. Charlie was just . . . being Charlie. It never occurred to him to think of anyone else. That, as his mother so often put it, was just the way he was. But Beth and her mother would surely not understand. So when I called them back to say the kids were found, and safe, I wanted to be able to say honestly that I didn't know yet exactly what had happened today.

I'd figure out what to tell them tomorrow.

I was almost calm by the time they came home. The kids were fine, no broken bones or bandages, and they were jazzed—getting to play with Grammie and Grampie was a special treat for an ordinary school day.

"What happened?" I wanted to know as he came in the door.

"What?"

"Why'd you pick up the kids? You said you had meetings."

"The last one was cancelled, so I went and got 'em."

"You knew the babysitter was picking them up. What did you think she was going to do?"

Shrug.

"Why didn't you tell her?"

Shrug.

"Or me? I could've told her."

No reply.

"Charlie, they were frantic! Why didn't you tell her? They've been looking for the kids for hours. I was about to call the police . . . " I was starting to get frantic myself, reliving it.

"They were fine. We went to my parents' house."

And he walked away, down the hall, to change out of his work clothes.

I tried again, as he settled into the sofa with the latest copy of his investment newsletter.

"Charlie, the babysitter and her mother thought she'd lost our children! Can you imagine how that felt? God! They were ready to call the police."

He turned a page.

"You caused that. You need to do something."

Silence.

"Charlie?" I pushed the newsletter aside.

"*What*?!" His lashing out always intimidated me enough that I'd leave him alone, thus giving him what he wanted. This time, though, it had affected other people, not just me. I couldn't just back away.

"You need to do something. God—to lose someone else's children! She'll never babysit again!"

No reaction. He turned the newsletter over to the back page and kept reading.

"Can you at least write her a note? Give her some extra money for her trauma?"

Shrug. "Okay." Another page turned.

The next day I asked him if he'd written the note yet. And the following day. I knew it wasn't going to happen. I was beginning to understand that he honestly wasn't capable of such a thing.

So I wrote the note. And delivered it.

He wrote the check.

seventeen

SUNDAY MORNING, ALMOST SUMMER. Uncle Mike and Aunt Carol stopped by on their way home from church. It was always good to see them, always good to see Charlie in animated conversation with someone. Laughing with his brother. We so seldom saw him laugh.

In our big, sunny front room, Carol and I talked mom stuff while Stasia and Alex came and went, occasionally stopping to chat with their aunt and uncle. Charlie and Mike sat at the breakfast bar on comfy stools with backs, leaning over some map or pamphlet, next to our bookcase.

Carol asked me about something that we needed to look up. As I stepped past the two men to reach for the book I needed, I overheard Charlie say, "So on day three we should make it to Lake Louise?"

Lake Louise. He'd talked about going there for years, ever since I'd known him. Canada. Glaciers. Mountains. Road trip. Everything he lived for. Mike pointed to something on the papers they were looking at. I glanced over his shoulder and saw maps of Canada.

Carol had another question. I pulled down the book I'd gone for and turned to her, my mind a whirl. Lake Louise. Charlie and his brother were going to Lake Louise. That's a big trip. He'd never mentioned it.

Mike nodded. "Yeah, we should have no trouble finding two campsites together. We could probably even fit all of us in one site, they're pretty big. Do you guys have a tarp to put over the tents? It rains a lot there."

Tents? You guys? All of us? My mouth continued talking with Carol, but the thought forming in my mind was horrible. I must have heard wrong.

I tried to continue listening. The kids were running and laughing, Carol was talking, the doorbell rang, the kettle began to whistle, they were folding up maps, Mike was talking about a lake, and a glacier, and PVC pipes that would hold up tarps to cover our campsite if it rained . . . and they had to leave.

Our campsite. We were all going to Canada. *I* was going to Canada.

I was torn between asking him right there, or keeping quiet and not letting the others know how dysfunctional we were. Privacy won.

Mike and Carol knew about the trip, and the kids probably knew, too. I was the only one he hadn't told. This took it to another level altogether. I couldn't think of a thing to say. How dysfunctional were we, really?

I waited until they had left.

"So, Canada, huh?"

"Yeah, it's gonna be great!"

"Were you planning on telling me?"

No response. Flipping through maps.

"Do the kids know?"

No answer.

"Didn't you think I might need to pack? Or plan stuff? Like jobs."

Silence.

When people asked, years later, whether we fought (they could see how different we were), I always said "no." No fights, no raised voices, no arguments. It's impossible to argue if one person doesn't say anything. Like the sound of one hand clapping.

Had I waited long enough? Was it time to strike out on my own? Oh, how I hoped . . . But now and then, I got a glimpse of how needy my two pre-teens were, how they seemed to need me more, not less, as they grew into adolescence. That would change, one day, but right now they were far from safe.

I still had no options.

We did go to Canada that summer, Mike and Carol and their daughter, Charlie and I and our two kids. We had a camping adventure filled with alpine lakes, scenic hikes, glacier walks, wildlife. The six of them had a great time.

I tagged along, like luggage, awed by the nature and wildlife. The rest, I forced myself not to think about. My kids were going to Canada on a big adventure with their aunt and uncle and cousin. They'd been looking forward to it for months. Mom wasn't going to ruin it for them.

. . . .

I HAD BEEN FEELING off for two days. Headaches. Nausea. Weakness. More headaches. Left hand out of commission after a marathon of heavy-duty, nonstop yard work all day Sunday.

Maybe it was just the inevitable effects of never having anything to look forward to. Of being forced to live alone, when I thought I got married for companionship. Of being forced to pretend all the time. Maybe it had worn down my defenses, weakened me. Physically and emotionally. Or maybe I was just sick.

I used to know when I was sick. Being sick was different from being normal. Maybe that was the real problem: in my life now, being sick was no different from any other time. The lines had blurred. It was depressing not to be able to tell the difference.

The real tragedy was that this wasn't how I wanted my kids to think of me. What on earth would they remember about their parents, later in life? That they never spoke? That they never had a smile for each other, or a word or a touch or anything at all?

And of course they wouldn't understand my safety concerns, the fact that I couldn't in all conscience leave them with him. They probably wouldn't understand that until they were parents themselves, or at least much older, maybe an aunt or an uncle.

And what of love? What would they learn about that?

Sometimes I felt I was worrying for nothing. They were strong, so maybe what they experienced at home wouldn't matter. Or it would teach them, through negative examples, what they should seek in life. You can learn just as much from a bad example as from a good one—sometimes even more. Maybe they would be enough like me to make that connection, and I should stop worrying about it.

If only I could.

• • • • • • • • • •

THE SECOND TIME I took the kids to France, they brought their climbing shoes. They'd both been going to the climbing gym for about a year, and we were going to spend time in the Savoy Alps, in southern France, with my best friend, Geneviève, and her husband Philippe, an experienced climber. The tiny shepherd's stone hut they'd transformed into a little, spartan *chalet*, or cabin, sat high in the mountains. We couldn't drive to it—we'd have to hike in carrying all our supplies. It sounded like a great adventure, and we couldn't wait.

This trip, like the first, had a linguistic goal. Charlie would have loved the setting of the chalet, but he and the two children would have formed an English-speaking bloc that would have canceled out the main reason for the trip. I assured him that any time he wanted to go, I'd be delighted to make the trip with him, just us. No kids. He agreed. We both knew it would never happen.

Our first day there, Philippe took my kids out to a small, local crag to see how they climbed. Afterward, he'd declared eleven-year-old Alex ready for a climb he had in mind. Stasia, thirteen, chose to stay home with Geneviève and me and their younger kids. We would all meet the guys later.

So far, Alex's climbing had been mostly limited to gyms, so this adventure was doubly special—not only outdoors, on a real mountain, but on an alp. *Un Alpe de Savoie.*

I trusted Philippe. My son was young, very small for his age, but Philippe was old enough to exercise good adult judgment. At least that's what I thought as we got Geneviève's two little kids and my daughter out of the car. I looked up and saw the rock.

"What's that?" I asked Geneviève. The unusual geological feature shot straight up from the flat ground around it, a three-hundred-foot tall, phallic-looking spire of cream-colored limestone.

"C'est le Monolithe."

My stomach clenched as she said it. I vaguely recalled Philippe talking about le Monolithe, where they would climb today. I know the meaning of mono- and -lith. How could I not have put that together?

Could that be the same one where . . .

Surely Philippe wouldn't have . . .

Surely I hadn't agreed . . .

Words failed me, in both French and English. I was mesmerized and horrified at the same time, drawn toward it, as moviegoers at a horror movie are drawn to the gore and blood, knowing terrible things are going to happen but continuing to watch nonetheless.

The others were instantly forgotten. I hugged my jacket around me and walked, alone, to the base of le Monolithe. It loomed over me, blocking out the sun. It blocked out everything but my fear. Philippe and Alex were so high already that I couldn't make out their faces.

This was my own damn fault. I should have asked specific questions. Details. I'd just left everything up to Philippe. Never again. If my son lived through this—if *I* lived through it—I'd never make that mistake again.

But he had assured me that the climb was at Alex's ability level.

"Regardez!" (Look!)

People had been strolling the trails near the base of the climb, and they'd begun to notice the two little splotches of color high, high up on the side of the rock.

I kept walking around its base, slowly, my neck sore from craning upward.

Sound travels perfectly in the crisp alpine air. Alex's French was passable, but I could hear Philippe shouting all his directions in English. No doubt just to be safe. The irony didn't escape me. But that didn't make up for his incredible lack of judgment. What did I really know about Philippe's experience? How irresponsible was I to entrust Alex's life to someone I knew so little about?

The crowd that was gathering had also noticed the change of languages, the English directions.

"Ça, c'est pas des Francais!" (They aren't French!) Mumbling, a lot of head-shaking. *"Ils sont fous, ces Anglais!"* (The English are crazy!)

I kept walking silently around the monolith, trying to keep my son in sight, trying to understand why a boy, or a grown man, would risk everything to hang on the side of a rock like that, trust his life to a thin rope and a few metal bolts that could easily pull out of the rock, sending my son hurtling to the ground.

Bright sun filtered through the sparse, leafy canopy, casting shadows on the side of the relatively new limestone. Puffs of clouds came and went. My mind partitioned that off; I would admire the scenery some other time. I saw only my son, tiny, high, fragile, and yet, obviously, not.

The voices of the onlookers hummed behind me, punctuated by the dialogue going on over their heads. I could feel the exact moment they realized what was happening.

"That's not a man!" one shouted. "It's just a little boy!"

This seemed to touch a chord among them. More head-shaking.

"Where's that boy's mother?!" A woman's voice, bringing back our playground dramas of only a few years ago. "How could she allow that?!"

I waited for the nausea to pass.

Silence. Something in the small crowd had changed. They'd noticed I wasn't moving, wasn't talking. Eventually they muttered, shook their heads and left. New arrivals took their places. The crowd flowed, talked, but I just stood there, looking up.

I smiled, nodded to them, looked up again, pointed my head toward the climbers. *"Oui,"* I admitted, *"c'est mon fils."* (That's my son.)

My son. The one they were all watching, gasping about, cheering for. My son, the climber. The one I would watch with pride from a meadow, so many years later, as he and his friend Hans broke yet another speed record on El Capitan, in Yosemite. The one to scale El Capitan without rope—the only one to have done so. My son.

Poor Alex—we used to joke that until he was about four or so, he probably thought his name was "Alexander-NO!" It was the only way he ever heard it. Grammie, Grampie, his aunts, uncles, our friends, any adults who got to see him in action were always jumping up to catch, to protect, to prevent.

High up on the side of le Monolithe, no one told him "no!" Clinging to the limestone, Alex was in charge, in control. This was what he'd been waiting for. Born for.

I could see it in his smile when he and Philippe touched down at last amid cheers and applause. He'd tasted freedom. He'd conquered his first big climb.

I knew this was just the beginning.

eighteen

"**YOU GOOD TO FIND** your way down, Mom?" Alex asked me as he finished coiling his rope before attaching it to his back, like a pack. He was a Greek statue—pure, powerful, lean—silhouetted against the clear cyan sky.

At twenty-four, he climbed all the time, on real rock. Magazines were beginning to write about his feats. Today, that feat had been to lead Mom up a multipitch climb, our first together since that day at the climbing gym. Now, we were about to walk off the back of this four-hundred-foot mountain.

The repetitive motions of piling layers of rope up on his shoulders mesmerized me. He did that so fast! When I did it, the ends never matched up, and there was always a loop or an end left hanging on the ground. His was perfect.

We were standing on top of Lovers Leap, high above the meandering trail we had hiked on to get up to the base of our climb. Alex had offered to lead me up something interesting that day. For him, fun and easy. For me, a challenge that had stymied me several times and left my fingers and toes raw. But we'd both made it up all three pitches.

His question filled me with dread. Find my way down? By myself? I was still reeling from having climbed my way up. Following him down was the original plan.

"I don't know—"

"It's right over there." He pointed toward the northeast end of the formation, into the woods. "Can't miss the trail. Just follow it down and keep this," he gestured at the formation we were standing on top of, "on your left. You'll be fine."

I was still trying to process being alone up there and whether I could, indeed, find the trail back down on my own. Doubt was probably all over my face.

"I want to try down-climbing East Wall," he added—the 5.7, three-pitch route we had just come up.

The higher the number, the tougher the climb. The scale starts at 5.0, and for many years, 5.10 was the hardest climb out there. But then someone came along, someone like Alex, armed with better gear, or better, stickier shoes, better training, and they moved things up. Thinking that would be the end of it, they called the first new level 5.10a. The next, 5.10b. Now, all the 5.10s, 11s, 12s and onward are divided into four sublevels, a through d. The hardest one, right now, is 5.15d.

"Down-climbing?" I knew the words but didn't have a picture in mind of what it looked like. Alex had a rope, but his partner was leaving to find her way down an unknown trail. How could one down-climb without a partner? Maybe he was meeting someone . . . ?

While we talked, I started changing back into my shoes for the hike down.

"Yeah, it's easy," he continued. "I'll meet you down on the trail where we hiked in. Okay?"

He kept the rope as we parted ways, leaving me to wonder what he was going to do with it. Maybe he was meeting friends who were also climbing up here today. I didn't know enough about his life or about climbing to imagine all the possible scenarios. He was living the "dirtbag" life, living out of his van and climbing all the time. Already, he had driven the family van I'd given him into the ground and replaced it with a basic van of his own. I saw him when he stopped back home to restock, attend a family event, or just get from Point A to Point B within California. Today, I'd expected us to be together the whole day.

But as concerned as I was for him, I was equally concerned for myself. He'd made it sound so simple, so offhanded, that I hesitated to mention any of my fears; maybe he was right and it would, indeed, be simple. I would walk down the obvious trail, he and his partner, whoever it might be, would climb down, and all would be well.

When I got to the woods, where he'd pointed, there was nothing that I would have called a trail. I headed in the general direction I needed to go—down—stepping over roots, fallen tree trunks, rocks, holes, sticks. As crowded as it was though, the "trail" I was following was definitely clearer than the woods around it.

After a while, it dipped down into a small stream bed that had only a trickle of water, then followed the stream down the mountainside. Stepping carefully over wet, slippery rocks and muddy patches, holding an occasional branch or tree for balance, I wondered whether I had left the actual trail somewhere up higher. But it did seem to be going where I needed to go, in a general, roundabout kind of way, so I kept following it down and around.

Suddenly, the trail left the welcomed shade of the conifers, and I found myself on top of a wide expanse of granite slabs. They sloped downhill, like a series of wide, giant playground slides piled on top of each other. This couldn't be a trail.

Where had I lost it?

Damn it! He'd said to just follow the trail. He hadn't said anything about the trail ending, or petering out, or becoming a massive blank area. Or being a stream. This didn't fit any definition of trail that I knew.

As I considered my options for getting down, at the back of my mind, I was still trying to figure out what Alex had meant by down-climb. Or rather, I was trying hard to convince myself that what I knew it meant was wrong. Had to be wrong. Must be wrong. Just like this stupid trail must be wrong.

The angle of the slabs was so steep in sections that I didn't trust my feet to stick to it. At times they did. At times they didn't, and I shuffled down in baby steps, grabbing small bushes when they were available, or leaning back to rest one hand on a slab behind me. Here and there I sat and scooted down on my behind and my feet.

And then, there it was—a clear, well-defined trail again. Maybe this *was* the real trail. Maybe I just needed to relearn a lot of vocabulary to be a climber.

But I knew what *down* and *climb* meant. And I knew what my son loved. And I hadn't asked, hadn't objected. I'd just meekly followed his directions and let him go do what he needed to do.

Down-climb. Every profanity I knew whirled through my head. I'd had so much trouble getting *up* East Wall! That empty, blank section where I'd given up finding a handhold and almost decided to dyno, or jump for one—how could anyone down-climb that?!

The trail, recognizable now, wound through dense, leafy tree cover and around Lovers Leap, which I now duly kept on my left. I pounded along, stepping faster and faster where it was possible, running all imaginable scenarios through my mind. But only one fit.

I should've stopped him...

I should've said...

No.

I should've at least asked more questions...

No.

My stride got longer, faster, as I raced down toward the spot where he'd said I would find him, where we'd started hiking up to our climb.

Oh, please, God, please don't let that mean what I think it means...!

What kind of mother would let her son do something like that? My pace became a run. The small trail I'd been following joined the Pony Express Trail at the base of Lovers Leap wall. The one we'd hiked in on.

As I jumped out onto the main trail and out from under the trees, I saw them. Alex and a friend were standing close together, pointing upward, talking animatedly, and laughing.

He was down. Safe! Standing. Talking. He was okay. I tried to force myself to take a deep, deep breath, but only little gasps would come. I hoped they would erase some of the telltale signs of the emotions I'd been wrestling with all the way down.

My feet slowed to what I thought might be taken for a normal, nonchalant pace as I approached them.

"Oh, hey, Mom. You made it."

He introduced me to his friend, another climber named Andy. Young, lean, and lithe, like Alex. A bright yellow helmet hung off the top of his small backpack, and he was wearing a climbing harness, which was crowded with metal and nylon gear. The two young men spoke a language I was only beginning to learn, climbing vernacular, so I just hung back and listened.

I had guessed right. My son had just climbed down the route that we'd climbed up together, East Wall, with his rope firmly coiled on his back. Useless.

As their voices murmured in the background, my mind tried to process what I was feeling. Four hundred feet straight up. Vertical. I couldn't tear my eyes away from that wall. Humans can't do that, can they? Just scamper down something like that?

Without falling?

If I'd tried to say anything, the dam would surely have burst, so I said nothing, just stared, listened. Tried to think.

Why couldn't he have been this crazy about baseball? Football? Tennis? Something that plays out on the ground, where gravity isn't a factor. We'd been careening toward this point all our lives together, since I'd found him standing on top of the six-foot-high slide in our backyard at ten months old. The signs had been clear.

What would I do about it?

I was at one of those forks in life, when you glimpse how the rest is going to go. When you seem to have options, but you know you really don't. All you can choose is an outcome. Once that choice is made, nothing else matters.

Andy was openly, energetically impressed by what Alex had done. From the little I overheard, it was obvious that such a feat wasn't common. I wondered whether anyone had done it before, but couldn't force myself to ask. It didn't matter right now.

This clearly wasn't a onetime event. Alex had been climbing with purpose since he was about eleven. Over a decade of his life, although I knew little about it. I was as supportive as I could be, at home, but I knew that I wasn't really part of this passion of his. Climbing was all he talked about, when he talked at all—at home, he was usually a man of few words. But even reading between the lines, I could plainly see that climbing was everything to him.

Today was a step for him, nothing more. Toward what, I couldn't even begin to imagine—but I knew with absolute certainty that he would hurtle toward that future no matter what anyone else thought of it.

Right now, I had to decide whether I would be part of it. That was the outcome I had to embrace, or reject.

The road forked in front of me. If my fear for his safety or, even more drastically, disapproval was all that he saw, I knew Alex would start to include me less and less in his life. He cared for me, and that care would cause him to distance me from that side of him.

But there was no other side of him. Climbing was his life. And I wanted to be part of that life.

So I sucked it up. I reined it in. I took that deep breath, a real one this time. My life from now on was going to consist of a lot of deep, deep breaths.

"Cool, dude!" Andy said in a sort of summing up, as he and Alex high-fived and he set off down the trail. "Props, big-time! See ya 'round."

"Yeah." My son turned to me, flush with victory and satisfaction.

"So, Mom, wanna go climb something else?"

"Sure!"

And we did.

nineteen

LAUNDRY WAS WASHED AND hung, billowing in a sunny, delicate breeze in our yard. The Japanese maple that I'd planted a few years back stood straight next to the wrought-iron fence, its graceful branches growing in exactly the direction I'd hoped, shading our tiny, south-facing patio, which we'd never been able to use because of the unrelenting California sun. I'd always imagined having breakfast out there someday. Today, breakfast was already cleaned up and put away, and neither kid had complained about it. A rare occasion.

In fact, no one had complained about anything today. Almost lunchtime, and no one had argued about anything, no one had refused to do anything I'd requested—even the Japanese maple was spreading its lovely shade exactly where I wanted it. I stopped at the patio door to drink in the possibility, no, inevitability of a shady, welcoming patio filled with friends and a table laden with good food.

Back in the house, I noticed that Alex had picked up the Legos that had been strewn across the floor of the family room. After only one request. I stopped to process that for a moment. It felt unusually gratifying.

My article had gone in to the *Sacramento Bee* on time—early, even—and it looked as if I'd have time this afternoon to work on the short story for the Japanese magazine. I was having fun with that. Sun dappled the family room, spilling happily into the hallway. Spring in the Sacramento area is an explosion of floral color, beautiful and appreciated, even though one doesn't have to wade through months of snow and slush to get there. It was just beginning today. Yesterday, there had been a cold, sideways rain that left puddles dotted across the cement and made the sunshine appear even more brilliant in its many reflections.

By the time I had finished making lunch for the three of us—Charlie was away at a conference that weekend—everything was still going right.

All morning. As I walked through the hallway, I found myself smiling at the photos of my brother as a one-year-old.

That stopped me.

Something strange was going on. Today had been perfect, absolutely flawless, yet also completely ordinary. What was going on? Why did I feel this way? Sure, I felt rested. And my eyes didn't burn, as they usually did from the climate. Neither did my nose. That hadn't happened in a very, very long time. That was part of it.

And then it hit me. Almost made me double over.

Last night was the first night since before Alex was born that I'd slept a whole, uninterrupted night. My husband's snoring hadn't woken me as it did many times each night. I hadn't woken to the feeling I was suffocating, as I did when my nose shut down completely several times a night. Anguish hadn't kept me awake, wondering about Charlie, as it so often did.

Alex was fourteen. I could have felt this way, this outstanding, this amazingly happy, for fourteen years.

My hand went to my mouth to stifle the sob I felt rising in me. It poured out of my eyes anyway. I'd allowed Charlie to rob me of fourteen years of happiness, of comfort. Of civility. Of respect. Of feeling anything with him besides frustration and exhaustion. I would never get those years back.

And I had allowed this to go on so long out of ignorance. Even now, I didn't know what to do. Professional help was beyond our budget, and he wouldn't consider it anyway. Why would he want to? By not talking, he was in complete control. He did what he wanted, the way he wanted, when and where he wanted. Never explained, never discussed, never justified, never replied. Just proceeded with life as if he were alone. And he would no doubt continue to do so as long as I stayed.

But the reason I stayed was also the reason I had survived. My smile returned at the thought of the two kids at the other end of the hall. The kids who had kept me sane.

Charlie had delivered me into a nightmare, but he had also given me my two biggest reasons to be happy. It was impossible to imagine life without them. They were my wonderful, lifelong absolute.

He had given me more than that, too. With Charlie, I had learned so much about the world. He was the best wilderness teacher, the best introduction to the mountains and their world. Without him, I never would have lived in Japan or become familiar with so many Asian cultures. I wouldn't have explored Australia's outback. I might never have become a teacher of ESL or taught English to students all over the world.

Charlie was at the root of all those gifts. The price had been steep, though. And he was coming home in two days.

Today, an intense happiness, a glimmer of hope, had washed over me, wave after wave, all day long. I wanted to hold onto this feeling! How was I going to live through the remaining years, until both kids no longer needed me for all the millions of little assists that parents give their children, unnoticed, unasked for, unwanted (the children think), yet so essential to their happiness and well-being?

Today had given me the answer: I would simply endure. I would remember today and how good life could be. Because if I began to pull on one string in the tapestry that was my life, the whole picture would begin to unravel. *If I hadn't . . . then we wouldn't . . .* Those sorts of thoughts are far too dangerous. The whole years-long, decades-long weaving of my life with Charlie's had culminated in two wonderful beings who gave the tapestry all its colors and all its life. It would be drab and meaningless without them.

For them, for those colors and that life, I would endure.

. . . .

ONE HUNDRED AND THREE. The thermometer didn't lie: I was really sick. I needed to go to bed. The flu-like symptoms had me holding the walls as I walked down the hall to the bedroom. I couldn't stop shivering. Or vomiting.

Stasia had gone to a party that evening. She and all her friends weren't far, at someone's house a few miles away. There were parents there, and she'd likely call for a ride home before midnight. I wasn't going to make it till then.

Charlie was on the living room floor, reading and listening to music. Before stumbling down the hall, I asked him to wait for her call. The phone was on the breakfast counter, right next to where he lay on the floor in front of the stereo. He nodded, and I staggered off to bed.

My fever broke some time during the night, and I woke in the early morning feeling weak but no longer nauseated. When I reached the living room, in search of a cup of tea or some toast, Charlie was still on the floor, still reading.

"What time did Stasia get home?" I asked him.

"She didn't."

"What do you mean? Where'd she go?"

Shrug. "I don't know."

"What do you mean, you don't know? Didn't she call?"

Shrug.

Our innocent (I hoped) little fifteen-year-old daughter was out somewhere, all night, and he wasn't even curious. I looked at the telephone. It was blinking several times. Still walking weakly, gingerly, holding onto the counter, I punched the button.

"Hello? Mommy? Daddy? Can someone come pick me up? I'm at Karen's house and ready to come home. Hello?"

My heart broke. Charlie kept reading.

"Didn't you hear that?" I was having a hard time—harder than usual—accepting this scenario in my mind.

"I was listening to music. I had earphones on."

"You were supposed to be listening for your daughter to call so we could pick her up! You said you would!"

Shrug.

I punched the button again. The little light on the phone was still blinking.

"Hello? Is anyone home? Mommy? Daddy? They're talking about going to Freddie's house, and I don't want to go. I need to come home. Is anyone there?"

I couldn't believe what I was hearing.

"How many times did she call?"

No response.

I punched it again.

"Hello again. Never mind. I went to Freddie's house with everybody, and I'll just sleep here. I'll get home tomorrow morning some time."

I could hear the reproach in her sweet voice.

In my heart, I was grateful for my daughter's friends. I knew most of them, and they were all wonderful people I trusted. But I didn't know them all. I didn't know Freddie. Or why she didn't want to go to his house with them.

"Charlie, what did you do last night? You said you'd wait for Stasia to call!" Did I really expect an answer? "Even when I'm sick you can't . . . ?" I couldn't think of any way to say what needed to be said. It was way too late.

But this removed any doubt in my mind about ending our sham of a marriage. As unbearable as the situation was for me, this drove home the point that I had no options when it came to my children. I couldn't leave my young teenagers in the care of someone who would cover his ears and read, leaving his daughter stranded all night, and not even care to check the messages in the morning.

My fever was coming back.

. . . .

I WAS SITTING IN the living room when Charlie came back after three days of reading essays for the Educational Testing Service in the Bay Area. He walked in, in silence, went through his mail in the entryway, and, without once glancing in my direction, turned and went to change his clothes. Came out with a book in hand, sat down, and proceeded to read for the rest of the evening.

Not one word, all evening. Not even a glance in my direction. Even after all the years of being on the receiving end of his silent treatments, it still astonished me.

When people in his family died, he said nothing and did nothing to mark their passing in any way. No sign to note their mark on this earth or on him. No closure. Nothing.

I told Charlie the next morning, as he passed silently through the kitchen, that my father was in the hospital again. He looked at me, didn't say a word, turned, and kept going. So much for respect, love, or concern. Unfortunately, Alex was sitting there when it happened. What were my children going to learn from him?

twenty

TWO YEARS EARLIER, MY parents were at my brother's house in southern California for Christmas. They'd come out to escape the bitter winter in Pennsylvania and would stay until the weather improved. Snow, ice, and hail storms raged across the country, so it promised to be a long visit.

But then my mother got sick. She was already in a lot of pain, starting from when she was diagnosed with polio as a baby. In spite of that, and contrary to the predictions of her doctors, she'd had an almost normal life. By the time she got sick, though, we knew that as victims of polio aged, more and more muscles atrophied.

My mother was in her seventies. Various doctors had diagnosed her with extreme heartburn, or maybe a hiatal hernia, or had simply shaken their heads and wondered why she had such pain in her abdomen. They didn't discover the cancer that would take her life until just two months before she died. Not until it was too late.

She couldn't sit in the car long enough to get home to her own doctor. Too many days across the country, in unstable winter weather. Too many unknown conditions—steps, access, slippery walking weather—in motels along the way. She was in far too much pain to handle a week of jostling and struggling through the storms.

Charlie saved the day.

"I'll drive your car home," he offered while we were down there after Christmas. "You can fly home. Be there tomorrow."

We often attribute our own motivations to other people. Of course, we think, in that situation they would feel this way or that way, because that's how we would feel. Which is how Charlie inadvertently won over my father.

Charlie didn't like my parents. He was outwardly courteous to them, but I'm sure they knew. His eyes lit up, though, as he made his "noble" offer. He was going on a trip! He'd escape the drudgery of this winter vacation. He could get away from the pressure of all the jobs waiting for him in both our house and the rental house we owned. Instead, he'd travel.

"Are you sure?" my father probed. "Those storms look pretty bad." Every picture on TV showed cars and trucks at every possible angle scattered all over the sleet- and snow-covered highways.

"I'll be fine," Charlie insisted. Of course he would. He was leaving on an adventure. A challenging adventure, made far more so by all the severe weather. Nothing could be more exciting to him.

"It's a good car, and I have snow tires, but those storms look really bad—"

"I'll be fine, don't worry."

"Are you sure you want to do this?"

My father saw only the danger, only the sacrifice of offering to do this for someone else. A whole week on the road, in horrible winter weather! Sacrifice was my parents' mantra. Parents sacrificed for their children so they could have a better life. Young people sacrificed their time so they could get a good education and advance in life. Teachers sacrificed their lives, their time, their weekends so that their young charges could succeed in their futures. Everyone sacrificed something they loved during Lent, for the future of their immortal soul. Seen through that lens, Charlie was offering an enormous sacrifice, and my father's fear lent even more cachet, more honor and value, to it.

But Charlie had always belittled their sense of sacrifice and duty as ridiculously old-fashioned—its religious origins alone made it a source of derision—and just generally too stupid for words.

Conversely, when my parents first met Charlie and his whole family, their big concern was that they were, in their eyes, heathens. They didn't seem to believe in anything. No higher power, nothing greater than themselves. To my parents, that was unthinkable. Now Charlie's single act of sacrifice had redeemed him to them. As my mother got sicker over that long, long winter and eventually died, my father often repeated his profuse thanks, to Charlie, to me, to anyone who would listen.

"What would we have done?" he often asked later, any time the conversation came around to that horrible time. "She would have died in some hospital in California, among strangers!" The worst fate imaginable—prevented only by my husband's noble sacrifice.

Charlie had done the impossible, driven through horrible ice storms across Texas and the whole south, to arrive at their house in Pennsylvania in snow and ice in the middle of the night—a hero! A bona fide, supersacrificial, lifesaving hero.

I never did or said anything that would tarnish that view.

· · · · · · · · · ·

IN MARCH, ALMOST AT the end of that winter, my father called John and me. It was time to come see our mother one last time. It was that close.

As I prepared for my flight, I couldn't help but think about my mother's dream book.

When I was little, she loved to tell me about the book she was going to write someday. She would use all her experiences and write a novel.

How wonderful it must be, I remember thinking back then, each time she'd go on about it, to do something so magical. A book! Whenever she talked about it, her face would soften, lit up with some inner light that promised happiness, her eyes focused in another world where things like that could happen.

As I got older, I started to get impatient when she'd talk about it. Even then, I knew that to succeed at writing, you had to actually write. Not just talk about it.

My brother arrived in the afternoon, while my plane landed in Pennsylvania close to midnight. John met me at the airport in the numbing cold, and we drove straight to the hospital. It was too late for goodbyes. She was unconscious.

Later, around two in the morning, I knelt in the dark next to the low window in my parents' home that looked out over the empty street. I could see, almost hidden behind the fir trees in the church grounds, the statue of Mary gleaming as white as the snow that had just started swirling about in the wind. Without a sound, slowly, the trees turned white as well, and the streetlight faded, surrounded by a silvery, snowy halo. Even the mounds of dirty, gray slush that already filled the street gutters were turning pure white.

It's the perfect night to die, I thought. *Take her now.*

My mother died that morning. And her book died with her.

Her story, which no one would ever read, had cheered me and brought us a tiny bit closer when I was little. It had given her dreams—beautiful, happy dreams that would have made a wonderful legacy.

It was one of the only times she'd allow closeness between us, a fact I'd always mourned, especially when I had my own children and discovered how rich, how rewarding, that closeness could be. Her story had been our bond, our little secret that was going to make us all happy. How I would have loved to read that story! But my mother had let it wither and die.

I vowed that night to never let my children feel such regret. I would see to it that my voice was shared. I would write my story. They would know who I was, and that I loved them, and life.

And then it will be the perfect night to die.

. . . .

"THERE, MOM." ALEX POINTED to the right of the narrow road we were driving on, toward a small brown sign. I slowed the rental car and turned into the driveway in an area of the Mohonk Preserve that Alex called the Gunks. We parked in the visitors center parking area, under a thick canopy of old trees.

The family reunion in eastern Pennsylvania wasn't until tomorrow. Alex, seventeen, and I were the only ones in our family free this summer to fly east. So, after visiting cousins in Vermont, we decided to detour to the Shawangunk Mountains, near New Paltz, New York, on our way to the reunion.

I'd heard the excitement in Alex's voice when, after studying the map, he asked if we could stop at the Gunks. My cousins in New York State had often mentioned the Gunks when I was little. So I knew that people went climbing there. Whatever that meant.

Alex, of course, knew exactly what that meant and was excited to see a climbing area he knew only by reputation. With one glance around the unfamiliar, wooded hillside surrounding the small parking area, he seemed to know exactly where to go. I didn't question it, just marveled and followed him. My son, not quite a man but definitely not a kid anymore, knew things that I didn't. As a mother, this fascinated me; as a person, this awed me.

We scrambled for about ten minutes up a rugged, zigzagging system of rocks that had been placed, like steps, to enable visitors to reach a flat path on the far side of the parking area and much higher than the visitors center. The steep, black earth on both sides of the steps smelled rich and damp, and by the time we reached the wide path, I was also damp from the exertion. There, we walked along an escarpment, a rock wall that rose next to the path about three stories high. In both directions along the path, the wall extended as far as we could see.

The rock wall loomed over us, dark but for the sun that filtered through the maples, oaks, beech, and other large canopy trees I couldn't name. This was my homeland, where I'd grown up, yet I knew more about the trees and shrubs of California than I did about those here. Somehow that seemed wrong, like something I needed to correct.

We didn't see anyone as we walked. The midday sun lit up the breaks in the leafy roof, alternately blinding and warm, or cool and fresh. From the path, we could see a lush valley that extended back toward the Hudson River. An occasional bark rose from one of the farms or houses scattered among the deep green. A curving stream glistened here and there.

I turned back to talk to Alex. He wasn't walking next to me anymore. I looked around for a second, back along the path where we'd been, up ahead—and noticed a movement, up high, above where I stood. Alex was on the rock, moving along with me but about a story and a half higher up the wall.

"Alex!" I exclaimed. "Get down from there!"

As the words left my mouth, I flashed back to Rockaway Beach, on Long Island. I'm five years old, knee-deep in the ocean, watching the waves carefully so I could get in the water. Aunt Helen is shouting, "Don't go too far!" Uncle Bob is shouting, "Be careful! Look out!"

I never learned to swim there.

"I'm fine, Mom," Alex said. He sounded much calmer than I felt. I squinted up at him. He did look fine. Completely at ease.

"Kind of high, no?"

He was following a crack, or small ledge—very small—that angled upward, so he was getting higher and higher as we kept going.

"I'm fine. This is really easy."

It didn't look easy to me. In fact, it looked really hard. And dangerous. But I wasn't a rock climber yet.

I was about to say *be careful*, but realized the absolute, ridiculous futility of that. Of course he'd be careful; that was him up there, his life, his safety. He was making the decisions here, not me. We both knew that.

Free-solo was not a term I knew back then. I had no idea what he was capable of, how comfortable the rock was to him. I only knew the signals my eyes sent me. Powerful, danger-fraught signals.

I had seen him at the climbing gym and at a few indoor climbing competitions. Thirty, forty feet high, rubber floor, lots of people to catch him if he fell, first-aid kits handy. Pretty controlled conditions. Here, the consequences were wildly different. Hard, sharp rock. Great distances. No one around. No access to transportation if anything happened. I was thinking like a mom.

I forced myself, just for a moment, to think like a climber.

"You sure?"

"I'm fine, Mom."

I looked down the path to see where we were heading. A large, tall deciduous tree had grown out from the base of the rock wall and straight up alongside it for twenty or thirty feet. Only a few minutes away. I knew those would be long, long minutes.

"Okay, I'll meet you on the ground, down by that tree." I gestured toward it.

"Okay." And he was off, scampering like a happy squirrel across the forbidding terrain.

No, I corrected myself, *across the rocks*. It only looked forbidding from my vantage point. Clearly not from his.

That was the first of many compromises I would make with myself over the next few years. When I'd been trying to figure out my nonfunctional marriage, my kids had helped keep me centered and sane. Now, faced with my son's growing love of high places, I had only my own resources to fall back on for resilience, for stability.

I'd soon find out just how resilient living with Charlie had made me.

twenty-one

I JAMMED MY HAND into the crack in the granite, made a fist, and pulled back. I could hear rock grind against bone. *That can't be good,* I thought. But at almost three hundred feet above the ground, I'd use anything I could find to keep my body on the wall.

My other hand yanked a piece of protective gear off my harness, the shiny blue #3 cam that I thought I'd never need for this climb. *Way too big,* I'd thought when I was on the ground looking up. *There are no huge cracks like that up there.*

Why did I want to lead this climb so badly and risk both our lives? Was this really the place for an almost-sixty-year-old woman who'd spent her life in front of a classroom? If I fell the three hundred feet back down to the start of this climb, it'd be my own stupid fault. Fine: "She got what she deserved." But I didn't want to take my son with me!

After our triumph on East Wall—mine in fighting my way up it for the first time, and his at having down-climbed it—Alex and I had hiked around the formation next to Lovers Leap, called the Hogsback, to another three-pitch climb: Knapsack Crack. I had asked him several times, whenever he came home from an adventure, whether he thought I could someday lead a climb. Be the first one up, on the sharp end of the rope. Put in the protection. Belay the second climber up behind me.

An awesome responsibility, it was dawning on me. I'd had no idea.

I plunged the blue #3 cam, like a huge metal molly bolt, into a crack in the rock and released the spring to lodge it firmly against both sides of the crack. I pulled on it, twisted it, did everything I could to be sure it would hold my weight if I fell. I attached the rope to it. We were safe . . . for now. Then I remembered to breathe.

I wasn't sure whether to be glad or furious that Alex had let me do this. Yes, I'd pestered him about it. But he knew what was up here, whereas

I had been climbing for less than a year. What was he thinking? I liked to believe he just trusted my judgment and was convinced I could do it.

Oh, God, I hope he's right!

I tested each piece as I placed it, hung on some of them, full body weight, just to be absolutely sure it would hold a fall. But beginners make mistakes. I'd read about that in all the climbing magazines.

My heart was pounding so hard I couldn't hear anything else. Didn't he care that we'd both die, or get really hurt, if I messed this up?!

I could see exactly what would happen if we came off the wall. We'd bounce three hundred feet straight down, hitting every jutting-out granite block along the way, to the ledge where we started climbing ... and then keep bouncing all the way down to the noisy river, several more hundred feet below. Unless, of course, we were impaled first on one of the many trees and stumps.

When I glanced down, midpitch, and saw Alex starting to climb far below me, while I was still moving, I realized with a throat-clenching jolt what he'd meant by "simul-climbing." As with down-climbing, I'd understood the word when he'd suggested it, but not necessarily how it would play out on the rock. Simultaneous meant that both of us were moving at the same time. If I fell, and my gear held, fine. But if I fell and any of my gear pulled out, then my mistake could take him down with me. Someday I'd have to find out from him why he wanted to simul-climb this. But the excitement of finally climbing on the sharp end had blocked out simple, clear thoughts like that beforehand.

Alex wasn't going to fall; he's a professional. This was easy for him. Babysitting. But I'd never placed gear before. The higher I got above my last piece, the harder my hands shook.

With my free hand I reached up and grabbed the top of a block that had a small lip. It felt solid, like I wouldn't slide off it ... but it was high over my head—and I've never been able to do a pull-up.

I yanked my fist out of my first-ever "hand jam," as I learned to call it that day. The bones were okay, but the back of my hand was raw, bloody red where the skin had been scraped away. I blew on it, hard, licked it to remove the tiny specks of dirt and debris that stuck to it, and kept climbing. One more handhold. One foot a tiny bit higher. Step up. Breathe.

I had climbed this route before, as Alex knew. I knew I could climb it. But lead climbing changes the stakes completely.

Fear can kill. It can make you do stupid things, rob you of your normally clear judgment. I've read the publications. *Accidents in North American Climbing*—a riveting, terrifying page-turner that details the climbing accidents that take place each year. Most fatal climbing accidents are due to human error. Someone on lead gets scared as weather worsens or night falls and does something stupid, something they know not to do under normal conditions. And people die.

A quick glance at my harness—only three pieces of gear left! I'd used all the others to get to this point, but I was still far from the top of the climb. I'd need all three of them to make the anchor at the top, to hold the rope as Alex followed me up.

I talked to myself, repeatedly told myself as matter-of-factly as I could that there was no option: I had to finish the climb without placing any more gear. That's called "running it out." I tried to ignore the common-sense thought that I was much too new at this to be running anything out. After all, if I'd had any common sense, I wouldn't be in this situation.

I looked up. More rocks. Blocky rocks to squeeze between, or climb over, or try to go around. I couldn't even tell where the actual summit was, but I knew that if I could make it as far as the small trees that I could almost see now, I'd be safe. We'd be safe. I'd be able to stop shaking, stop thinking.

But I didn't want to stop thinking. Thinking, and more importantly, thinking clearly would get me to the summit. It would prove something. I'm not sure what, but it was the reason I was up here, I was sure of that.

As the route approached the summit, it got lower-angled, more rounded rather than straight up. I leaned in, hugged the rock, and told myself that I'd just reduced the pull of gravity by a tiny bit. I had to keep reminding myself to breathe. I stepped up, pulled hard, stepped up again.

And again. And reached the stunted, gnarled pine at the summit. It was the most beautiful tree I'd ever seen. It allowed me to start breathing regularly again.

I took the three pieces of gear off my harness, one by one, and made a perfect three-point anchor, thinking it through clearly, my hands calm and still now.

I allowed myself a smile, finally, looked around, and checked the gear and the knots one last time before belaying Alex up. He didn't need the rope. He could run up this wall without it. But the job of the lead climber is to make a solid anchor and belay her partner up. So I did.

"Way to go, Mom," he said as he topped out just a minute or so behind me. "Nice work."

We slapped a vigorous high-five. I knew he would never have any clue how hard that had been for me. And he was a kid. I wasn't.

As Mom, my main job, for years, had been to anticipate all the bad things that could happen and protect against them. To put soft rubber corners on the coffee table so the baby wouldn't hit his head. To put locks on the drawers so the kids couldn't find the medicines or sharp knives. To put childproof locks on the cabinets so they wouldn't pull out the ceramic cups and break them and cut themselves.

If I had a squad car, it would say in big letters on the side: Anticipate and protect. That's what I'd done, for years. Now I was supposed to just turn that off?

I had started working on shutting down my urge to protect a few months ago, when my tribe started taking me outdoor climbing. I was still working at it, and probably would be for a very, very long time. But for now, I shook out my hands and arms and relaxed into an oh-so-satisfied smile as I surveyed the view from the climb I had just led.

I'd won. I'd beaten the fear and done what had scared me more than I've ever been scared before.

This was no doubt a tiny fraction of what my son must feel, out here, up here, on his climbing days. Just a fraction, but enough to make me glad that I had kept my peace earlier that morning. I recognized a bit of the gleam in Andy's smile as he'd congratulated my son on having down-climbed East Wall. What a feat! An accomplishment that other climbers surely dream about.

My tiny lead on the Hogsback had been my own triumph. Today was a milestone: I'd graduated from standing in a classroom, and sitting at a computer, to the first level of an internship in climbing, an endeavor that was so much more than just a sport. I was only now beginning to understand its depth, and the extraordinariness of what my son did, every day.

Choices. I'd made some right ones today. I'd backed off when I'd needed to, and in doing so had grown closer to my son than I could have in any other way. I would do whatever was needed to keep it that way.

In many ways, my two climbs today had been a marathon. When Stasia ran thirty-five miles in green forest, or biked a thousand through the desert or over mountains, she dipped into the same well I had. Like her brother when he did things on rock that other people only dream about.

I could go home or choose to run one more block.

I could insist on my role as Mom or I could let him lead me up the wall.

Life is all about choices.

twenty-two

ON ONE OF THE many weekends when Charlie was at a conference, my brother and sister-in-law came for a visit from San Diego. Since we lived about ten hours from each other, visits were rare. This time, they were on their way somewhere else, farther north than Sacramento, and stayed one night. We hugged before they went on their way north in the morning, after a breakfast punctuated by laughs and family reminiscences—then I was able to reflect on the strange day we'd just spent together.

It had been a thoroughly pleasant, relaxing visit, maybe for the first time since I'd gotten married. No treading on eggshells, as I usually had to do. We all actually had a good time together. Even the kids seemed to enjoy their company—a surprise for all of us.

I knew it was because Charlie was away. Without him, there was no one to run interference for. No one to make excuses for. No one to try to please despite the "obvious obnoxiousness" of the guests. Now that there was such distance between us, I was becoming more and more aware of how rigid he was. Anyone who didn't do things the way he thought they should be done wasn't worthy of his interest or courtesy.

How had I not seen it before? Love truly is blind. Now that love wasn't part of the equation anymore, it was sadly clear. And clearly sad.

• • • • • • • • •

I CAREFULLY PLACED THE red glass ball that said *Wesołych Świąt*, "Merry Christmas" in Polish, on the tree I had just assembled. All day, I'd been slowly transforming our ordinary house into a fantasy of keepsakes that evoked an emotional Christmas landscape. I would happily dwell there for several weeks, among the decades-old, brightly colored ornaments of real glass, the photo ornaments the kids made in first and second grade, outlined in red felt, my great-aunt's hand-stitched table-cloth with green pine trees across a field of red, my mother's homemade throws, my grandmother's antique, gold-edged ceramic table serving set, covered in a web of tiny, fine lines. Some of them were beautiful, some were undoubtedly a bit worse for wear from the past few decades. But their beauty, for me, lay mostly in their emotional value.

The phone rang as I picked up the next glass ball. I put it back and picked up the phone. My brother had said he'd call.

John was going skiing with his family at Mammoth, in the Sierra Nevada, for Christmas. He would ski every day, some days with his daughter. His wife, Maria, would make hot chocolate in the RV they parked right near the ski lift. Or she would enjoy the lodge and its comforts, maybe ski a day or two with them.

It sounded like a Currier and Ives fairy-tale Christmas. I made the appropriate speech sounds as I listened, trying hard not to feel what I was feeling. Knowing that was small of me, but feeling it nonetheless. It wasn't jealousy, exactly. Jealousy is a bad thing, evil. This wasn't that—I was sincerely happy for him. And overwhelmingly sad for me. For us.

"So what are you and Charlie doing this holiday?" John asked finally.

"Oh, the usual," I mumbled. "Dinner at his parents', and probably the Christmas Day dinner here at our house. The usual big crowd."

He knew our teaching schedule; he was a teacher, too. He knew we'd be home for a couple weeks.

"What do you and Charlie like to do for fun?"

Time stood still. Not sure for how long.

"For fun?"

More time standing still as I thought, searched, tried, desperately sought . . .

I must have mumbled something, because John continued talking, telling me about their holiday. I was, after all, highly skilled in making people think everything was fine. I'd had decades of practice at it.

Fun.

My mind raced as I tried to recall the last time we'd had fun together, just the two of us. Australia. Camping through the outback. Japan. Visiting Odawara Castle during cherry blossom festivities had been fun.

Exploring Hakone, near Mount Fuji, together. Before that, camping and hiking southern California's deserts, or the Sierra Nevada. Joshua Tree.

But never at home. Never with people, except his nuclear family. Always on the road.

John and I were still chatting. I half-listened. Christmas offers lots of opportunities to be with people, chances to talk, to have fun.

Our fun had always been traveling. Then we settled down, with a house and kids. And that was that. The end of life.

I'd thought I'd been in love with Charlie, way back when. Maybe it wasn't that at all. Maybe I'd fallen in love with California. With my new world. My new freedom. Or maybe a bit of all of those.

I had surely been bowled over by love, back then. Twitterpated. Dizzy with it, awed, unable to think clearly. His voice had captivated me first, on the phone. When we met, his hands drew my gaze. The artist in me had always been fascinated by hands, and his were beautiful, strong, capable. His eyes were pools of India ink, and he exuded a calmness I had rarely encountered, and envied. He was gorgeous, a hunk. I'd never known a hunk before. And a hunk who wanted me! Could I possibly have been any happier? He talked and talked, about places I could only imagine, and that we later went to see together. To camp. To hike. To explore.

He was my new landscape, and I was in love with the exploration. Had there ever been any more than that between us? John—and probably everyone else—assumed we were living a normal married life. Having fun doing things together, talking about things together. I'd been that good at pretending.

John and I continued our nice, normal conversation, but I don't remember any of it. Only his question. And the anguish in my heart.

Life as I'd known it for too many years had just changed. I'd pretended, excused, protected everyone for long enough. The kids were old enough. Strong enough. They would probably handle it better than I would. I was done.

It was over.

twenty-three

A BLUR. THAT'S THE only word for our lives during the years we spent slogging toward divorce. The kids were not kids anymore: Alex graduated from high school while we were thrashing things out and became, somewhat half-heartedly, an engineering student at UC Berkeley—although later I discovered that his main source of education was a beautiful climbing crag within the city. And Stasia had her own adult life in Portland, ten hours north of Sacramento, as a teacher and in a committed relationship. She seemed happy, and still had the power to transmit joy to everyone around her.

I don't remember when I finally mustered the courage to tell Charlie I wanted a divorce. We had been communicating exclusively by email for quite a while already, so naturally that was where I spelled it out for him. He was incredulous. He was about to lose his housekeeper, his maid, and his cook. To whom he never spoke.

He didn't see the problem with that.

The housekeeper, the maid, and the cook did.

I was going to be in Poland, on a teaching scholarship, during the summer that I wanted to tell the kids, and then in New York and Pennsylvania to visit my father on the way back. Charlie and Alex were flying to a wedding in Michigan from California. Stasia was going to fly from Portland and join them. Or something like that. Whenever we all had time off from school, our lives were a constant coming-and-going—flying, driving, moving. So things were already a blur even before divorce was added to the equation.

As the logistics worked out, both kids would be with Charlie while I was in Poland and on the East Coast. So he would tell them. I just hoped he wouldn't skew the story too badly. He really didn't see any problem in our marriage. I hoped they would see through that version, to the truth. They had, after all, been keen observers through it all.

By the time the dust had settled from all of our respective trips that summer, and everyone had found their way back to California and Oregon, unpacked and repacked and gone back to school and work and life, it just seemed . . . somehow surreal to bring up the end of our non-marriage, with the kids or with anyone. Charlie and I had never had a life together. Nothing was really going to change, neither in Alex and Stasia's lives nor in ours. I would still see him occasionally at the community college where we both taught, and he would continue to spend evenings there, or sometimes nights, as he often had, and go on even more conference trips. All without a word. Business as usual.

And I knew that both kids would still see their dad. Nothing would change there, either. He would always be their fun guy, always ready for a trip, anywhere, for any reason, anytime. Nothing would deter him from that. Charlie would continue to drive Alex to climbing competitions all over California and take the kids camping whenever he could.

We had no lawyers. They cost a lot of money, and Charlie had never changed his tune about that. We made all the decisions about the divorce ourselves, by email, and used a legal group to put it all together into the appropriate paperwork and file it. Every decision took forever. But he was living in his mother's house by this time, so it didn't matter to me how long it all took. He was gone, and I was beginning to savor the peace that had settled over my home.

Stasia took it upon herself to be my cheering section, for which I'll always be grateful. Not verbally—none of us talked about this invisible, behind-the-scenes change. We all knew that the only thing that was changing was the quality of my life—that was probably what she was thinking about when she made my music CDs.

We had always shared a love of classical music, but this was different. She burned two CDs for me of popular modern songs, and every one had the same theme: overcoming. Being strong. Making it on one's own. Crafting beginnings out of endings. "I Will Survive" by Gloria Gaynor. "Red Rubber Ball" by Paul Simon. In Stasia's world, the morning sun was always shining like a red rubber ball.

And the one that always stopped me in my tracks, whether I was driving somewhere or cleaning the house or working on an article: "The Way" by Fastball.

Like the people in the song, Charlie had always craved the highway; his shadow was always "wandering off somewhere."

Where, indeed, was he going without knowing the way? But he never needed to know the way, never needed a destination—just *going* was the goal. Being on the road. Being free. Whether it was from the obsessiveness of autism or just an overwhelming, all-consuming fanaticism, he was only happy when he was on the road, or planning to be. When we'd settled down, with children and all the accruing responsibilities, his life had ended.

I was giving him back his freedom. Finally.

. . . .

"MRS. HONNOLD?"

I juggled the phone to my other shoulder as I continued typing. The bills had to be paid, no matter who was on the phone. I was expecting a call-back from one of the several companies I was working with to clean up the aftermath of our three-year-long divorce process. Things were still far from the way I needed them to be, financially, physically, emotionally. But the hardest part was over. It had officially ended only a month ago, but I still answered to my married name. It was easier than explaining.

"Yes?"

"Is your husband Charles Honnold?"

That got my attention. I stopped typing.

"Yes?" Had I overlooked some paperwork? Some detail? Was he changing his mind about something? Usually he contacted me by email, himself, about those.

"This is the Phoenix airport."

I glanced at the clock. Charlie was on his way home from a conference in Washington, DC. His plane was due in to Sacramento in a few hours. Had he missed his flight?

The plane got in on time, but he wasn't on it. He was, as the lady on the phone informed me, at the hospital in Phoenix, where the paramedics had taken him. If I wanted more information, I needed to call the hospital.

I did. While I waited, I thought about the irony. One month divorced—would I still be expected to care for him if it was really serious? I didn't know. I'd never been divorced before. Never been close to anyone who'd been divorced. When it came down to it, except for the paperwork, I really didn't know anything at all about divorce.

Finally, after several wait times, a doctor came on the line. I didn't catch his name. It was indeed serious: a heart attack. Even through his thick East Asian accent, I could make out those words.

"How is he?"

Hemming and hawing, clearing of throat. Never a good sign. "It is not good."

"Is he conscious? Can he talk to me?" *Come on, Doc. Give me something solid.*

"I am afraid he is dead."

I didn't breathe for a few moments. That couldn't be right. How could he be dead? We just got divorced. He was coming home from DC to move the rest of his stuff out of the house.

Divorced. Dead.

· · · · · · · · · ·

"MRS. HONNOLD?"

I almost dropped the phone. His voice had the same sincere, forcibly kind intonation I'd just heard a few days ago from the doctor in Phoenix. Where Charlie had sprinted for his last airplane connection. It felt like years ago.

This call came early in the morning. I could come to the Sacramento airport today, the man said, and pick up the box of ashes that had just arrived from Phoenix.

No one I asked would go with me. My friends, who had helped me through the long, long years of anguish, indecision, and eventual divorce, wouldn't come for this. I don't think I really expected anyone to come along for such a grim ride. Would I, if I were the friend? I wasn't sure.

No, this was something one did alone. Especially after living alone together for over two decades. Even after our non-marriage had finally ended.

Today I was as alone as I'd ever been while we were married. That seemed appropriate. I glanced at the empty passenger seat of my little car. I had covered the seat with a towel before I left the house, just in case. In case of what, I had no idea. I'd never done this before. I had no clue what to expect.

What does a shippable box of ashes look like? Ashes I could picture, but my mind refused to come up with any solid guesses about what kind of receptacle would hold them. I'd never known anyone who'd been cremated; it wasn't permitted in the world I'd grown up in. I'd been to dozens of funerals as a child, and they always ended at the cemetery, with the casket lowered into the ground. We often threw spadefuls of dirt onto the casket as it lay there, several feet below us, the clods of earth making dull thumps as they hit the shiny box. Ashes made no sound at all. They swirled around in the breeze and eventually became part of the earth, somewhere. In movies, Grandpa's ashes always sat in an urn on the mantelpiece. Would they give me an urn, at the airport? A cardboard box? A plastic bag?

The man at the counter was expecting me. He had very kind eyes, and when he spoke I had the impression that he wanted to give me a hug. But there was that counter.

"Mrs. Honnold?"

I nodded, and he disappeared behind a wall with an open doorway. He returned a few seconds later holding a small box wrapped in a shiny, dark-colored ribbon. It looked like a very demurely wrapped birthday present, big enough to contain a small, round teapot.

I just stared at it. My mind had shut down. For a few fractured moments, I didn't know where I was, or why I was there. He held the box out a little closer to me and asked a question. I think I said something in reply. Finally, I reached out with both hands.

I was braced for the weight of a metal urn or tiny casket, but it weighed nothing at all. The box almost went sailing across the room. Apparently the only thing inside was ashes, probably in plastic.

Back in the parking lot, I placed the box on the towel I'd laid on the seat next to me. I got in the car and put the key in the ignition, but didn't turn it. I sat there, not moving, both hands on the wheel. Shallow breaths made ragged little sighs in the quiet car as the windshield fogged over. I'd been hollowed out, gutted, and there was nothing left to feel anything with. Or maybe there was just so much to feel, so much emotion unexpressed after all these decades, that the overload had shut me down.

I was in a weird time warp. Time, and events, seemed to move differently. After so many years of not knowing what to feel, how to deal with the unending silence, anger, frustration, confusion, I found myself stranded in a never-never land, an empty universe that I didn't know how to fill.

I'd been gutted, and my emotional well had gone dry. I was dying of thirst.

The sun hadn't moved much across the building when I finally drove away, so I probably sat there only a few moments, maybe minutes. But it was a lifetime.

I drove the same freeway on the way home. I made the same driving motions, I saw the same vast shopping center and empty fields and light rail station and equestrian center that I always did on the way home.

Nothing was the same, though.

Just when I thought I understood the new landscape I had planned for so carefully, for so long, everything changed. Now I would be moving through a wilderness I'd never been in before, alone, with no map, no guide.

I arrived home—at the house that was now *my* home, mine alone—and put the box on the large kitchen counter, where I always put everything as I came in from the garage. That wasn't where it belonged. I looked around the open space that encompassed the kitchen, living room, family room, and dining room.

His ashes did not belong on my piano. Definitely not in the dining room, either. Should they be the centerpiece on the one table in the living room, until his family decided what to do with them? Maybe if it had been his space, but it had always been mine.

My eyes settled on the fireplace insert. That was where he belonged, for now. The fireplace had always been his. He loved making fires and tending them. It was a skill he'd been proud of. For many years, instead of having the heater serviced—which cost money—he kept a fire going all winter with free wood from the family cabin at Tahoe. It made most of the house unlivable for me for six months of every year. He loved it, though.

I placed the box on the flat top of the cast iron fireplace insert. Definitely where he belonged, at least until his family took him somewhere else. I already knew there wouldn't be a funeral—many members of his family had died since I'd joined the family, but there had never been a funeral. No wakes. No ceremony of any kind. No closure, until months or years later, when the family would get together to remember the person who had died.

So I knew that box might sit there for a long time.

As I stepped back, I thought that this would be an appropriate time for a few tears. Still, no tears came. I had already shed them all. The well was empty, and that feeling of emptiness would no doubt stay with me for a while.

This wasn't the ending to our marriage that I'd envisioned.

twenty-four

"LOOK! THERE!"

I pointed toward the woods to the right of the car as I braked slowly to a stop. Gary and I were in Yosemite National Park for a climbing trip, driving down to Yosemite Valley to join our friends from Sacramento.

"See them?"

Gary was from Ireland and had never seen a bear, not even in a zoo. As if on cue, three adult-sized bears lumbered out of the lower woods to the right, ran across the road in front of us, and scampered up into the higher woods to the left. Each was a different color, varying from tawny gold to deep, dark chocolate brown.

"Wow!" His gaze followed them as I started driving again. "But they're not black."

I laughed. "They're black bears. That's the name. The species, or something, not the color. They can be a lot of different colors."

"Wow."

Every time I drove into the park, no matter who I was with, Yosemite would gradually overwhelm me. After hours of highway driving, the fragrance of the forest would take me by surprise as soon as I opened my window at the entry kiosk on the park's edge. It made me want to get out of the car, right there, to walk and breathe it in, let it heal me, cure me of my city and suburban living.

The road into Yosemite National Park started in California's flat, fertile Central Valley, at sea level, winding up to about six thousand feet past occasional towns, endless fields of dry grass and cattle, and rolling hills. Then it snaked down again through a tunnel of greenery, heading down into Yosemite Valley, which sits at about four thousand feet.

Sun cut through stands of valley oaks, live oaks and black oaks, buckeye and laurel in blinding swaths of brilliant yellow-green. Occasional cottonwoods towered and swayed, dwarfing the other trees. Filtered sunlight from the conifers sent sparkling spotlights onto the chaparral underbrush. The vast woods around me always seemed magical, probably because I knew what awaited me in the Valley.

The first time Charlie and I drove into Yosemite, I'd had no idea what to expect. When the road twisted and a vista opened up of a vast rock wall on the other side of the river below us, I asked, excited, "Is that it?"

He just shook his head with a smile and kept driving. Then the road turned again, and the vista expanded to include an even more impressive wall across the river, with some land, that I could have called a valley, far below us.

"Is that it?"

He shook his head again and kept driving.

"You'll know it when you see it," he told me.

He had said the same thing when we'd driven into Sequoia National Park to see the redwoods. He was right then, and he was right about this. As the road made one more twist and we entered Yosemite Valley, I gasped.

He slowed as I craned my neck and my whole body to see both sides at once.

El Capitan dominated the north side of the narrow valley, a wall of creamy, smooth granite that rose straight from the flat valley floor three thousand feet into the sky, uninterrupted. It awed. Humbled. Stunned.

The entire long, skinny valley was lined with granite walls, buttresses, and towers, most of them nearly as high—but not as straight—as El Cap. At the far end of the Valley rose the feature that I recognized from photographs in magazines and calendars: Half Dome.

I couldn't say anything that first time. Or any time after that. Yosemite Valley has always had that effect on me. Its massiveness gives it a power that precludes mere mundane conversation. It is a cathedral, the most impressive cathedral imaginable. Ordinary chatter dies out in its presence.

As Gary and I continued into the park, I wondered if I was up to the challenge of rock climbing in a valley that contained a wall of such majesty. I knew that was silly—Yosemite offers all kinds of climbing, in all grades and levels of difficulty. Nonetheless, it was daunting to drive past The Captain and on toward our campsite. It made one feel tiny. Insignificant.

The insignificance I felt looking up at El Cap was compounded by my memories of Charlie from that first trip, and the ones after. Like the time he'd left me stranded, as it started to snow, two thousand feet above the Valley. It was a beautiful, clear day when we'd started out, and I'd followed Charlie and his family to the top of the Mist Trail.

"I'll go that way and see if that's the trail we want," Charlie said as he left me waiting on top. The rest of his family had scattered down different trails and apparently knew where they would meet later. Yosemite was like their own backyard to them. But I had no idea where I was or where to go. They all knew that.

He never came back for me.

As the snow thickened, I headed down alone, as fast as I dared on the slick, wet trail. An hour and a half later, as the snow clouds passed, I reached the trailhead in the sunny valley. Charlie and his siblings and some of their children were sitting in the afternoon sun, laughing, talking happily about the grand adventure they'd all just had together. More memories for next time. No one seemed to notice that I'd come down alone. A lot later.

My adventure hadn't been so grand. Many "family adventures" would play out that way, over the years, and I'd sworn I would never go back to the places where I'd suffered from Charlie's neglect. A thick, ever-growing patina of anger and frustration can mar the beauty of a landscape—even one as splendid as Yosemite—like fresh, creamy milk suddenly gone sour.

Yet, under all the layers of things left unsaid, of insults unintended, of actions unnoticed, nature can still heal. I was beginning to discover my own resilience as I revisited these places with my new climbing friends. They were helping me replace the old, harsh memories with happy ones. Many of the places I thought Charlie had forever ruined for me—Tahoe, Joshua Tree, so many!—had begun to blossom again, in a fresh, new palette. My acquired distaste for those places had nothing to do with the place.

Six of us were camping and climbing this weekend. We all walked into the area east of El Capitan called the Manure Pile Buttress, a name that hearkened back to the early days of the Valley. Then, the only transportation into Yosemite was by horse, and they used to pile the manure here, far from the campgrounds.

As we all walked to the wall, about ten minutes from the road, there was a rustling in the woods near the trail. At the base of a tree, in dappled sunlight, a bear had been napping. Our voices and the clinking of the gear on our harnesses had awakened him from his midday siesta.

We were all bear-savvy, since our main climbing places were in the Sierra Nevada. But in Yosemite, the bears were protected and had no fear of humans. And they loved human food. Signs all over the park warned people of the dangers this posed. Bears who became too accustomed to "breaking and entering" often had to be relocated, sometimes even put down. Killed. For our mistakes.

This one must have suspected lunch was on its way, as he came shuffling out to see what he could rustle up. We threw rocks at him, shook our gear and just made lots of noise—none of which had the slightest effect. He was used to humans and their noise. And he'd been banded—his ear sported a large yellow card marked #90, indicating that he'd already had encounters with humans that put him on the watch list.

So we stashed our lunches and other scented items in the bear box provided by the park, a vault-like steel box with a bear-proof latch, assuming we'd seen the last of Bear #90.

Then we spread out as three pairs, to climb. Michelle and Gary worked on the corner climb, a route called After Six, at the extreme left of the long wall. I was belaying Michael on After Seven, a few feet to the right of them. A few more feet to the right, Steve was belaying George up a thin crack climb called Nutcracker.

Suddenly, I heard George's voice from about twenty feet up his climb. "Dierdre! Bear!"

I looked down. It was right next to me! Our sleepy bear had spotted my water bottle, clipped to the outside of my small backpack, which leaned against my leg as I belayed so I could sip if I needed to. I had read that bears in Yosemite could recognize water bottles and sometimes tore into cars where one was visible. I'd sort of half-believed it.

But here he was, right at my leg. He grabbed my water bottle in his teeth, and bottle and attached backpack went flying off into the woods.

I was belaying. Michael's safety, even his life, was in my hands. There was absolutely nothing I could do. George's partner lowered him quickly off his climb, and they both chased the bear, and my backpack, shouting and throwing stones. They just bounced off the bear's thick fur. George picked up some hefty rocks, as big as he could toss. Some must have gotten the bear's attention; after a minute or so, George came back out of the woods carrying my pack. My favorite water bottle now had six large punctures through which all of my water was pouring out.

Resigned, we emptied all our pockets and stashed our snacks into the bear box, keeping only what we needed to munch on as we worked hard out in the sun. A plastic bag of homemade, organic trail mix was tucked safely into the pocket of my hoodie, and I dipped into it now and then when I was able.

Michael had almost finished the pitch, but it was a demanding crack climb that required a lot of finger strength and trusting one's feet to just stick to the rock face. He was climbing cautiously, thoughtfully, and the sun was blazing down on our side of the Valley.

Sweating, I managed to shrug out of my hoodie while he was at a good, solid stance. I dropped it on top of my foot and we continued our work.

Suddenly, George's voice, again: "Dierdre! Bear!"

Bear #90 was observant, and patient. He grabbed my hoodie off my foot and ran into the woods—where George chased him, again. I was still linked to Michael and couldn't move.

From the corner of my eye, I saw him shake the jacket, flipping it back and forth like a dog does with a floppy toy. Finally, the prize— my trail mix—flew out of the pocket, and the bear ran after it. George, my champion again, brought back my jacket, covered in bear slobber but otherwise okay.

That night, we made a campfire. Someone in our group had brought a box of wood, and they'd coaxed it into a raging fire in the stone firepit at the center of our group campsite. We had each brought a small chair of some sort, folding lawn chairs, beach chairs, collapsible canvas chairs. One person sat on a stump that was next to the firepit. Michelle had brought small individual bottles of red wine and I'd brought Kahlua, which we drank out of little plastic cups.

It was magic. Our faces were hidden by the darkness, occasionally illuminated for a few seconds as an ember fell or the fire flashed. A spark would fly up, then disappear into the velvety blackness like a firefly on a summer night. Voices floated out of the dark, disembodied, but made gentle by the crackling of the fire and the softness of the night. Each of us was a mere shape, indistinguishable from the towering conifers that surrounded us or the shadows cast by the flickering fire.

They had no idea, these people, these new friends of mine, what a miracle they'd wrought. That I could be here, in Yosemite, laughing and forgetting—that alone would have been unimaginable just a few years ago, when my so-called married life was ending. As we hunched around the fire and exchanged stories in the dark, about ourselves, our families, our past, and our adventures, now and then I would remember where we were. And where I'd been, not so long before.

We kept shifting our little chairs around as thick smoke billowed up from the firepit. Acrid, stinging smoke, sharp enough to bring tears to anyone's eyes. It was a fine excuse. I used it, over and over.

twenty-five

THE TIMING OF CHARLIE'S death had a strange effect: death superseded divorce. No one ever mentioned the divorce after he died, and I felt like a widow at fifty-three. Both of my children were grown and lived on their own, so the divorce hadn't affected their daily lives. When we spoke on the phone, it was mostly about estate documents they needed to sign or mail or otherwise deal with, and all the paperwork and details and decisions we had to make every day. I could tell they were okay, but there was little time for more. I had two full-time jobs, teaching during the day and estate work all evening. Life went on. But not the same life.

In August, just weeks after his dad's death, Alex asked me what I would think if he didn't go back to UC Berkeley, where he had just finished his freshman year.

Berkeley—what parent would not want their child to get a diploma from Berkeley? When it came to books and learning and education, my kids grew up with some heady examples. Three of their four grandparents had been teachers. Their parents were both teachers. We'd all been both impressed and delighted when Alex had gotten his acceptance letter from Berkeley.

Things were different now, though. I could only guess how the loss of his father had changed his thinking about staying in school. But I knew Alex had been less than happy during his first year there. When he came home, instead of talking about his classes, or his friends, or his life there, he described in detail the bouldering crags in the Berkeley area. And, as I would learn much later, he often went to the crags instead of attending classes. I was beginning to understand that, in his world, climbing would always win out.

So his question was twofold: How would I feel if he dropped out, at least for a semester, and went climbing full-time?

What could I say? There was only one answer to such a question. I gave him my blessing, and my Chevy van, and off he went to make history.

• • • • • • • • • •

WHEN CHARLIE'S FATHER HAD died, just a few years earlier, I'd lost a good friend and my favorite flute duet partner. Within a year, still processing that as I filled out forms and wrote extensive divorce documents in Latinate legalese in the evenings, I lost my own father. He was the last remaining connection to my past in New York. Laying him to rest next to my mother in the beautiful, sylvan cemetery outside Hazleton, Pennsylvania, marked the end of any vague dreams I might have had about returning to the East Coast, to my home. From all of Charlie's complaints about money, and knowing how paltry my own pension was going to be, I knew I'd never be able to afford to live there again.

Still, I couldn't bring myself to sell my father's house in Hazleton. It was only a couple of hours away from the border with New York, and my mother's father had built it, with his own hands. The house was a direct connection to everything I'd left behind and the old country my grandparents had left behind them. It could be home. I might never be able to afford New York City again, but I might, someday, go back to live in Hazleton, at least temporarily. It was Escape Plan B.

With the children grown, I no longer needed the capacity of our large family van, so three days before my new semester was to start, I left Hazleton driving my father's little red sedan to Sacramento, alone. To do it in three days, I had to drive about a thousand miles each day. I did it on autopilot, alert to the road but nothing else. Numb. As I turned, finally, onto my street, in a stupor of fatigue, I saw the driveway piled high with Charlie's things. He was moving out.

The following summer, when he died with the ink barely dry on our divorce papers, I was in the throes of remodeling the Pennsylvania house from across the country. I didn't have a cell phone to make the job easier, and Hazleton was the kind of place where people stayed in their house for generations, so there were no property managers. I had to do it all myself.

In the divorce, I'd also wound up with our rental house, which Charlie had neglected to the point that the city had condemned it. The living room was open to the sky. Squatters had lived in it. Every day, I worked with handymen and suppliers, on both coasts—by phone in Pennsylvania, and in person in West Sac—after my eight- or nine-hour teaching day at the college, to repair both homes.

After Charlie's death, there was no time to seek help of any kind. I wrote all the estate documents. The kids were too young, his mother was too old, so I became the default executor. Wills. Trusts. Enough paperwork to wipe out a small forest. More hours spent on that than on my teaching job. There was no time to grieve. No one helped. No one knew. I saw no one, talked to no one but the kids and my students, as I moved numbly from task to task.

Every evening, sometimes quite late, when I could no longer focus on what I was writing for some estate document, I would take Juno, our Alaskan sled dog, out for a long walk through the silent suburban neighborhood. Our stride became my mantra—wordless, exhausting, relentless enough to deaden some of the emotional fallout and numbing pain. With Juno's long legs and body built for pulling, it usually turned into a trot, for me, and then often a run. I ran to escape.

One evening I came home breathless to find Alex, stocking up between trips.

"Alex!" I called out as the dog and I staggered through the door. "Guess what!"

"What?" He slouched into the kitchen as I caught my breath.

"I just ran a mile with Juno!"

Growing up, I'd lived more than twenty years in a house completely filled with smoke from my father's nonstop cigars and my mother's "self-defense" cigarettes. I could be the poster child for secondhand smoke. For my entire life, anything more energetic than sitting had left me breathless. I knew Alex couldn't understand the import of that simple statement, but I had to tell someone.

He shrugged. "Cool. If you can do one, then you can do one and a half." Another bite of cookie.

His logic was unassailable. I considered it. Then I checked the map, routed some future walks. Several evenings later, I came home and announced with some pride, "Juno and I just ran a mile and a half!"

"Cool." Another shrug. "If you can do a mile and a half, you can do two." And on and on.

Stasia was already a runner, ticking off miles and miles each week. She's crazy about it, and gets crazy if she can't do it for a while. But she and her brother were in their twenties. I couldn't even remember my twenties.

The feeling of accomplishment was seductive. I found myself looking at the clock in the evening, hoping it was late enough and I'd done enough work that I could go run. Running became my escape, something I did just for me. Maybe the *only* thing. It reminded me of when I was young, riding off on my bicycle to explore neighborhoods. Time had no meaning when I was on such a quest. Now, no matter how exhausted I felt in the evening, I would tie on my running shoes and go play. Explore. Be me again, not someone else's requirement of me.

But that was only part of it. All my life, I had known that running was out of the question. My lungs couldn't support it. Now, to my amazement, I had jogged along with Juno for a mile—a whole mile! Unthinkable. And then more. And more. I couldn't argue with my son's logic: if I could do one, or two, who knew what else I could do? The possibilities teased me, seduced me, dazed me. I wanted, needed to find out just how far this could go.

When I reached three miles, I started exploring online. What did runners really do? I knew the city closed down streets now and then to accommodate them. I knew that special running shoes cost a lot more than sneakers. That was about all I knew.

Then I saw an ad for the Run to Feed the Hungry, to help the local food bank for Thanksgiving. It sounded outrageous at 6.2 miles, or 10K. Sure, I ran around the neighborhood with the dog a little, but . . . *six miles*?!

It was for a good cause, though, whether I actually ran the mileage or not. So I paid my money and signed up. To train, Juno and I ran every evening, and once in a while, I'd go running and leave her home (she stopped a lot). I ran in jeans and sweats, knowing nothing yet about what "real" runners wore. There was no structure to my training. I just ran, whenever I could. As far as I could. I always ran alone, late at night. Since I'd signed up for a six-mile race, I tried to increase my distance, little by little, but the deciding factor in this, like in everything else in my life, was how much work I'd gotten done. And how long I could stay awake.

Alex was going to Spain for a climbing competition and returning the evening before the run. When I mentioned that I'd signed up for it, he said, "Sign me up, too."

Really? The morning after a twelve-hour transatlantic flight? I would have been a sleepless wreck after that. But he seemed sure. I signed him up.

Thanksgiving morning. I put on my jeans, my T-shirt, flannel, and big white sneakers (I really didn't know anything about running). I woke Alex, who had slept in his clothes after his late-night arrival, and off we went to my very first road race.

I had grave misgivings when I saw the huge crowd assembled at the start. Thousands of people! High-energy runners, *real* runners, in their spandex and turkey costumes—all of them clearly better informed and better prepared than I was.

Trepidation battled with excitement as the gun went off. It was unlike anything I'd ever experienced. All those people, out there to help people, by the thousands, single-minded and—judging from the music, the media, and the sheer energy in the crowd—clearly having a blast.

I wasn't.

For me, it was anything but fun. I struggled to breathe. I'd never done anything physically competitive in my life. I was out of my element.

Alex ran alongside me and told me about Spain. As I gasped for air, trying to ignore the pain that was taking over my body—this was harder than just jogging at night, and I was pushing myself to go faster than I ever had—he talked about his adventures there. I couldn't imagine how he could breathe enough to talk while running! His tales were fascinating. He entertained me with descriptions and anecdotes as he ran backwards in front of me, alongside me, in circles around me, occasionally zigging or zagging up someone's lawn.

He became my single focus as I forced myself to keep going. When I knew I couldn't manage one more step, I'd look at Alex and try to picture him having those adventures. When I needed to stop, he stopped with me, carried my sweaty shirt, kept up his recounting of the week before. I made myself concentrate on his words.

When we passed the halfway mark, I still didn't think I'd finish. I can't count how many times I might have stopped, had my attention not been on something besides my physical misery. My throat hurt from trying so hard to suck in air. Blisters were forming painfully on my bunion and my heel. A jagged pain was building in my knee. I was too hot. The waistband of my jeans was digging into me. My sunglasses kept sliding down my nose. This was not fun.

Somewhere between the fourth and fifth mile, something changed. I was still following Alex's voice, and I still couldn't breathe enough, but my own footfall began to replace all the other sounds around me. Suddenly, with a clarity I'd never felt before, I knew I'd finish.

When I glimpsed the huge red and white sign at the finish, several blocks ahead, I realized my life had just taken a major turn. I had no idea where it was going to lead, but I knew there was no going back. An unexpected, overwhelming feeling of power gripped me, forced tears down my cheeks.

I was a runner! A fifty-five-year-old beginning runner. I'd have to buy some real runner's clothes, some good shoes. There was probably— certainly—lots more I needed to know. But I'd just learned the most important thing: I could do this. In my mind, I could hear Stasia's sweet voice cheering me on. I knew a tiny bit of what she knew. It drove me forward.

I was teetering on the brink of an enormous crevasse, a gaping, yawning endlessness filled with possibilities. All I needed was the courage to leap into it. If I could do that, what else might I be able to do someday?

I'll never know for sure whether I would have finished if I hadn't had Alex's voice to follow the whole 6.2 miles. Maybe the stubbornness—or is it tenacity?—I've since discovered as a rock climber would have surfaced then and pushed me to the finish line. I'll never know.

But I'll always be grateful for that voice.

twenty-six

"HELLO, MOTHER?"

A groggy, mumbling voice—my son's voice, almost unrecognizable—on the phone. He sounded like he was on drugs, or drunk, but I knew he never did either of those. His climbing buddies called him The Monk.

"Where am I? Why am I all covered in blood?"

I caught the phone as it fell out of one hand.

"Alex?" I tried to breathe enough to keep talking. All I could hear was my heart pounding. "Where are you?" Hadn't he just asked *me* that? "Are you okay?" How could he be okay, covered in blood?

"Yeah..." He hesitated. "W-Where am I?"

My mind was racing, but I slowed down my voice so he could concentrate on it. He wasn't drugged, or drunk. He was covered in blood. Possibilities flashed through my whirling brain.

"Aren't you on Tallac?"

He had left the night before, Christmas night, so he could try out his late dad's new snowshoes on an ascent of Mount Tallac, which rises prominently above South Lake Tahoe to almost ten thousand feet.

"Oh. Yeah."

"Are you still on Tallac now?"

"Yeah. I guess I fell..."

His voice kept fading out, whether from atmospheric conditions or his own condition. Not a good sign, either way.

As I tried to keep him talking and find out the extent of his injuries, I ran down the hall with the old landline handset clutched in my hand. I charged into his sister's room, where she lay sleeping off the festivities from Christmas day.

"Stasia!" I woke her and handed her the phone as she rubbed her droopy eyes. "It's Alex. He's hurt. Keep him talking. Don't let him fall asleep!"

As fast as I could grab my brand-new, one-day-old cell phone, I dialed 911 and explained what was happening. After some background noise, they transferred my call to Search and Rescue (SAR) at South Lake Tahoe.

While I waited, the serendipity made me shake: Alex had been able to call me only because I'd given cell phones to all three of us for Christmas, the day before. With my son always out somewhere climbing mountains, I thought he should have one so he could call for help, or call me.

I never imagined he'd put it to use the very next day.

"Ask him what he sees to the west," a metallic voice commanded on my cell phone. They were trying to locate him.

I relayed the question to Stasia, who was fully awake now, and she asked her brother. Apparently he was aware enough to look around, think clearly, and reply coherently. We continued this four-way attempt at locating him for quite some time, back and forth across two phone lines, until I heard men mumbling on the SAR line that they knew where he was.

They'd found him! I forced myself to breathe again. He was near the top of Tallac, coherent enough to help, and we'd ascertained that he could walk, but he could only use one arm and was shivering from the cold such that he had trouble talking through his chattering teeth. And he was still covered in blood—liquid, on a nine-thousand-plus-foot mountain in the winter snow. He was slowly freezing to death. I gripped the phone a little harder as I listened to the far-off conversations among the SAR guys.

I heard a discussion, muted and hurried, about a helicopter. Yes! They would fly up there, pick him up, and all would be well.

Both Stasia and I talked with Alex while SAR organized and planned. We chatted about his climb before his fall, about the weather, about his injuries. I knew it was imperative to keep him awake. If he fell asleep or lost consciousness he would certainly freeze to death.

At our home in the Sacramento Valley, the sky was dark and threatening, true midwinter weather. On the mountain, Alex described the same kind of conditions, but much colder and much, much windier. Days later, we would read about the fierce storm that had blown down from Alaska on Christmas night. Its violent winds had probably blown Alex off the peak of Tallac early that morning. And would freeze him solid if the helicopter didn't get there soon.

More muted chatter. Then: The helicopter couldn't land in the wild winds. It was too heavy. I clutched the little phone harder. Now they were talking about skiing up to get him.

Skiing! Up Tallac!? They would get to his frozen body the next day, or that evening!

Hope became despair. I watched Stasia chat with her brother, all smiles as they shared the story of his adventure, and thought, *She may never see her brother alive again.* I wondered whether she had thought of that, but decided she was probably too young for that to occur to her. Who thinks about imminent death at twenty-one?

I did, though. I couldn't imagine life without either of them, and I didn't want my sweet little girl to have to suffer through the loss of her brother. I had learned a lot about my survival skills over the last couple of decades—I knew life would go on. But I didn't want that lesson forced on her so young. They had both lost their dad, suddenly, that year. I told the universe that that was enough for them to endure right now.

My son was freezing to death, but his sister kept him laughing and talking while SAR worked hard to find an alternative. And they did.

The helicopter used by the California Highway Patrol was smaller and much lighter. The consensus among the metallic chatter I could overhear was that it might be able to land. It wasn't far away, somewhere in the Sierra Nevada already. Before long, it arrived in the vicinity where Alex was stranded.

The helicopter bounced wildly in the wind, but was finally able to land. Once SAR told me that, they had more important things to do than chat on the phone. I later learned that once they landed, they'd had to cut off Alex's brand-new down parka, which was soaked in blood, and that he had blacked out once or twice during the procedure. If he'd stayed conscious, they would have flown him to South Lake Tahoe, just at the bottom of Tallac. But head wounds are tricky, and all indicators pointed to concussion. So they took him instead to the trauma center at the hospital in Reno, Nevada, on the opposite side of the lake.

Stasia and I packed a bag with some of his clothes and snacks, as fast as we could, and headed up Interstate 80 to Reno. Once we got on the road, though, I realized what day it was: the day after Christmas, when everyone rushes to the stores to exchange or return their gifts. Every exit off the freeway had a line of cars backed up onto the road, slowing traffic down. Wherever the road passed a shopping center or mall, we slowed to twenty or thirty miles per hour.

Didn't they know my baby was being sewn back together and waiting for me to get there? We alternated between twenty and eighty miles an hour, the three hours passing in a blur, not of speed but of imagination. When we finally got to the trauma center, they directed us to Alex's room. I hesitated just a second before pushing the dark green curtain aside.

Alex was on a gurney with the back raised, so he was half-sitting, half-reclining. His right arm was in a cast from fingers to elbow. His eyes were ringed with black and purple. Between them rose a monstrous purple-and-yellow lump the size of a baseball. He was smiling and laughing at something the doctor behind him had just said. They could have been having coffee together.

The floor of this "coffee shop" was slick with blood, which made walking tricky—and strewn everywhere, stuck in all the streaks and puddles of dark red, were tiny down feathers. At that moment, the doctor was carefully picking feathers out of the wound on the back of Alex's head, so it could be sutured. They danced around the air, settling and then bouncing again, finally sticking to some surface or gliding to the sticky floor.

She had already done that for all of his other wounds, and his broken arm. Once she'd finished suturing his head—he also had a concussion—he could go home, she said.

Go home? I couldn't believe she meant it. It was hard to look at him—his face was a mass of cuts, scratches, and that horrible purple-and-yellow lump between his brows. His arm was in a cast, his hair matted and bloody, despite having been cleaned up. And he had sutures in several parts of his body. Go home? Was this person really a doctor?

But once she finished sewing up the back of his head, Alex sat up, slid off the gurney, and was, indeed, ready to head home with us. He was, if not cheerful, still in full possession of his powers of observation and his caustic wit. He and the doctor knew someone in common and had been chatting like old friends, making jokes as if he hadn't just been airlifted off a wintry mountain.

Which, thankfully, gave me time to regroup emotionally. I'd held it together to keep him awake on the phone, but I still hadn't recovered from the shock. Heck, I still hadn't recovered from the phone call about his dad, just a few months ago. And then I'd held it together for his sister, while I'd prepared myself for the worst—I had no idea what to expect when we arrived at the trauma center. Apparently the damage was all external and relatively superficial.

In retrospect, his handling of it was probably predictable. Over the last few years, his exploits had proven, at least in part, the unusual extent of Alex's endurance. He can go and go, far beyond most people's physical limits. In 2015, over a decade after the Tallac event, he and Colin Haley pushed their limits to get back to the town of El Chaltén from the Cerro Torre, a series of peaks they'd gone to climb. A severe storm forced them to rappel down the opposite side of the mountain chain from where they'd gone up—and away from all their gear, food, and supplies. Once down, they had to walk (using that term loosely) for twenty more hours, postholing through snow and in harsh conditions. After having climbed the Cerro earlier that day.

If I'd known then what I know now about his extreme endurance, that day in 2004 would have been far less terrifying.

As we headed to the car, around ten o'clock in the evening, I finally got around to wondering about the van. Alex had parked it in the woods and slept in it, to get a very early-morning start. Was that just today? It seemed like a lifetime ago.

I asked him if he thought he could find it in the dark, after all he'd been through. The storm that had blown him off Tallac wasn't over, and winter up here lasted months. If we didn't bring the van home with us, it might freeze into the forest floor and not be movable until spring. Some moonlight peeked through the towering pines and firs, but the sides of the road were pitch black, which didn't bode well for finding anything in the woods.

"Sure." His reply was quick. Of course he could. Knowing what I know now about his abilities, I wouldn't have even asked. But he was only nineteen then, a kid.

So instead of taking the interstate home, we followed the two-lane highway down the west side of Lake Tahoe. Normally, the shores of the lake teem with tourists. But this was the night after Christmas, and not a light shone anywhere. We couldn't find any food or drinks; nothing was open. A bit of caffeine would have been really welcome . . . or some real food for someone who had spent the whole day on the mountainside in the snow and freezing wind. Something to supplement the snacks we'd brought him. But there was nothing.

Alex directed us to a small road that wound uphill, away from the lakeside highway. Then onto an even tinier road, then off the pavement and onto a trail into the woods. I was beginning to wonder if he was as aware as he'd seemed.

I knew we couldn't drive much farther into the woods. The storm that had blown him off Mount Tallac had been raging all day, depositing ice in shaded places. My little Dodge sedan was skimming and dancing over the rough, slippery terrain. Alex pointed deeper into the woods.

"There."

The forest-green van nestled among the trees, dwarfed by huge conifers, surrounded by ice. The freely spinning wheels of my car made it obvious we weren't going to get any closer. I stopped, hoping I could back out of the tiny, icy clearing. I had no chains for my little car. I never drove up to Tahoe in the winter, so I hadn't thought of that when we were packing up in a whirlwind to get Alex.

Stasia took the keys from her brother. She would try to rescue the van, even though she had no experience driving in ice or snow. I probably should have done it myself, but right then, I needed to stay with Alex. I rolled down my window to try to defog the windshield a bit, and we watched her skate gingerly across the forty or so feet, holding onto branches, sometimes flailing her arms to stay upright. In another situation, it might have been comical.

The van's engine started quickly, and she let it warm up for a few moments. Then slowly, expertly, as if she did it all the time, Stasia rocked the heavy van back and forth, back and forth. The tires were sunken into the ice. It took a few minutes, a lot of crunching, but she worked it free and slowly rolled out and stopped right in front of my car.

After we congratulated her on her new skills, Alex got into the van with his sister at the wheel, and I followed them home, close behind.

If this day had been an action movie, this would have been the quiet after the car chase, when everything's over and the protagonist, finally realizing what just happened, breaks down into sobs. The ride down Highway 50, which twists and turns along the American River on its way down to the Sacramento Valley, reflected the peripatetic state of my mind. No sobs, though—I was driving, at night, on a twisty mountain road, and couldn't afford that.

The coincidences were staggering. When my cell phone company sent the new phones for Christmas presents, they sent the wrong ones. I had ordered plain and simple phones, for emergencies, but they'd sent the latest technology in flip-phones, with little screens and the ability to take photos. When I complained, the cell phone company explained that they could never get them exchanged in time for the holidays, so I could have them for the same price as the ones I'd ordered.

Alex had the cell phone with him, he said, only because he wanted to take pictures of the wintry mountains for his friends. Hiking Tallac in the winter . . . no one in his right mind did that! The photos would be unique. If he'd had the phone I'd originally ordered, it would have sat in the van waiting for him. As he froze to death.

And he had to have a place to carry the phone. If the brand-new parka that I'd given him for his outdoor adventures hadn't had a special cell-phone pocket inside the front flap, he said he wouldn't have carried the phone up with him. The protected downy pocket probably also saved the phone from being smashed as he rolled down the mountain, and again when he was stopped by a pile of boulders—the same ones that connected with his forehead.

And his brand-new phone worked perfectly during a winter storm at almost ten thousand feet. Not only did it work, but he'd had the presence of mind, despite his injuries, the blood, the freezing wind—all that—to call me. Despite the fact that he'd just regained consciousness and was disoriented.

As I followed their van down from the mountains, I shook with the serendipity of it. If not for each one of those tiny details—so many could have so easily not happened!—he would have frozen to death up on Tallac. They wouldn't have found his body until spring.

Serendipity. Coincidence. Luck. Angels. Call it what you will, some force or power I couldn't comprehend was hard at work that day.

As we settled in to our warm, peaceful, uneventful house late that night, Alex chided me for the big mistake in my handling of the whole thing.

"You shouldn't have called 911," he insisted. "I could've walked down myself. And I could've driven myself home," he said, gesturing with the cast on his arm.

He was probably right. He probably could have done all those things. The world has had ample proof of the superfeats Alex is capable of.

But he did black out—twice—while the Search and Rescue crew was prepping him for his ride in the helicopter. He might have been able to drive, but if he'd blacked out while driving, he might have been killed or killed someone else. But a nineteen-year-old doesn't think that way.

Mom, however, does—and he lived to complain about it.

· · · · · · · · · ·

WHEN STASIA ASKED ME to drive her to Napa for her first marathon, I took my own running gear with me. I'd only been running—jogging, really, I didn't think of it as *real* running—for a few months, but had figured out that I needed real running shoes, and maybe some clothes that didn't chafe or get soaked with sweat. Since I had running gear and we were going to a marathon, I tossed it in the car, thinking that maybe I'd jog a little while I waited for her.

The idea of running 26.2 miles didn't register in my brain. At that distance, you could probably run across the whole country of Liechtenstein. The entire principality of Monaco. Closer to home, 26.2 miles went through five cities, from Folsom all the way to Sacramento—the course of the California International Marathon.

Unthinkable.

In junior high school, Stasia had talked and talked about the teacher she had who was going to run a marathon. I didn't know exactly what that meant, only that the city would shut down many of our streets that day. It all seemed unnecessary, just to allow a bunch of people to go running. Couldn't they just run on their own? To Stasia, though, it was clearly an inspiration. Her teacher, a young woman, was going to run right past the store we always went to, just a few blocks away, so Stasia was going to go wait for her and cheer her on.

Now I remembered how excited she got that day. And I felt it again, for this upcoming race. My daughter was going to run so far that ordinary people found it extraordinary!

The day of the marathon was gray, cold, windy, and wet. But Stasia, who was by then teaching in Portland, Oregon, was very experienced at running in the rain. Her enthusiasm for running in general, rain or not, was contagious. She was excited that her mom was running, too, and anytime I visited her, we would drive to one of Portland's many lush green parks and go running together. Well, not really "together." She would run whatever distance and speed she needed to fulfill her week's running plan, while I ran or jogged as much as I could, and we would meet at the end. Sometimes our paths would cross in the woods or trails, and her beaming smile would flash a brief beacon of encouragement.

"Go, Mommy!" she would shout as we passed each other, and I would run a little faster, a little lighter.

But running in cold rain hindered my already meager running skills. After I dropped her off at the northern end of the Napa Valley, I drove back down to the south end and parked.

The route I'd planned for myself was about six miles long. Doable, no matter how slowly I ran—I hate running in the rain—and I'd still be able to see Stasia when she ran in at the finish.

I had watched her get ready that morning. Special tights that don't bind, even in the rain, special socks that don't ride up or down, special shoes that don't weigh anything, a special lightweight, water-resistant jacket—it seemed that everything she owned was different and special. I had no clue what some of it was for.

After my run, I changed into dry shoes, got my umbrella out of the car, and walked to the finish line. As I watched the runners come in, I thought about the carbo-load dinner the night before. There were speeches, stories, lots of laughter. But I was an outsider. It was like going to someone else's house for the holidays, where everyone talks about past events and silly family anecdotes and all you can do is smile and pretend you belong. Now, as I stood in the pouring rain, I began to realize how far outside their circle I was. My daughter had just done something that I couldn't even begin to comprehend.

But I wanted to! I wanted to feel the depth of joy that I saw on their faces, even those contorted in pain, as they realized they'd finished. I wanted to know what that kind of determination felt like. Why they did this. Why she did this.

As we drove home—when she wasn't dozing—I listened to some of her impressions of the race and her experience. Just a few comments, nothing deep—it was clear she was still processing it herself. But to have done something that hard, a feat that required that much processing, seemed to me mysterious, inspiring, and amazingly tempting.

The next week, I signed up for the California International Marathon, the race from Folsom to Sacramento. To friends who asked, I said that, well, yes, I'd signed up . . . but who knew if I was actually going to do it? But *I* knew.

As I began to train, I told myself that I wasn't going to waste all that money. It costs a lot of money to run in a marathon—another surprise. But it had nothing to do with money. I knew I had to do this. My heart clamored to feel what it was like to be one of those runners I'd watched come in to the finish line, some walking or stumbling, blood trickling down the front of a few of the men's shirts, tears canceled out by amazed grins.

I scheduled in training runs, even though my job-and-a-quarter at the college, writing, and running the household single-handedly left no time. And the death of my father, my last parent, had left a gaping hole in my heart. Tying my running shoes became a symbolic act. I was girding myself against life. With those shoes, I could do anything.

Running is balance, and in my out-of-balance life it was something I could control. I made charts. I ran on a schedule, and began leaving the tired, old dog at home. As I ran, I could forget all the emotional pain, the frustration, the wasted years. Life seemed intent on stopping me. While I ran, my good friend died in a freak accident. My dog died. A lifelong friend's twenty-year-old son took his own life. Numb, I continued to run.

. . . .

THAT DECEMBER, WHEN I started running my first marathon in Folsom, I still didn't quite believe that I belonged there. I was fifty-six, and everyone I saw around me, stamping and stretching and getting ready for this grueling day, was young. A lot younger than me. But I'd been training for about twenty weeks and was pretty sure I was going to finish. Fairly sure. But I still had misgivings. I was just a jogger. I was out there to have fun. If I finished at all, it would be at the back of the pack, with the grandmothers. Maybe they would find me still jogging in as they swept the course afterward. The runners all around me, stamping and flexing and stretching as we waited in the predawn winter chill on the hill in Folsom, all looked like serious runners. I was sure I didn't.

They all looked like they had a real, quantifiable goal. I was just out there to see whether I could do this. The few I talked with had already done a marathon; they knew they could finish.

The beginning, maybe the first quarter, of the California International Marathon is downhill. I thought that was great planning. I flew, and the running seemed effortless. I remember grinning as I sped through Orangevale. I was running a marathon! I was even passing other runners, a big surprise. But gradually, the course flattened out and the running became work.

At mile three of the marathon, I began to suffocate. I immediately thought of my irregular heart—a lifelong problem—before I realized I just wasn't sucking in enough air through my tears. They poured down my throat, my face, a complete surprise.

As I pounded out the mindless rhythm and struggled to keep breathing, bits of things I'd read about grieving and mourning flashed through my mind. True, I'd never had time for either. But what did that have to do with running?

A few miles farther, I noticed something oddly familiar about the wide avenue we were on. Could this be the same street I always took to go shopping, to the bank, to work? It looked different. It took a few more miles before it struck me: without cars, filled only with people and their soft footfalls, the busy, traffic-filled road I knew had been transformed. The trees that lined it swooshed in the breeze and offered a birdsong background for the heavy breathing and cheers that surrounded me.

After we crossed the river and entered Sacramento, I was forced to dig much deeper. Up to that point, I'd counted my progress in cities. Whole cities! They'd flown past as I'd pounded out the mindless rhythm and struggled to put one foot in front of the other. As I raced over the bridge and into downtown Sacramento, toward the Capitol, my pace slowed, measured now by streets, not cities. Fifty-Sixth Street. Fifty-Fifth Street. Fifty-Fourth Street. At that point, I figured I was done. Numbers were creeping past, slowly, deliberately, like on the odometer in a car. Fifty-Third Street. Fifty-Second Street. From one side of the intersection to the other, I wondered whether I should just go home and rest.

That's when I learned to really dig. I did one more street. Then just one more. Surely I could still run *one block*. Then I would run just as far as that building on the corner. Then as far as that little park. It looked cute, I wanted to see it. Maybe I'd enjoy some of the oranges that nice man was holding out for us to grab on our way past, just in the next street. He turned out to be another professor from the college where I taught. Our eyes locked for just a moment.

"Way to go," he said. "Impressive!"

I couldn't talk at this point, not enough puff, but his words helped get me to the next decade of streets. He thought this was impressive. One downside to training by yourself is a complete lack of rah-rahs or motivation. So his words carried more import than I think he knew. I kept going.

Minigoals tricked me all the way to the finish.

Stasia was twenty-three when she ran her marathon. I was fifty-five. I went on to do three more.

I get it now. Stasia made me believe. Until that day, I was a bystander. Now, I was running toward a new life. I understand why the car decals given out at the marathon say "I believe in 26.2." I used to think that was just hokey marketing.

Now I know. It really is all about believing.

TOP LEFT: *No sleeping on the floor for Alex: the higher up, the better*

TOP RIGHT: *Christmas family portrait, 1986: Charlie, Dierdre, Stasia, and Alex*

LEFT: *Alex's first outdoor climb—at age eleven: the Savoy Alps, France* (Photo by Philippe Poirier)

RIGHT: *Stasia (six) and Alex (almost four) in the French Alps*

BELOW: *Stasia and Alex, circa 2015*

ABOVE: *Some of the climbing tribe: Gary, Dierdre, Michelle, and Steve*

LEFT: *Dierdre, Stasia, and Dierdre's climbing mentor Mark Cicak at Smith Rock, Oregon* (Photo by Sean McCartney)

RIGHT: *Feeling pretty good at the end of the Lake Tahoe Half Marathon*

BELOW: *El Capitan*

OPPOSITE PAGE: *Practicing on the Heart lines on El Capitan* (Photo by Karalyn Aronow)

NEXT PAGE: *Jumaring on El Capitan, September 2017* (Photo by Karissa Frye)

twenty-seven

THE PHOTO IN THE magazine was black and white, and grainy. It didn't stand out much. As a non-climber, I found it unimpressive. But it was my son in the photo—very small, not really recognizable—and I'd seen comments online about the feat that prompted the article, so I bought the magazine. If people were talking about it, it must be worth keeping for him.

The route was called Bushido, and Alex had free-soloed it. I wasn't completely sure what that meant. As Alex came and went at home, between climbing trips, he sometimes explained climbing terms to me—sport climbing, trad climbing, aid climbing, solo, free-solo, send, redpoint, pinkpoint, rope solo, and on and on. It was a new list of vocabulary words that, lacking meaning in my own life, were difficult to memorize in a meaningful way. Much of it was lost to me after he left again.

Free-climb and free-solo sound almost the same. As vocabulary goes, pretty similar. In real life, worlds apart. In free-climbing, ones uses ropes and safety gear. Only in free-soloing are you completely on your own, no rope, no gear, no security.

Sport and trad, I really tried to distinguish. But I'd never climbed and had never seen either in action. Climbing is a sport—in my mind, it was all sport—and I had seen Alex climbing in competitions at the gym. Climbing in the gym was different, I supposed, from climbing outdoors. Alex would explain what trad climbing was, and I followed what he said, but then I wouldn't see him again for many months, as he traveled the country climbing. When he came home, it would all be a jumble again in my memory.

Not that my memory was faulty. But during those months and years while Alex was away, my brain was on overload. Everything had changed, very fast. My father, my father-in-law, my (recently ex) husband—all gone. My son had come perilously close to dying. The one house I'd been remodeling on the East Coast had turned into three after I bought the other two parts of the triplex my grandfather had built. The remodel in West Sac was also extensive—we were recreating the house from the floorboards up, inside and out. And I was still teaching, not to mention correcting papers and planning lessons and taking care of my own house, yards, trees, pool, and all the demands of my little suburban estate.

Still, most of my concern was for my children, who had lost so much in the last few years. I knew I'd be fine.

So when a magazine featured an article or an ad or some other notice about my son, I would buy a few copies, for Grammie, Stasia, and me, and then get back to work. I would think about what it meant later. When I had time.

When I wasn't dealing with electric companies on two coasts, or gas companies, or heating oil companies, or buying large appliances or building materials by phone, or talking with the insurance agent about all three houses, or the tree roots heading for the garage floor ... Then, for a few seconds, I would stop and remember the people I'd lost. But only for a few seconds. Then it was back to work, or to fall unconscious into bed in the middle of the night. Five thirty came very, very early each teaching day.

Moonlight Buttress was another name I'd read about in a magazine, just after Bushido. Reading the articles was similar to reading Latin, for me. With my knowledge of French, Spanish, and Italian, I could pick out basic meanings in Latin texts or inscriptions, or in the legalese of estate work. I could get the gist, but not most of the finer points. These articles about my son were written in a jargon I was just beginning to learn. I got the tone, the amazement in the writer's voice, but I just assumed that Alex was a very, very good climber, so much better than most others that the magazines saw fit to display and rave about his feats. I knew I would pick up the language as I read, the way I'd picked up Polish as a little girl. All I needed was time.

Even if that was the one thing I didn't have. It was only after I read about Half Dome that I forced myself to pull out of all the jobs I was doing and really focus, read, think, and wonder.

I don't remember how I learned of Alex's free-solo of the northwest face of Half Dome, the vertical cliff that looms over Yosemite Valley. The feat that landed him on the cover of *National Geographic*, and so many other media. Maybe the complete lack of recollection about it was self-induced, a survival tactic. In my journal, I simply wrote:

> *"Alex is famous again. He's become the first man, the first person ever, to scale Half Dome free solo, no harness, no rope. Just crazy! :-)*
>
> *Wow!! Hard to know what to say. I'm extremely proud of him. He pushes himself, studies hard, accomplishes what other people can only dream of. Wow."*

. . . .

I PROBABLY DIDN'T HAVE time to write more. Clearly by that point, though, I was beginning to understand in a vague, shadowy way what free-soloing meant. It is also equally clear that I had no clue what it *really* meant, in the world of climbing. In my son's head. In the history of human physical and mental achievement. The most stupendous, unthinkable, history-making climb of all time. Soon to be followed by several more, equally far beyond the normal scope of human ability.

Now, as a climber, I still can't wrap my mind around what he did. Back then, though, that blissful ignorance protected me. I'm not sure at which point I allowed his accomplishment to finally fully penetrate my mind. Deep, down to the core. Maybe after the *60 Minutes* film crew left my house at the end of a several-day session filming Alex at home. Maybe it was after the film crew from Spain and southern California left Sacramento. Or the *National Geographic* crew. Or after I saw some of the videos . . .

It was a gradual dawning, not so much a realization as a slow, creeping incredulity. Was I understanding this right? Is that really what he did? The videos made it pretty darn clear. That was what he'd done, and the rest of the world was in awe.

Me? Awe, for sure, but lots of other mom stuff mixed in. Every time I went to a showing of one of his videos, the same question was thrown at me: "How can you stand it?!" Or, as one middle-aged woman whispered to her friend, sitting next to me at a showing of one of his award-winning movies, "How would you like to be that kid's mother?!"

How, indeed. It was something I had to figure out, fast.

Alex has always had the foresight, the understanding, or consideration, to never tell me about his climbs before they happen. As he explained in an interview or two, no one but the climber can evaluate the risk of a climb. The consequence of free-soloing is clearly evident—John Long said it succinctly in the *60 Minutes* show about Alex: "You fall, you die." But the risk depends on many different factors—weather, humidity, the climber's condition both physically and mentally, the condition of the rock, the distractions on site, many others. Those, we can't judge. Only the climber can. That's where trust comes in.

Eventually, all parents have to trust their children's judgment, whether about money, job, childcare, homes, or so many of the other things life throws at us. Climbing is Alex's job. I trust his judgment. And try not to think about the consequences.

But I do, of course. Who could block those out? Who could stand at the base of El Cap or Half Dome and not be seized by the terror of those god-awful consequences?

More people die from lightning strikes or car accidents or bathtub falls, than from climbing. But I don't do numbers. I know the insidiousness of statistics. They're meaningless, if you're the one exception. Or your son is.

Or your daughter. When Stasia leaves on one of her thousand-mile bike adventures, with only her camping gear for company, the same thoughts bubble up in my mind, despite her enthusiasm and preparedness. Bad things often happen no matter how carefully we prepare. Like the day her bear spray came loose, fell off her bike, and exploded. On the eve of the night a bear would visit her tent. No one can prepare for things like that.

Or a handhold peeling off the rock face and falling two thousand feet.

Shit happens. We like to believe that we're in charge, but I'd sensed, years earlier, that the notion we can exert any control over life is foolish, a vulnerability. The point had been driven home, over and over, that often the best I could do was just to hang on and cope.

For Stasia, it could be the last bike ride over the last mountain, or through one bleak desert too many, over one precipice too weakened by rain or an out-of-control truck or a swollen stream. My imagination was rich, too rich.

And the whole world knew of Alex's adventures. He lived all over the country in his van, and magazines or online sites would inform me of the feats he had just accomplished and how they had moved the world of climbing toward new realms of possibility. Again. His motives were pure—a challenge to himself, a transcendent experience—but the path to get there often challenged the rest of us, too, to let go of fear. To stop imagining.

As Mom, imagining—foreseeing—and preventing, was my job. But I had to try to let that go, try to envision another role, another way to see the importance, the beauty, of what Alex strove to do. So each time I saw them, I slew that fatted calf, baked the banana bread, potted another plant, did whatever we both loved and that brought us closer for a moment. Because when we kissed and hugged good-bye, I knew that each time might be the very last.

It's always true, of course, that each time we step across a street or walk to the store, we might meet our end. Ample evidence of that in the newspapers every day. Nonetheless, my children seemed determined to up that ante. Each time I stood and gazed up at any of the walls Alex has free-soloed, the point was driven into my heart with a fearsome certainty. Each time could surely be the last.

Early in his career, when I began keeping magazine articles about him, that awful rationale was buried somewhere deep in the unruly quagmire of my imagination. Someday, *someday*, that collection of articles, and especially photos, might be the only thing that Stasia and I had left of him. Each time I added to his binder, I tried—so hard!—*really* tried to not think about why I was doing it. Why it was so important.

Then, after enough binders, it became habit. Eventually, an archive. Every famous person has an archive, for press purposes, or reference.

The archive grew, as did its use and its reasons. No longer just because Stasia and I might need it.

They both choose their epic adventures out of need. Not to appease, not for anyone else, but to grow. To take a step forward. To live a life each has chosen. It's obviously in the genes I gave them. But what would I do with those genes, now that I was on my own?

Life had simplified things for me. I no longer lived to keep the peace at home. No longer had to protect anyone. That crevasse I'd leapt into as a new runner, that gaping endlessness filled with possibilities, was offering me more choices. How would I respond?

The marathon I'd run was a beginning. My first climb at the sharp end of the rope was a baby step. I was just beginning to understand how little I knew, how little I'd done, just beginning to realize how many possible paths led out of that crevasse, and how tempting, how exciting each one would be.

Which, and how many, would I choose?

twenty-eight

"SEE THAT, MOM?" ALEX shouted down to me from his belay ledge on the rock wall near Yosemite Falls.

Not only had I seen the lightning strike he pointed out, I'd noticed every one of the seven or so earlier ones. Not a big fan of electrocution, I pondered the wisdom of continuing our three-pitch climb, a 5.6 route called Munginella, but Alex assured me we had plenty of time. Since he practically lived in Yosemite Valley for part of every year, I deferred to his experience—against my own better (parental) judgment. It had only been five months since that first day at the climbing gym, and I was just starting to learn to trust my son's instincts in all things climbing. I was still too new at this to have any of my own.

I didn't climb much, maybe two sessions a week at the climbing gym, a couple hours each. But fitting that in was remarkable. In the five years since Charlie had died, while teaching full-time, I'd bought two houses, remodeled four houses, and written and submitted all his estate documents. I'd moved offices at the college, sold rights in several countries to one of my language texts, sold all of my grandfather's houses in Pennsylvania, and become a long-distance runner. Numerous medals from marathons, half-marathons, and shorter races decorated the wall of my office.

The zen-like world of climbing, twice a week, maintained my sanity. Running had taken second place to this new life, and helped me stay in shape for it. Every week, I arranged all of my other obligations around those sessions at the gym. On weekends, my outdoor climbing days in the Sierra were a mini-vacation. Having spent so many years without anything to look forward to and no one to talk to, I hoarded all my hours with my climbing friends. Our time together was long-awaited therapy. It let me heal.

And getting outdoors with my son filled in so many gaps in my education. I learned how little I knew about the mountains. About my own possibilities. About him. And learning about him here, in Yosemite, was a little bonus. But this unexpected morning storm had cut our lesson short.

My peripheral vision caught another flash, on the opposite side of the Valley. A storm had been slowly rolling around the Sierra peaks for over an hour, rumbling like an empty stomach.

I squinted upward. The flake I was arguing with stood out from the wall about a foot or so. Too wide to reach around, too high to step over, too everything. I stood there and talked to myself far longer than my son had the patience for, I knew, although he never said so.

I tried again. Fell again. Another raw knuckle to ignore. The damn flake was beginning to make me doubt my meager credentials—if I couldn't get over this little thing, I was no rock climber. No matter which angle I tried, which movement, the next holds were just centimeters out of reach.

Crack! Another bolt, on our side of the Valley this time.

"Come on, Mom, you got this." Alex's voice was a study in control. Was he trying really hard, for me, or was he always this nice to every newbie, gumby climber he happened to be saddled with?

Crack! Blinding this time, right next to our climb!

In a few seconds that I have absolutely no memory of, I was over the flake and moving really fast. I was rock climbing again. All it took was an act of God.

A feathery, insistent rain followed me up the rest of the pitch. It chilled us while we exchanged gear for the last pitch at the belay ledge. I didn't voice any of my fears about the possibilities, unwilling to make them real.

The rain finally slackened as I belayed Alex up. *The worst is over*, I thought as I balanced on the fast-drying sandy ledge. But as I followed him up, the sky blackened and rain began pelting my back, drumming on my helmet. After a few holds that turned out to be less slippery than I'd feared, I thought, *Okay, I'm wet, but this is easier than I expected. I can do this. No biggie.* But the storm had rattled me, and once safely at the top, my instinct was to just curl up tight against the wall and wait it out. Then another bolt struck nearby. Alex had no trouble convincing me to try the walk-off, even though it was now a rushing river of mud.

Where I come from, summer rain is soft, inviting, a tease to the senses. These were icy whips that startled and battered. We slithered slowly down the trail, as much on our butts as our feet, grabbing whatever we could to keep from sliding off. After a few dozen or so feet I started repeating, *I can do this. This is okay.* I pictured standing on flat ground again.

Then Alex stopped. I couldn't hear what he said over the pounding, roaring rain. He pointed ahead. The wide granite slab that the trail crossed was gleaming under the rushing water that covered it. Completely. No question of getting across such a waterfall. It was a dead end.

"We'll have to rappel," he shouted over the roar.

I couldn't believe I'd heard him right. Was it safe to rappel in driving, freezing rain? I was too new to know. I'd just learned to rappel, had only done it once. I looked straight down: definitely too far to scramble through the brush. We'd only descended about one pitch. Another loud crack of lightning helped make up our minds.

While Alex anchored us to a pair of rappel rings, I tried to keep my teeth from chattering too hard and remain vertical in the rushing mud we stood in. I did try to get my harness ready, but my hands were shaking too hard to be of any use. The rest of me wasn't good for much either. I just stood there, like a clueless toddler, as Alex attached the rope to my belay device. I vaguely remember apologizing. I knew I should have been doing something, but couldn't get my fingers to cooperate.

"Okay, Mom, you go first."

Me? First? Did he really know what he was doing? But I couldn't get my chattering teeth to form the words, so I just followed his instructions.

He'd found a relatively empty, straight section of wall for us to lower down, had secured my rope, checked my knots—done everything. He was good. All I could do was shiver as if I was going to shatter. All I could think was, *My son does this all the time. Just another day at the wall.*

"You know what to do?" he shouted against the wind.

I nodded, grabbed the rope, turned around, and stepped off. The one time I'd rappelled hadn't prepared me for this. My feet skidded around in the mud. Each time I braked the rope, water spurted up from the sponge that the rope had become. Icy water tossed in my face did not help my concentration.

By the time Alex reached the ground beside me, the rain had stopped. Chastened, humbled, and exultant, I waited for him to untie and coil the rope, and we headed back to the base where we'd left our packs sitting between a tree and the wall.

I saw a lot of color as we approached the bags—red, green, black. Some kind of long, vivid-colored snake had curled up on the wall to dry out, right above our packs.

Neither of us knew what it was. Neither of us wanted to find out the hard way whether it was venomous. Alex went first, dashed between the tree and the wall, grabbed his pack on the fly and kept running. Really fast. I did the same. The snake didn't move. We stopped, breathless, and put on the packs for the walk down.

As a mother, I marveled at this process of swapping leads. Parents and children often wind up changing roles in life, as they get older. But never, I thought, is that transformation as obvious as when they climb together.

. . . .

AS CLIMBING BECAME MORE and more important in my life, I often found myself thinking about Merlin the magician, from the story of King Arthur. Merlin lived backwards. He youthened. Became younger. Went backwards in time. How I envied that! Each time I got slowly out of bed, waiting to see which knee would crack the loudest, which toe would hurt most, or which part of me would make the most noise until I shook it out, I thought of him.

I ran my first marathon two years after Charlie died, and my second the following year. During my last training week before the second race, I caught my toe, flew through the air, and broke my hand (and lacerated various other parts). If the weather's right, I can still feel it.

My fourth marathon was also my last, and probably not such a good idea. The piriformis pain that resulted from it plagued me and made running impossible for many months. That was the year I started climbing.

That injury was just one more in a series of injuries that regularly reminded me that I was no longer young. The big toe I'd smashed in a biking accident when I was young didn't improve my gait as I ran, and later would stop me from wedging my toes into a crack in the Sierra granite. As a kid, I'd landed on cement instead of in a snow drift and smashed my sacrum; this made chimney-type climbs impossibly painful. The knee I'd wrenched horribly in the Swiss Alps the year after college had never really gotten back to normal, and plagued me whenever I hiked strenuously up to a climb, and was even more painful on the way back down. The list of small disabilities went on and on. I was definitely not youthening.

Those few years of running had made my legs stronger, especially my thighs, and that proved to be beneficial for climbing. But climbing also required upper-body strength: forearms, fingers, hands. Suppleness. Cardio fitness. Lots of things that challenged my body after a lifetime of damage.

But each time I topped out, whether on a wall, a mountain, or even just a one-pitch climb, in the Sierra or the Gunks, in France or Greece, or anywhere I've gone climbing, each time, the pains were forgotten. Each time, I re-experienced what the writer Daniel Duane called, in his article "El Capitan, My El Capitan" in the New York Times, "the human sublime."

I could never fully express to my non-climber friends or colleagues the effects that sublime had on me. It had subtly taken over my life, affording me occasional, momentary glimpses of so much more than what teaching or writing or anything else, even music, had ever given me. I couldn't even explain it to myself. But my body was definitely feeling the crunch of time. It was time to step up my program.

A year ago, when climbing was still fresh and new to me, I'd begun scouring all the climbing sites online for information about the most appealing, challenging, and beautiful climbs within my range of difficulty. There were so many! But the most beautiful, the most impressive-looking, the most daunting-looking, the most visually out-standing ones were all in Yosemite. Three and a half hours from my house. No need to find a sponsor willing to send me around the globe, like my son had. The best climbs were in my backyard.

So I made my list. I never called it a bucket list—what a depressing thought, that bucket! My plan was simpler: to climb them all before I started on my seventh decade, before my joints or lungs or heart or all of them started to object too loudly.

The first on my list was Snake Dike.

twenty-nine

THE BOULDERS STARTED TO come crashing down on my climbing partner just as she was about to high-step out of the creekbed. Amy and I were hiking toward Snake Dike, the classic 5.7R climb on the shoulder of Yosemite's iconic Half Dome. Not the vertical, daunting northwest face that the tourists gaze at from the Valley floor. That was my son's territory. Way too hard. But on the west shoulder of the formation, several technical climbs make their way up the blank-looking, lower-angle slab wall that rises for ten pitches to the top. Snake Dike snakes its way up, following a pale orange-colored dike that protrudes from the otherwise uninterrupted white granite.

Amy braced, pushed back against one of the cascading boulders, while I pushed against another. They stopped. We froze, arms straining, afraid to move and set them in motion again. Alex, our guide, rushed over to help. As my fingers lost their grip, Amy jumped up, and the boulders crashed harmlessly into the stream bed.

Probably happens all the time, in Alex's world—but for me and my friend, the "elderly ladies" he joked about leading up Snake Dike, this day was anything but ordinary. Like me, Amy had spent her life working a desk-oriented day job and raising two children a few years younger than mine. She'd already been climbing for many years, so she was more comfortable on the rock than I was. But neither of us had ever done anything as extraordinary as climb a formation as iconic as Half Dome.

Last month, when Alex suggested we do Snake Dike together, I thought he was joking. Climbing eight slabby pitches, up to 8,836 feet, seemed a bit much for someone with a one-year beginner's tick-list. But Snake Dike *was* on my to-do list.

As we hiked in, the weirdness of the situation hit me, as it had on Munginella in the thunderstorm: how many parents ever get to put their lives in the hands of their children? Amy and I, both of us moms, were about to follow Alex up like little kids, trusting him to keep us out of harm's way. I wondered whether I'd feel so confident if the media hadn't told me incredible tales of his abilities.

After hiking four hours, I looked across a series of large, exposed flakes of rock to the start of the climb. No holds I could discern. I know the physics of it: the more shoe rubber on the rock, the more likely you'll stick. As we traversed the low-angle slabs, I imagined what would happen if I tripped—hurtling two thousand feet down to our campground. My body handled the traverse just fine, but my head . . . that, I've learned, is where climbing really takes place.

When I was little, I never thought about what would happen if I tumbled out of the maple tree in our backyard. Or off the garage roof. Did Alex have fears like that? Or would that make climbing impossible?

At the last flake, I raised my leg to step up . . . and froze. I recognized the sound immediately. A few days earlier I'd mentioned to Amy that I'd seen lots of rattlesnakes, but the only ones I'd ever heard were in movies.

Alex sauntered over, picked up a stick, and poked it under the flake where the rattler hissed.

"Alex!"

He laughed. "They're slow, Mom."

I wondered how he knew that—and what else he knew that I didn't.

I worried that this day might turn into an epic. In the climbing world, an "epic" is a day where everything that can go wrong, does. But the boulders hadn't done any real damage. And the rattler just hissed and slithered away. Not an epic. Yet.

We ate at the base of a slab that rose straight above us. Until today, four pitches had been my max for an outdoor climbing day. I'm not sure what made me think I could do ten—especially after a monster hike. And then there was the hike down. Something about Alex's off-handedness when we'd talked about it, his extreme, casual assuredness, made me believe.

By this point, though, we had no choice. At the summit, a photo crew from *National Geographic* was scheduled to shoot stills of Alex on the face of Half Dome, which he'd free-soloed the previous year, for their magazine. He was committed to this climb. Once we reached the top, he'd go to work.

I was just beginning to understand what his feat on the face of this rock last year had meant. But even now, looking up at the blank, white, curving wall that stretched up to the sky, my earlier understanding of what he'd done paled in the face of the real thing. The real deal. I probably wouldn't really understand it for a long time. But I was beginning to understand the level of commitment required for such a feat.

Amy and I were just as committed, within the constraints of our respective worlds, to climb Snake Dike. We both went climbing at the gym whenever we had the chance, usually only after work hours, and when other life obligations allowed. Amy still had two needy teens at home, and I had a lot going on as well, but when it came to climbing, Amy was as determined (stubborn?) as I was.

Tying in, we watched in amazement as Alex added our water and gear to his already full backpack.

"You can't!—" I started to say. But at home I'd seen him fill a haul bag so heavy I couldn't even knock it over—then easily walk out to his van with it. Somehow, while I wasn't paying attention, the scrawny little boy had become a powerful man. Daunting as this climb looked to me, the famous northwest face of Half Dome was far harder—and he'd free-soloed it. I tried to imagine the mental control he needed to do that. My son has a level of control that I—and maybe most people—will never comprehend.

As I started to belay Alex up, I suddenly had trouble breathing. The task ahead had finally sunk in. It had just gotten real. I needed to manage the fear that was beginning to squeeze the air out of me. Feeling it was normal; anyone who ventures out on real rock feels some fear, if they're paying attention. Allowing it to control me, that was the issue. That, I refused to do.

My son does this all the time, I thought as I followed him. Alex seems to feel no fear. And yet I've often heard him saying how scared he was on climbs. It didn't seem possible, as I watched him scamper casually up one of the world's most intimidating features. Maybe it goes away, if you do it often enough. If you've free-soloed a rock like this, then climbing it on a rope probably doesn't have that kind of grip on your head.

My head, however, was firmly gripped. My world now was nothing but the stark white granite in front of me. I was alone. Nothing else existed.

We leapfrogged up the wall. Each time Alex reached an anchor point, he pulled up all the slack in the rope so Amy and I could start climbing up to join him. I belayed him from below as he climbed above us, he belayed us up to him from the top. I knew my belayer was a climber so strong he once broke his closet door off just opening it. I knew he could hold me. Didn't matter. I was the one climbing. I was alone.

By the top of the third pitch, as I clipped into the belay anchor, I finally convinced myself to turn around and see what I was missing.

None of the so-called exposed climbs I'd done had prepared me for this. Curving walls, nothing below or to either side. El Capitan, the monster wall my son has climbed so many times, where climbers break records or die, was a distant speck. Yosemite Falls, which I'd seen up close so big and full just the day before, was now just a tiny white sliver.

But emotion had to wait, as did the icy feeling that was twisting my stomach—Alex obviously didn't feel it. I was in awe of the control required to reach that point. First, focus. Find a hold, step up. Keep moving. *You can do this! Don't stop!* I've never talked to myself as much as I did on those remaining pitches.

Then I looked up. Alex was untying his rope. *Our* rope!

Snake Dike ends below the summit. He'd told us that. My head knew we'd walk unroped up the last two low-angle pitches. The reality was quite different.

Alex began scampering up the slab. Amy, an experienced climber, followed him easily. I had to sit down several times, head down, and try to drag in enough oxygen to keep going—a combination of exertion, emotion, and elevation. We'd gone from 4,800 feet to almost 9,000.

Wobbly, I convinced Alex to stay tied to me. Tired as I was, my imagination hadn't slowed down a bit: if I tripped here, I'd bounce down a thousand feet of rock before rolling through a few thousand feet of forest to the campground. We wouldn't be anchored while simul-walking, but I knew he could hold me if my oxygen-deprived body got clumsy.

As we topped out, the photo crew was lowering camera people down the northwest face, already ablaze in alpenglow. They were ready for my son.

This is his day job.

Would I be able to go back to mine? That random thought came out of nowhere as I watched him get ready to go to work. For me, work was a safe, quiet world, devoid of fear, of danger, of excitement. Would I be able to go back to it with any enthusiasm, now that I'd been so far removed from that tidy little world?

I did a shaky 360. Alex stood at the very edge, munching an apple. Beyond that I saw . . . nothing. Distant gray-blue ridgelines topped with snow. The deepest cerulean sky I'd ever seen. A few puffs of white—we were up in the clouds. On the summit.

My body and mind were at war. Completely spent physically, I could barely move, but I wanted to dance, shout, hug everyone! Wanted to spend the rest of the day up there, just savoring this once-in-a-lifetime experience. Instead, I settled for a quick hug with my son, before the crew commanded all his attention. Then I sat down, as near the edge as I dared, to watch them all set up, and pulled out the remains of my lunch.

By five thirty, the hours-long photo shoot was about to begin. But Amy and I had just spent eleven hours getting up here and didn't want to hike down in the dark. In eerie silence, we began the cable descent on Half Dome's northeast side. We slid and slipped down the near-vertical cable corridor, amazed that tourists do this, and glad, at this late hour, that they were gone and we were alone. The granite between the cables gleamed, worn slippery by all those feet. Although the darkening sky made us want to rush, we took precious moments to attach our daisy chains.

About two hours later, in the dark, we joined the John Muir Trail. At first, we used only one headlamp at a time, to save our batteries. But after sloshing through ankle-deep water we couldn't see and hesitating at countless rocks that looked like bears looming over the trail, we turned both on.

I've hiked in semi-darkness before, reached parking lots at nightfall. But treading through hours of switchbacks, exhausted, without even a glimmer of moonlight, brought out new fears. Fear of the dark is common, but add to that the complete, total moonless dark, the knowledge that Bear #90 and his cronies were out there, the big cats that were most active at night in this wilderness, the fact that we were alone ... The litany raced through my mind, on and on and on with each step.

We sang, to alert the bears to our presence, and laughed about Bear #90. We swept the woods on both sides of the trail with our headlamps. We rattled our metal gear. We made noise. We wanted anything out in those woods to know we were coming and give us a wide berth. And the activity calmed me.

Each time the thought popped into my mind that I needed to stop moving, just for a little while, just a few minutes—we'd started at five in the morning and it was past eleven at night—I imagined being in my tent, nestled in my sleeping bag, warm, cozy, healing. I could feel its soft down envelop me. I could smell it. My mind replayed some of the incredible sights I'd glimpsed today—when I was seeing anything at all besides the rock in front of me. The thin ribbon of Yosemite Falls. Illouette Falls, which I'd never even heard of before today. The panorama of snow-covered peaks that were the backdrop all around the summit. I knew I'd dream about those, curled up inside my bag in my warm tent. Which was just a whisper away from the tent in the next campsite, so close to other people ...

I longed to see or hear other human beings! We glimpsed another headlamp now and then, far below us. Small comfort, but some. I convinced myself that any small comfort was plenty, and we marched on.

Climbing, though, is not about comfort. Self-help books talk about getting out of your comfort zone. This entire day had taken me so far out, I knew I'd never be the same. And I knew I'd never see my son the same, either.

Alex's definition of an epic climb included disasters, dangers, and unpredictable outcomes, but this day *had* been epic for Amy and me. And it had nothing to do with rattlers or climb ratings. To trust your child to hold your life in his hands, hour after hour, requires a faith that normal living rarely prepares us for. Climbing exposes that faith, pares away what's unnecessary. Alex would probably never put away his clothes at home. That's unnecessary. But if I ever need anyone to save my life, he's my guy.

This climb changed me, too. Now I knew fear can be ignored and fatigue is in the mind. If you think you can, you can. It's as simple as that, and not so simple at all.

Alex's climb up the northwest face and ours up Snake Dike were both on the same dome but worlds apart. My head and I had some serious dialogues up there, and I wondered whether Alex has also had a day when everything changed for him. Surely, that free-solo must have been one.

At midnight, Amy and I reached camp, calves and thighs sore, but with more energy than I'd expected. We dragged food quietly out of the bear box, ate, and then salved our suffering feet. The campground was completely silent—but sleep was still a long way off. I couldn't help thinking about the endless nights so long ago when I'd lie on the floor with Alex the toddler, trying to make him stop climbing and go to sleep. I wondered if he realized how unusual his life was—and is. Since he left on his adventure, in 2004, I've been discovering bits and pieces of a young man who has surprised me, and the world, many times. Today, I got to put some of those pieces together.

Alex and I were both students in the same grand classroom. He was postgraduate, and I was a freshman. Thinking back to my years in school, I recalled that every class I'd taken seemed to have at least one person, one colleague, who taught me more than any professor ever did.

This amazing young man, who'd guided us up the wildest, most challenging adventure of my life in the classroom of Yosemite granite, was that colleague.

thirty

I STOPPED TO REST my arms, hanging about twenty-five feet above the soft, spongy floor of the climbing gym. I shook out one arm and hand while holding on with the other. Changed sides, repeated.

Two weeks. Two interminable weeks. That's how long this climb, only a 5.10c, had been frustrating me, mocking my climbing skills. For pro climbers, like my son, 5.10c is not even hard enough to be a warm-up. But I wasn't a pro or a seasoned climber; I was just lumpy old Mom. At least, that's how I had felt each time I went to the climbing gym lately.

The route was a lead climb, which made it feel harder than its grade. That meant I was the one putting up the rope. If I fell, I'd sail through the air, swing big, then have to be lowered. And start again.

Which I'd done, over and over, for two weeks. Each time, I made it to this point, where the horizontal part of the route joined the headwall that went straight up to the anchor. Each time, I'd try one way, retreat, try another angle, retreat, while hanging my full weight from my hands. Try again, retreat again. Up, down, up, down, until I just got too tired to keep holding on. My fingers would just open. And I'd fall.

My project. Two weeks, so far.

I looked up at the holds, just beyond my arms' length, on the other side of where the horizontal line met the headwall. It looked so doable! The moves were obvious—my middle-aged body just refused to do them.

Lots of coaching had been shouted up at me over the last two weeks whenever I got to that spot.

"Drop your knee!"

"Try to raise your right foot a tad!"

"Put your left foot on that chip, behind you, and step up."

"You got this!"

"Go for it!"

I tried everything they told me to do. And, each time, I fell anyway.

I was trusting everyone's judgment but my own. After all, they knew climbing. They all climbed better than me. But they didn't know my body. Today, I would listen to nothing but my own body. This morning, I'd concentrate only on how it felt. The gym was quiet; there were only a few people there and no one I knew but my belay partner, Michelle. She knew me, knew that I needed to concentrate. Quietly, attentively, she fed out the rope, and I knew she would have me if I fell. The calm helped me focus on what I was doing and how I was doing it. Nothing else.

I pointed my foot, using only my toes to make my body a little longer, reach a little higher. The move strained the arch of the foot that was pushing me up, and it started to cramp. Ignoring the twisting, gripping pain, I reached above me, then around the corner upward. The tips of my fingers could feel the hold, the one that had eluded me for so long. Just oh-so-slightly out of solid reach.

I changed feet, shaking out the poor cramped one, and twisted in the opposite direction, the opposite of the way I'd tried it each time, the opposite of how everyone else had instructed. The way they'd been coaching me had just never felt comfortable. Too awkward for my reach, for my feet, for my arms.

I dropped the knee nearest the wall and reached up, behind and over my head. The dropped knee gave me just the inch or so of extra height that I needed. My fingers closed on the hold.

In a few seconds, my feet pushed me up onto the headwall, and I flew toward the top anchor. It was over! I clipped the rope into the two top 'biners and grinned all the way down as Michelle lowered me.

I'd sent my project. No fanfare. No coaching. No photos.

No big deal. Unless you're a sixty-something mom who started climbing recently. A 5.10c was, for me, as challenging as 14b (okay, maybe 13b) to real climbers. After sitting at a desk or standing in a classroom, or in a kitchen, all my adult life, 5.10c was definitely the top of the spectrum. At least for today.

I had sent this 5.10c six years after I started climbing. I'd never thought of myself as old until that moment. Age was just a number, and numbers are meaningless in my life. I do languages, not numbers.

When I first started going to the gym, Alex told me that, as an older climber, I shouldn't boulder—do short climbs without a rope. He was right, as I've acknowledged after suffering the consequences of falling now and then, or jumping back down, even on the soft padded floor of the climbing gym. The sore hip. The protesting knees. So for the first five years following the rope up was my climbing world.

Outdoors, I was content (I'd thought) to follow my son or my friends up the rocks to vistas I'd never imagined. Happy to just be their second and clean the route behind them.

Until recently. Once in a while, as my climbing friends and I played on top rope after top rope, pushing our limits in technique and strength, I'd glance over to the lead-only wall in the gym. In my new little climber's heart, I wanted to know how it felt. I needed to raise the stakes in my own climbing, to see if I could put up my own rope. If I could ignore the danger and go for it.

Lead climbing was my climbing marathon. I trained for it whenever I could fit it in. I hung from the fingerboard as long as my fingers could take it. Push-ups and pull-ups still eluded me—probably always will— but I worked on them nonetheless. But with all the time constraints in my week, most of my training was just climbing.

And watching. Studying how other climbers do those routes. Where they rest. How they extend their reach. Where they don't or can't stop, and where they do. I'd learned to conduct an orchestra by watching, studying, thinking—maybe that would work here, too. Or at least help a little.

Passing the test to get one of the coveted lead cards seemed impossible. The routes they tested people on incorporated overhangs that were too hard for my hands and arms. But running marathons had taught me that nothing is impossible if you decide it isn't.

I'd run my second marathon with a cast on my forearm, having broken several bones in my hand two weeks prior. Two weeks! Even as I was lying on the ground, lacerations dotting every prominent body part, hoping nothing was too damaged, I knew I'd run it anyway and not waste all those weeks of training.

During the marathon, the friction against my clothes caused the abrasions and lacerations to start bleeding all over again. And I learned that after hours of running, a cast will eventually become soaked from the inside, which makes it ridiculously heavy. So I came in at the finish, holding my casted arm up in the air (to balance out my shoulders, which were suffering from the extra weight on one side), with blood trickling from my knees, shoulder, elbows, wrists, and everywhere else I'd scraped the ground when I'd fallen.

The marathon was in honor of a fallen policewoman, and uniforms were everywhere. As I limped in, out of kilter, bleeding but grinning big, several policewomen came running up to help me.

"You're the toughest runner I've ever seen!" one exclaimed. She appeared quite alarmed at my condition. I, however, was elated to have finished.

I went on to run two more marathons after that, and each one taught me about not giving up, but none more so than my second marathon. I hate waste, and I wasn't about to waste all that time—eighteen weeks of intense training. I'd already learned the hardest lesson of all, from the cruelest and most effective teacher. Surviving a non-marriage for decades had layered my psyche with thick callouses of will and tenacity, exactly what I needed to finish a marathon with my arm in a cast. And to climb walls.

So there I was, my lead card hanging down from my harness as I topped out on my project, the lead-only 5.10c. Grinning like a kid.

For someone like my son, it's hard, maybe impossible, to see the kind of climbing I do as courageous. I appreciate that. He and athletes like him are a different species. And yet, I've learned things about courage that might easily have gone undiscovered all my life if I'd never decided to start climbing.

That decision changed everything.

· · · · · · · · ·

AFTER SNAKE DIKE, THE second item on my climbing to-do list was Matthes Crest, a mile-long walk across the sky on the crest of a geologic fin. A five-hundred-foot drop on both sides dares you not to think about it. And near Matthes was a beautiful, lumpy, pyramid of a climb called Cathedral Peak, my third choice, that stabs the sky in a very small, sharp point at 10,916 feet. But despite my plan to climb Matthes second, it turned out to be the third.

Alex and I headed out toward Matthes Crest at first light on a low, cloudy morning. We had both parked at the trailhead in Tuolumne Meadows, around 8,500 feet, and before we started hiking, Alex went through my pack to see whether he could make it lighter. A lighter pack means a faster climb, and my son holds many speed records in climbing. So by headlamp, he emptied my bag to see what "junk" I was carrying that I didn't need.

First he pulled out my harness. To save time, I had already clipped what I thought I'd need onto it. He took most of it off.

"You don't need this, Mom."

He removed two small carabiners that I always carried, just in case.

"In case of what?" he challenged, knowing that I was so inexperienced at this that I couldn't possibly come up with a good scenario to warrant carrying extra metal. So they stayed on the floor of his van.

"Mom, you really don't need this today." My nut tool. I never followed a trad lead climber without the nifty little metal tool that helped me remove the nuts, or small metal chocks, that the leader sometimes placed in small constrictions to hold the rope. They can be notoriously hard to get out, especially if either climber has weighted the rope. And I often did, as I hung on it and tried to figure out what to do next.

"But sometimes I have a really hard time getting nuts out—"

"Don't worry, I won't place any nuts. I don't even carry them. Don't really know how to place good ones." That joined the 'biners on the floor of his van.

"You don't need this, Mom." He held out my rappel backup. I was confused. What goes up must come down, and whenever I rappelled, I always used the small cord backup so that I could go hands-free on the way down, if I needed to.

"No rapping today?"

"No, we'll walk off." He continued pulling things out of my bag. "Mom, do you really need two water bottles? It's not a long climb."

To him, of course, it wasn't. To me, though, it was Everest. The hardest thing I had ever done. To him, it was babysitting. He wouldn't even put on his climbing shoes today. This was his rest day.

"It's really dry up here," I explained. "When I'm gasping through my mouth, my throat gets really dry." He'd seen me do this many times on hikes and climbs.

"But you have one on your harness!" From his viewpoint, ridiculous indeed. From mine, a lifesaver. I just nodded.

"I'll probably need 'em all."

"I'll take these, then." He put my two extra water bottles into his pack and continued his search. "Do you need this food with you, or can you just snack when we get to a ledge?"

I knew my pockets were filled with crag food—energy gels and chews, whatever I could easily pull out of my pocket while my hands were busy.

"Okay."

He added my food to his pack, too. When he was satisfied that I was as light as possible, we started hiking. Small circles of light from our headlamps bounced around the trail, the tree trunks, his legs and mine, until the new day rendered them useless.

As the trail left the creek and began moving more significantly upward, I began to slow. To gasp. I had just come up to this elevation the previous day, after a week of teaching, and it was too soon to be doing such a hike. I slogged on, slowing now and then, stopping sometimes to suck in air or to bend forward and rub or massage my thighs, which were feeling the lack of oxygen.

None of that was lost on him. My condition, or rather lack of conditioning, plus the cloud cover that wasn't dissipating in the morning light, convinced Alex that today wasn't the day for Matthes, which was almost a seven-mile hike. The same trail passes Cathedral in only three miles, so that became our destination. Shorter, easier, less hiking—better odds all around.

I think I grinned my way up the first few pitches. The holds were obvious, the rock was beautiful, white and clean and inviting, and I climbed as if I knew what I was doing. I even worked my way up my very first chimney section easily, finding just enough places to push down with my hands while stepping up with my feet on opposite sides.

It didn't start to snow until I was at the hardest section, just below the top. If I'd seen photos online of the summit blocks at the top of Cathedral, I might not have attempted it. The rating clearly said it was an easy climb, but that obviously didn't account for the five or six summit blocks at the top, a series of white vertical walls separated by air, each one a bit higher than the previous. Each time I let go of one to leap across to grab the top of the next, I had to cross a black abyss. Then another. And another. My brain balked. It balked even harder when it saw snowflakes, sometimes hail, bouncing off the hand I was grabbing with.

I didn't have the courage to leap across those infinitely deep, black spaces. My arms were just not strong enough to hold me, if I did. But this was a multipitch climb, with no bolts, only the protection Alex put in, which I then pulled out. There was no turning around. I had to do it.

That paradox has been the most demanding lesson of climbing, for me. Alex often chides me for shouting up at him, as I follow him on a climb, "Alex, I can't do this move!" or just "I can't!"

To him, those words are final. When he says he can't, he means it. The climb is over. When I say it, it just means "hold on, while I catch my breath and figure this out." I shout it even though I know, in my gut, that I'm going to have to do whatever it is my mind thinks I can't do. My desperate cry is just a way to expel the "can't" from my body and my mind, so that I can get on with the business of climbing. Because, like my running shoes, when I tie on my climbing shoes, I know I can do anything I decide to do.

So I decided to leap across the first void. I did find the courage, and my arms did hold me there. Panting, incredulous, but definitely on the second block. And then the third, and on and on to the last leap off the last block onto the tiny spit of rock that is the summit of Cathedral. No bigger than a very small dinette tabletop.

We sat there, side by side, as I drank some water and ate my sandwich. The next climber coming up behind me—it's a popular route—took a picture of us. My smile was plastered on; I was still processing. Then Alex started to untie his rope. The other end of my rope.

"Okay, Mom," he said, "take off your rope, jump off the back, and walk down."

Walk down? It seemed to me we were high up in the air on a tiny nothing. I leaned back just a little and glanced over the opposite side from where we'd come up.

Yep. We were on a tiny nothing. A mostly vertical wall headed straight down from where we sat, maybe a hundred feet or more. Vertical, white rock. Lots of blocks. Cracks. Chunks. Lots of stuff to break bones on, if footing failed.

"Don't take the rope off, Alex."

He humored me, again, as he had up on Snake Dike. We stayed connected. He backed slightly off the front, where we'd come up, as he lowered me slowly down the other side, down the wall until it flattened out just enough for me to stand. Then he took off the rope, coiled it around his shoulders, and ran down to join me.

So Cathedral Peak became the second climb I ticked off my list. Matthes Crest, the one that almost killed me, would wait until the following year.

thirty-one

I WATCHED MY FRIEND Amy disappear over the top of the gendarme, the tall, wide, lumpy spike of rock that stood in our way, stopping us the way a real *gendarme* stops traffic with his arm raised. As I lost sight of her, it hit me. I was alone up here now. I'd have to figure things out for myself. I was the fourth climber on one rope, tied in at the end, two hundred feet from my son, who was leading. I couldn't see any of them. When the rope moved, I would have to ignore all the air on both sides of me, and just go. Ready or not.

A little intimidating.

Just minutes ago, we had all sat recovering from our seven-mile cross-country hike from Tuolumne Meadows to the base of Matthes Crest at 10,423 feet. As we ate, drank, and waited for the food to renew our depleted bodies, Alex had mentioned, quite offhandedly, that he'd never had four people tied into one rope before. He was sure it would work, though. None of us said anything. He was the pro. We all figured he knew what he was doing. We trusted him.

But everything I'd read about tying in with multiple climbers on one rope said that the best climber should always be at the end of the rope. That was definitely not me.

And yet, Amy had just disappeared, leaving me alone back here, up at the top of the world. Almost eleven thousand feet, with an uninterrupted view of the high Sierra backcountry. Snowy peaks scraped the sky all around me, miles away. It doesn't get much more alone.

I unclipped my phone from my harness to get a picture of the once-in-a-lifetime view. At that moment, the rope came taut and almost jerked me off balance. With a drop of about five hundred feet on each side of me, I definitely didn't want to lose my footing.

I slapped the carabiner with my phone back onto my harness and realized I hadn't paid close enough attention to where Amy had put her fingers and feet as she worked her way up the gendarme. Cracks and blocks and other features offered countless ways to get to the top of it—and I knew there would be many more like this on the way across the crest. Some would be manageable, some would be a lot harder. I'd have to choose my own route. I couldn't ask Alex or anyone for guidance; they were all gone, way ahead of me, moving slowly and steadily over and around the gendarmes that lay in wait.

No words in any language I know could convey the grandeur and the ferocity of such a landscape. Climbers who are interviewed at the top of things like Matthes, or El Cap, can be forgiven for dropping the f-bomb so often. It is a struggle to find appropriate ways to express how a place like this makes them feel. There aren't any.

You can die up here, in so many ways. The wild majesty of the place will still be there after you're gone. It doesn't care. And if you acknowledge that, you'll do okay.

So far, I was doing okay. Picking my way, oh so carefully, until the rope pulled taut and demanded speed. Hasty decisions can get you really, really beat up on a crest, where any fall, of any length, will whip you off your feet and bounce you down across the side of the crest. You won't fall to your death on a rope. But you might wish you had.

That scene played through my mind over and over as I sidled around blocks, or ledges, or whole gendarmes, gripping like crazy or just easing across, toes pressed into cracks or gripping ledges, or just hoping the sticky rubber on my climbing shoes really would stick to the rock.

We had to down-climb a bit in a few spots, picking our way down off obstacles, while remaining on the crest. Then off again, horizontally. When we finally reached the summit, or the highest point on the crest, it seemed like just one more gendarme.

We stopped there to savor the view and our accomplishment, and to take pictures. My son, veteran of thousands of photo shoots for magazines, videos, posters, and all manner of media exposure, had advice for us all.

"Take off your helmet, Mom, it shines."

"Steve, take off your glasses—they reflect."

"Turn toward the sun, Amy."

And he was always right. He knows. All the way across the crest, he had leapt and run and scrambled with ease, like a mountain goat, completely at home up here. On the other climbs we'd done together, I'd only seen him climb straight up, overhead. I'd never had such a strong impression of him gamboling. Playing. Bounding about like a little boy having the time of his life.

We all were. But ours would end the next day, when we all went back to work. To real life. This *was* his real life.

We spent only a few minutes at the summit, and, as always happens when I climb with Alex, emotions had to take a back seat to practicality. A climb isn't over until the climbers are all back on the ground, safely, or in their car, or at their campsite eating supper. I knew it would take days, weeks, maybe months to process all the impressions that had battered my brain up here. Right now, I had to keep it together and concentrate. Alex lowered us a couple hundred feet or so on the rope, until we could stand, as he had done on Cathedral, before coiling up the rope and following us down. Then we began to hike the seven miles back to our cars.

Seven miles is a long hike when it's all uphill and most of it is cross-country. Instead of trails, we picked our way over rock slabs and boulders and tree trunks, through rocky streams and mosquito-infested forest. The Sierra backcountry is rugged stuff. During the hike in, adrenaline and the excitement of the unknown helped propel me upward, on and on and on.

Going out, though, was different.

All my adrenaline and emotional energy had been spent up on the crest. Every last bit. Picking out each step now, over rocks and roots and stumps and holes and all the obstacles that lay in wait, took all of my remaining concentration and strength. I could feel it draining away, as if I were losing blood with each step. After three or four miles of that, I had nothing left.

My footsteps slowed. Everything else, everyone else, faded away. I was aware only of the muffled sound of my footfall, and the fact that each one demanded more of me than the last. Soon I'd have no more to draw from.

Hunger gnawed at my middle, but I didn't want to stop to dig out the remaining half of a bar from deep in my pocket. I knew that if I stopped, that would be it for me. I'd be done.

Another step. Another. We were on real trail now, and on both sides, tree stumps littered the forest floor. If I sat on one, I could rest . . . No, just one more turn in the trail, and then I would sit a while.

No, another turn just a few feet ahead. I could do one more turn. Then I would look for a stump . . .

This section of woods had no stumps. One more step. A little slower. Another step.

I had done the impossible today. Matthes Crest. Alex had told me many times, all year, that I could do it. All the vast, incredible vistas played through my mind as I tried to empty my thoughts, tried to ignore the thirst and the rumbling in my gut and the pain in my thighs and the thought that right here might be the perfect place to lie down and rest. The others were somewhere else, behind me or in front. Hiking at different speeds, we had spaced out along the trail. No one else was visible. No voices. I was alone.

I always made it out on my days with Alex in the Sierra. Always. No matter how long the day had been or how far out of my comfort zone he'd taken me. But today felt different. My footfall became more erratic, and slowed even more. The trail turned again, and ahead looked just as far as behind. The trail blurred.

I dragged a foot forward, stopped, dragged the other. Stopped. This section of forest had no stumps to sit on, no rocks to lean against. I had never felt this used, this spent. This empty.

Light was waning. It would be night in an hour, maybe a bit more. Perfect. The timing was just right. I would lie down, and by the time it was night and the temperature had dropped enough, I would be sound asleep. I could have fallen asleep standing right there. Even if I did shiver while freezing to death, I'd be in such deep sleep it probably wouldn't wake me. There was nothing frightening about the idea, or implausible. Complete calm settled over me.

A flat spot caught my eye, not far from the trail. Just right. Long enough for me to curl up in, and there weren't any rocks. My feet stopped moving.

I couldn't remember ever having wanted anything as badly as I wanted to rest. If it turned out to be forever, so be it. I'd done the impossible. I'd earned it. Forever sounded pretty good right now.

The trail was curved slightly away from the flat spot, too. The others probably wouldn't disturb me, might not even see me here in the gloaming light. By the time they got to the car it wouldn't matter.

My feet refused to move. They no longer knew where to take me. I just wanted to stop moving. I couldn't see anything but that sandy, slightly hollowed spot. No trail. No trees. I was ready to be enveloped by the cold dark, to not feel anything anymore. I didn't think of it as dying. It would be just another step, something that happened along the way. The three of us had learned about that together, so I knew the kids would be fine. Both of them were strong and understood the outdoors, its beauty and its dangers.

They'd be fine. And yet . . .

My feet stopped moving toward the flat spot.

They'd already lost one parent. Resting now would be selfish. Resting forever, now, would be unendingly selfish. I was ready, but they might not be.

I dug into my pocket, pulled out the half bar. My fingers shook as they unwrapped it. It held no appeal, but it was the only way I could get out of this dilemma. I had to eat. To drink. To take one more step. For them.

Those few bites of bar were too big, and I was too tired to chew. I tried sucking them into small, moist pieces that I could just swallow whole. As I stood there working hard on that, Steve caught up with me. Together, we drank some water, and he offered me one of his trekking poles. Although I wanted to express my gratitude for that generous, saving act, talking required too much energy. I hope he knew.

I jabbed the pole into the sandy trail, caught up with it in two shuffling steps, then pulled it up and jabbed it again, leaning on it, letting it lead me. One pole each, we limped the rest of the way, silent except for our rough breathing.

As I limped along, my mind was back in that flat spot near the trail. I was unsure what had just happened. Nothing, really, and yet everything was different. I knew that I would not have woken from that sleep. That should have scared me. It didn't.

Was it simply extreme fatigue? Lack of sugar and fuel in my system? Dehydration? Or had something more than that taken place in my brain, pushed by fatigue, that I didn't yet understand? If I hadn't had kids, I might have given in... but then, if not for them, or at least Alex, I wouldn't be out here. I was back to that tapestry that I didn't dare unravel.

So I tried to rest my overtired brain, to force it to empty and not think, so I could focus instead on my slow three-point shuffle, back to the car with my son and my friends.

Being alive had become important again. It probably always was.

thirty-two

AMONG THE GLISTENING WHITE GRANITE DOMES of Tuolumne Meadows is a blue-mirror lake dominated by hulking, low-angle Tenaya Peak. For climbers, it's an endless fourteen-pitch trudge or an easy fourteen-pitch scamper. Depends on your point of view.

My climbing friends and I had come up to Tuolumne to camp and climb and celebrate my survival for that year—what other people might call a birthday. That had become a September tradition in our tribe. But this wasn't just any year. This is the year I would begin seriously, legitimately working toward my seventh decade. My sixtieth birthday.

The day before that milestone, today, I wanted to tick off the last of my four peaks. Tenaya. The end of my list. At least, the current list. Who knew what adventures the next decade would hold?

Six of us had followed Alex as he bushwhacked through the woods to the start of Tenaya. Then the trail had turned upward and become the beginning of the climb. We all scrambled up behind Alex, eager to get this done. But Alex held speed records on lots of climbs, and he got farther and farther ahead of us.

Eventually, the distance also began to increase between me and the other five, all decades younger than me. We had just come up from the Central Valley yesterday, and my lungs hadn't had a chance to acclimate. It reminded me, again, of my parents' smoking habits when I was growing up. They hadn't known any better back then.

I stopped now and then to gasp and rest. Stark, snow-white granite blinded me as far as I could see, above, all around. I stopped and snuck a glance down at Tenaya Lake, a glassy, deep navy blue, far below me at 8,150 feet. That's when it hit me: we'd been free-soloing the start of Tenaya.

"Alex!" I shouted as loudly as I could with the little breath I had left. "Time to rope up!"

We were about three or four pitches up. It was exhilarating, and frightening. If anything happened . . . But nothing had happened, and I'd had a taste, a tiny, child-sized taste, of what free-soloing was. It had been several years since Alex's free-solo of the northwest face of Half Dome, but I still came up short trying to imagine it. I probably always would.

Three of us stopped to rope up—Alex, on lead, then me, then Michelle at the end of the rope. Not wanting to stop and take the time for anchor building or gear swapping, Alex decided we would simul-climb it.

The last time I'd simul-climbed with Alex was three years ago, and I hadn't realized what that would mean until after I'd done it. This time I did. But when we climb outdoors, Alex is in charge—so we roped up, I tried to suck in some air, and Michelle and I tried hard not to let the rope belly out, where it might wrap itself around some knob or sink into a crack . . . which it did, of course, stubbornly, over and over. She quickly learned to wrap it around herself as she climbed.

Tenaya is easy technical climbing, but very long—I had never done twelve pitches in one day. I was climbing the easy pitches fast, but struggling to take in enough air at that elevation. The last two pitches are a choice; left (easy scrambling), right (also easy), or center—overhung 5.8. As Alex put it later, the real rock-climbing experience.

When I got there, after twelve pitches of gasping, I was beat. That moment will always be vivid, even visceral for me: I'd happily negotiated the last bit of easy crack and slab, infinitely relieved that I'd almost reached the top of such a meaningful lump of rock. I'd nearly done my fourth, my last-of-the-decade, goal peak! I was ecstatic—then I stepped around the bulge and looked up.

Tears welled in my eyes. "Oh, shit!" flew out of my mouth, followed by some more rock language, some of which I had no idea was even in my repertoire. I knew I was in trouble.

But somewhere, even deeper, I knew I wasn't.

Alex and I share many characteristics—bone structure, stringy hair, skinny face. Love of climbing. One trait in particular, though, is the one that gets me through moments like this. We're both as stubborn as we need to be. My mother had told me often enough that I was stubborn growing up, but now I realized what a good thing that can be. Rock climbing taught me the value of being stubborn.

Some more rock language came spilling out of me. I was exhausted, spent, used. Scared. Rough rock loomed over me, up and out and over. Alex could have gone around, like the others had. The easy way. But that's not him. Or me.

My mind flashed back to the sudden desperation of my first glimpse of Cathedral's crazy summit blocks. *I can't do this!* I remember thinking. *I'm not strong enough / good enough / daring enough / all of the above.* But I have a summit photo on my kitchen wall that proves otherwise.

I looked up again, squinted against the tears and the sun. This wasn't any wilder than that, I told myself. I tried to picture the summit of Tenaya, and me standing on it. With Alex. I knew exactly where I'd put this photo—on my kitchen wall, next to the one of Alex and me smiling on Matthes Crest.

I shook out my arms and hands, took as deep a breath as I could manage, and started up the last pitch. Easing out over the boulders that hang out in the air, I began to step carefully across the little fissures and gaps. I tried to climb as if I were on lead, so hanging on the rope wasn't an option. I left plenty of souvenir bits of skin as the tips of my fingers got filed down against the crystal-studded rock. But when I thought I couldn't possibly step up high enough, I did. When I was sure I'd never make it over the next bulge, I did.

And then we were all up there, slapping high-fives and whooping and gaping at unimaginable views. But the view that really counted was one that no one else could see. Gazing at the crazy crest of Matthes in the distance, and Cathedral's sharp point, even the slouching silhouette of Half Dome, all I could see was the impossible. Done. Again. This was how birthdays should be.

I'd spent more than a decade dreading my birthday. To my husband, it was a day to rush through the kitchen and leave a gift on the table—usually a CD wrapped in newspaper—before leaving without a word. Or to sit at his parents' table for my birthday dinner. With them, he found words, pleasantries. But none for me.

One year we went to Ashland, Oregon, a trip organized by the college, to attend the Shakespeare Festival for my birthday weekend. On the actual day, everyone on the trip wished me well. I got a small gift from teachers I considered friends. The only person on the trip who didn't mark the day, with words or gift or in any other way, was my husband.

Now, friends and my children always made the day special, gave it meaning. Birthdays had become something to look forward to, an adventure celebrated with my new climbing friends of all ages.

· · · · · · · · · ·

WHEN I MADE MY original list of four peaks—Half Dome, Cathedral, Matthes, and Tenaya—I tacked on one more that I told no one about. It was probably beyond me. Too high—12,589 feet. Much higher in elevation than anything I'd done. Too remote—a seven-and-a-half-mile strenuous hike in. I already knew that could kill me.

Too everything.

But two of my climbing friends from Sacramento had enticed me as they talked about their adventure free-soloing Mount Conness, in the high country up from Tioga Pass in Tuolumne. They were both closer to my age than most of my climber friends, but they'd been climbing all their adult lives. Conness would be a challenge for me, maybe even impossible. So for years I considered Conness more dream than reality, or even possibility, and contented myself with finishing my four peaks— and figuring out what the rest of my life would look like.

I hadn't had the luxury of thinking about that during all the years I'd spent coping with silence and loneliness. But that was over. The kids were on their own, and the houses, with all their accruing chores and errands and paperwork, had dwindled to only two. My occasional articles, stories, or other writing projects or books didn't make any appreciable money but kept my writing career limping along as I ran the French section of the foreign language department at the college. I still played the flute with the college orchestra and occasionally performed in the region, either on flute or piano. Life had become manageable.

Now and then, though, the doubts would creep back in. Why had I waited so long? Why had I let him treat me with such disrespect, ignore me, for so long? As inevitable as the answers always were, the questions could still ruin my morning, my whole day. I would probably always wonder whether my decisions had made my kids' lives, and my own, better, or worse.

I could have left him while the kids were little. But I had worried for their safety, living half of the time with him. And I had been teaching only part-time, which would not have paid my bills if I left. They would have wound up in daycare, or with their grandparents—not terrible options, but I had wanted to raise my kids myself, not pay someone else to do it.

I could have left him when they were pre-teens, but I had still worried about their safety; when he had left our daughter stranded all night and hadn't even checked the phone, I had known that worry was well-founded. It still made me shiver to think of all the things that could have happened that night and so many others.

So many doubts! The water that had flowed under that bridge kept eddying back, drowning me with doubt. Over and over, I tried to persuade myself that the miserable mess of a non-marriage that our kids had witnessed would not color their life choices too much.

Climbing helped me make sense of it. When I was climbing, the past, the future, none of it existed. The complete focus required by an endeavor so physical and so mental at the same time forced all other thoughts out of my mind. It was my zen state, my zone. And each time I came back from that zone, all the rest seemed a bit clearer, at bit more understandable. A bit more forgivable.

So after Tenaya, when my friends talked about Conness, their photos and ones I'd found online showed a clean line of alpine granite that called out to be climbed. It was so beautiful! Pure, white granite that curled around a green-tinged alpine lake, a glacier to the north of it, features that cried out to be held—it was a dream that I hoped to be able to pull off. I had to do it. Or at least try.

I asked my son if he thought I could manage it.

"Sure." His usual reply. I knew what he meant now. Of course I could—if I wanted it badly enough.

In the two years since Tenaya, I'd been getting stronger. I still had skinny chicken arms, still couldn't do a push-up or a pull-up, but I no longer completely discounted the possibility of summiting Conness. I climbed twice a week at the gym, or more if I had a partner. I took my climbing outdoors far more often and had begun learning the value of climbing different kinds of rock. Besides the few areas within a day's drive of Sacramento, I'd also climbed at Smith Rock, in Oregon, and in New York, New Hampshire, Vermont, and had made many forays into the climber's wonderland of Yosemite.

But climbing was the easy part. Life had always been the hard part. Over the last few years, though, a kind of peace had settled over my life, and with it had come a different kind of strength that gave me direction and purpose. Since I no longer spent my days agonizing over how to fix something that I, alone, couldn't fix, I was free to see into a future. And more and more, I couldn't imagine a future that didn't include climbing.

So two years after Tenaya, we arranged it. As with many of the high-country climbs, the logistics were the most daunting part. My climbing friends in Sacramento often didn't know where a climb began, or how to get to that point—sometimes a serious, miles-long hike with lots of opportunity for getting lost. Or what gear they'd need. Or they worried about me.

"I don't know," they'd hem, haw, and try to talk me out of things. "That climb's probably too hard for you."

Or, "I can't hike that far in one day. We'd have to camp out there."

Or a whole gamut of solid, bona fide reasons why older people who spent their life in an office or a classroom shouldn't go try something like that.

But Alex and I immediately put it on our calendar.

Andrew, a friend from Sacramento who was younger than me but older than Alex, had also wanted to climb Conness, so he jumped at the opportunity. We made a simul-threesome, as I'd done on Tenaya with Michelle. Alex led, I tied in about two-thirds down the rope and cleaned the gear that Alex placed, and Andrew tied in at the end of the rope. One of Alex's friends came along to shuttle the gear between us, free-solo, taking it from me as I cleaned it out of the rock and carrying it back up to Alex, who would reuse it as we got higher. And higher.

Conness, I would whisper to myself. It invoked all the adventure that had become my new life. This was me, now. I was doing this. I had done my

four peaks, and I was climbing Conness. A trace of doubt still lingered—
that was a hold-over from my previous life, from years of being stymied
by an unsupportive partner in all my dreams, like conducting or building
a social life in West Sac. But I was doing this. I hoped.

Alpine climbs, like Conness, are different. The complete absence of
life creates a background of importance, of singularity, of focus. There
was nothing up here but climbing, nothing but rock. We'd left all greenery, anything growing, way below, at the last windy—oh-so-windy!—col
that we'd gone over. Each time we'd crested a col, or saddle between
taller rocks, on the way to Conness, the fierce wind had pushed us back.
To get over, we had to really want this.

As we pulled ourselves over the last one—sixth? seventh?—we stopped
for our first glimpse of the creamy white granite of Mount Conness.
Its clean, sharply defined edges scraped the sky as it rose, and rose. I
couldn't think of anything to say. It looked impossible. So many things in
my life had seemed impossible, for so long. And as often happened when
confronted with impossible-looking climbs, my vocabulary became
severely reduced.

"Wow!" was about all I could manage. So I said it over and over, with
differing inflections of awe.

My arms and my mind were tired before we even started our climb. I
hate wind. It renders my eyes useless, makes breathing and just about
everything else more difficult. It wears me out, physically and mentally.
Today would be a test of how far what my mother had called my stubbornness would get me.

For several hours we crept higher and higher, amazed at the stark
beauty. How could an absence of life be so beautiful? Contrast was the
palette up here. The white granite seemed to crackle against the incredible deep cyan blue of the sky. The startling chiaroscuro of shadows and
gleaming rock vibrated all around us. *If only I could bring my paints up
here!* I thought over and over.

Soon, though, the deep blue turned an angry slate, and then stormy
dark gray. The wind had not abated. Something was about to happen, despite the glorious weather reports from earlier that morning.
We climbed faster and faster, not stopping to eat or drink. The others

exhorted me to move quickly, but their words and cheers were unnecessary. I was already at my max, going as fast as my weakened, erratic lungs would allow. I'd seen the sky, too.

Thunder rumbled, far away, but too close. We were four lightning rods, creeping upward, and I was the only reason we were still on this rock. Me, the slowest climber. They cheered me on, encouraged me even more. I didn't say anything. I was too busy, too out of breath.

Lightning flashed, somewhere, not far enough. Again. Thunder growled, scolded us to go even faster. If someone died today, it would be my fault. That pushed me a bit faster. But you can't climb without sufficient air to deliver oxygen to the muscles you need, and I wasn't getting enough of either. If someone died today . . . That thought didn't help my lungs at all. My body had only been growing older since I started climbing, and I understood why my friends had tried to discourage me from Conness. But I wanted to find out if I could climb it. Conness was so big, so beautiful! So out of reach. Had I become a climber worthy of it?

When I reached the top, gasping, Alex was pointing toward the way down on the other side.

"Go, Mom! Over there—down!" Icy rain battered us, mixed with sleet, ice, and snow.

"But I—"

"Go, Mom—I'll sign the book for you." I could barely hear his shouts over the roar of the wind and the pounding rain. For weeks I had looked forward to signing my first alpine high-country register at the summit of Conness. We had talked about that. Alex knew. But we all knew what could happen to lightning rods, creeping across the top of a tempting peak in a major storm.

And "down," it turned out, was hours away. The clouds had already lowered until they were on top of us, enveloping the rocks. As we scrambled through cloud after cloud and lightning struck all around us, the whole inside of the cloud lit up: we could no longer tell where the lightning was striking.

This was information I never thought I would learn firsthand.

It rained harder, colder, sideways, or swirling or driving into our faces. All the tiny rivulets we'd hopped over in all the meadows on the way up had turned into raging torrents. I was soaked in near-freezing water up to my knees.

No one spoke. If the terrain hadn't been so harsh, we would have run. I picked my way as carefully as I could while going as fast as I could manage. We flew along, unable to hear anything but the water slapping our hoods and our faces. Night fell, and still the storm raged around us.

The two friends, who didn't have waterproof jackets, took off faster than I could follow, to meet us at the van later. Alex stayed with me. His clothing wasn't waterproof, either. But he stayed with me.

The distance wasn't any farther than I'd hiked on previous outdoor climbing days. But fear of death by lightning, fierce wind, treacherous footing, and icy-wet cold—along with the sustained effort of twelve very fast pitches after more than seven miles of hiking—had worn me down. For the last hour of slogging at top speed through the pitch-dark forest, I held on to a loop on the back of Alex's backpack.

Alex calls that cheating. I called it survival.

He and I are the alpha and the omega of climbing skill. He has no idea how far out of my comfort zone he takes me or how hard it is for me to go where he goes. But I go. I try. He respects that, I think, even though he's often incredulous at how shattered, how drained it leaves me.

We climb for the same reasons. I think—I hope—he understands that. I know he understands pushing limits: he free-solos the hardest vertical climbs imaginable. It's just that me pushing my limits doesn't look anything like him pushing his. He rolls his young eyes. That's okay. I still need to push them.

Being up here helps me forget. Sciatic pain. Arthritic knee. Tennis elbow. Crooked, unyielding toes. Deficient lungs. The limits of my body. None of that matters up here. The rock is ageless, unyielding. It gives no quarter. My mind is emptied of everything but the next handhold or foothold.

Being up here helps me understand my children, and also myself. Helps me see what I'm capable of. Or not. Essential knowledge, for an informed life.

Sometimes when I climb, I think of my mother. Not about our differences, or the faults that kept us apart, but about the gift she gave me: to really see this beauty, to appreciate its grandeur, and understand its scope. To bask in all aspects of it. We had often sat at the window together, or on the porch, watching as thunderstorms raged around the mountains of eastern Pennsylvania or through the urban canyons of New York City. She taught me about wonder, and awe, and to open myself to all the faces of the events of my life, even the ones that could kill me. And to see it all as an artist did, in all its color and beauty.

Conness brought all of that to the fore: the beauty of the climb and of the storm, and the strength I found inside to reach the summit, and make it back down. I would love to climb it again. In better weather.

. . . .

AFTER CONNESS, THINGS WERE different. I dragged myself through that first week, got myself to work, taught my classes, and went home— nothing more. I cancelled everything else I had scheduled. After five days, I'd hoped to go for a morning run to see if I still could. I'd signed up for a 10k the following week months ago. Didn't seem likely. But that wasn't the reason I felt different.

The writer Bill Bryson put it so succinctly in his book, *A Walk in the Woods*: "You don't hike the Appalachian Trail and then go home and cut the grass." After Conness, there would be no grass cutting for me, or much of anything else, for an undetermined period of time. Until I could come back down from wherever it was my spirit had gone.

Each time I summited with Alex on one of our extraordinary climbs together, I came home different. This was not a feeling one got from a great day at a job or a wonderful day with the kids. Even an exceptional day of teaching didn't do this to me. Didn't take me to this place where I'd never been and then bring me back unable to recognize who I am. Or who I'd been, before.

This was different. *I* was different.

I couldn't even begin to imagine how my son could come down from the walls he's scaled, with or without ropes, and still process what we call "real life." How did he manage that? After facing death, hanging over an abyss of thousands of feet, and conquering it, how could it possibly seem important to sweep the kitchen floor? To buy groceries? To pay the gas bill? And yet, somehow, he did.

Physically, climbing took its toll. There's something about thirteen hours of flat-out, more than 100 percent strenuous effort that one can't just put aside. Andrew, who climbed Conness with us, said that we'd burned about eight thousand calories that day. And once we'd started climbing, we didn't stop moving long enough to eat or drink more than a quick sip or bite, not until we got back to the shelter of Alex's van that night.

Before I'd become a climber, in my previous life, I would have bonked. Hit the wall. Had a meltdown. Stopped moving altogether, that night or the following day. Instead, I went to my daughter's the next weekend. I was still dragging a bit, but being with her is always good medicine if I'm hurting, or wondering.

She wanted to go running (she always does). I went with her to a beautiful park with sylvan trails, thinking I'd walk and just enjoy nature while she did her run. Turned out I was still able to run—nearly three miles, more than I expected to. I was slow, at first, and breathing was rough. But I did run.

And the following week, I ran the 10K.

Ten kilometers. A bit over six miles. Something really was different. After Conness, I'd thought I'd be down for days, maybe weeks. Instead, I got up that morning, dressed like a runner, ate my hard-boiled egg with some cheese and fruit juice, tied on my shoes, and went running, with hundreds of others. We were all out there to combat some disease that everyone who had signed up, and paid, agreed is worth wiping out. But really, deep down where there is no fibbing or pretending; each one of us there was doing combat only with ourselves. To run a personal best. To run 10K faster than the last time. To be better, in some meaningful way. Something more meaningful than cutting the grass.

On Conness, the battle had been fierce: the new me against the old me. The same battle I fight each time I climb. I no longer recognize the me who couldn't imagine going up Mount Whitney when Charlie first showed it to me. Who was that timid, cowed person so devoid of imagination? Of courage?

Each time I quest into the unknown, with or without my adventurer-children, I go so far beyond anything remotely comfortable or familiar.

After each adventure, my life changes a little more, my world expands, like a sprawl of saplings that might someday become a forest. And it becomes that much more impossible to ever go back. For over twenty years, my body had been trapped by my circumstances, hadn't known the exhilaration of exploring what I was physically capable of. Now, that thrill was back. I was back. I'd stood on the top of the world, and would continue to strive for summits that the old me would never have considered possible.

Now I know they are.

thirty-three

ROYALTY ARE OFTEN CROWNED in cathedrals.

Yosemite is a cathedral, of rock. This impression, or something like it, usually hits new visitors the moment the road twists and they get their first glimpse of El Cap standing guard at the entrance to Yosemite Valley, with Half Dome in the far-distant background. Awe overwhelms, then disbelief, and humility. Towering granite walls line both sides, so close that when you climb on one side in a clear, sparkling morning, it seems like the other side is almost within reach.

Each time I arrived in Yosemite, I tried to imagine being up on the face of Half Dome, alone, without a rope or any protection. The way Alex had done it. It was a futile effort; my mind just wouldn't allow it. The same mind, or heart, or whatever part of me it was that had insisted on protecting my babies, that part could not admit the possibility at all. It was protecting me. To comprehend such exposure . . . well, there's no telling what that might have done to my psyche. The refusal was a protective measure.

The memory of Snake Dike was ours, forever. But the northwest face, that was his alone. No one could really get it. No one but him.

When climbers I knew talked about other climbs in Yosemite, they sounded magical, and forbidding. Even gut-clenching scary. One of those is called Royal Arches. I'd heard many climbers speak with reverence about the climb, sometimes with awe, or anger at having failed at it. Always with respect.

Royal Arches is named for a series of arches that appear chiseled into its namesake wall, a rippling wave that rises up the north side, just behind the oldest lodge in the Valley, across from Half Dome. The route doesn't actually climb the arches, but rather twists along beside them, eventually turning left midway up, shifting away from the formations. It goes and goes, for fifteen or sixteen pitches, depending on which route is chosen for the descent.

Sixteen pitches—climbers call that a big wall. In the same category as El Capitan or Half Dome, but easier climbing. Within my reach, maybe.

Climbing is locomotion, like walking or running—it's a way to get from one place to another. The more pitches, the greater and more fulfilling the journey. I wanted to explore all of Yosemite's verticality, as I'd explored so many parts of the globe horizontally. Only my skill limited me.

I'd dreamed of climbing Royal Arches since the first time I'd heard about it. A climber friend in Sacramento, Steve, had climbed it, but had horror stories about coming back down. And a climb isn't finished until you're back on the ground.

Sixteen pitches. To travel that far on a Yosemite wall would be a true voyage of discovery. I would discover whether I was really a climber, worthy of these big walls. Year after year, the idea grew, in intensity and importance. It was always there, in the background, whenever anyone talked about going to Yosemite. Whenever I read about big walls.

My stomach had lurched when I heard Steve talk about the near misses he'd had on the way down from Royal Arches or when I heard other climbers talk about the pendulum pitch. Would I be strong enough to hang off the bottom of a fixed rope and pendulum from one side of a slab of wall to the other, to reach the next move? There was only one way to find out.

It had been two years since I'd climbed Conness. Two very full years. On the Greek island of Kalymnos, limestone had helped me discover the fun of lead climbing—I'd led something every day I was there. In the northeast, I'd sampled the granite ledges of New Hampshire, the legendary escarpment at the Gunks in New York, some small local crags in Vermont and Massachusetts. Climbing in Nevada and Oregon had helped round out my experience base, and other sports, running and hiking, helped improve my general conditioning. With friends, I'd hiked up Mount Whitney, the highest peak in the contiguous United States.

I was still teaching, but my reality had shifted. Teaching was still a part of who I was, but it no longer seemed real. It was an interruption to something more real: climbing.

After so many adventures in other parts of the world, I was back in Yosemite. Alex was resting that day, so he agreed to lead me up the big wall I'd dreamed of for years.

The day before, I climbed with friends on Swan Slab, a grouping of smaller rocks and walls at the foot of the wall that becomes El Cap, farther to the west. My lungs still needed to acclimate to the four-thousand-foot difference between Sacramento and Yosemite Valley. Getting in some moderate exercise and a good night's sleep at elevation is the best way to let the body get accustomed to the thinner air.

We climbed, ate, and slept at elevation, and then the day finally dawned: I would climb Royal Arches. Or at least try.

I wanted to climb just with my son. But nothing about Alex's life is the usual, the expected, and the whole *National Geographic* crew came along for the day. They'd been following him around for over a year, preparing a movie about him. Alex had made his peace with that, but I found their constant background presence an annoying intrusion. Nonetheless, their subject, my son, was leading this climb, for his mother, so they were there to record it.

I tried to ignore them, but that was like trying to ignore a roomful of mosquitos. There were so many of them. So I tried instead to focus on Alex, on everything he said about the route we were getting ready to start up.

In his memoir, Tommy Caldwell, a world-renowned climber and one of Alex's friends, refers to "the intimidation factor" of Yosemite's towering walls. If it feels that way to the initiated, to the world-famous climbers, that factor should be multiplied by many times for someone like me, who started climbing at an age when muscle can be counted on to dwindle rather than develop. Or at least that's what I'd always read and heard from professional climbers like my son: according to them, I would never get much stronger than I was that day.

But they were young. What did they know about getting older? About striving, even as you age? About *my* body? I didn't believe them for a moment.

Both my body and my mind had undergone extreme changes over the last decade or so. As a new runner, then an experienced runner; as a new climber and now, years later, as a fairly experienced one, I'd watched my body, and my closet, go through several mutations.

And my kitchen. Fueling a body for extreme sports requires more thought than eating for teaching or writing. I was in the best condition I'd ever been in, maybe in my whole life. I could feel it. And I was about to put that to the test, on my first big wall.

First, though, needs must be met. Before attempting the Arches, I had to go empty out. Find a private place out in the woods and lose whatever liquid I was still carrying around inside me. There would probably be few, if any, places on the wall to do that, especially with a film crew climbing all around us.

So I put my wind jacket and backpack on the ground and escaped into the woods for a few minutes. As soon as I returned to the base of the climb, someone from the crew handed me a microphone with a long wire.

"Slide this up under your shirt," he said, "and clip it at the top."

Carrying a mike was definitely not on my list of necessaries for today's adventure.

"No one needs to hear me—"

"You won't even know it's there," he prodded, holding it out to me. "You'll see."

Alex always wore a wire when he climbed for film. It didn't bother him. If he could do it. . . . I slid it up inside my shirt and clipped it to my collar, hoping he would go away. But he didn't. He held out a hand-sized, heavy-looking black metal box.

"Put this in your pocket."

The transmitter for the mike. This was getting complicated. There were far more important things I needed to be doing.

"I can't. My pockets are filled with food." As always on a multipitch climb, I had real food, a sandwich and some fruit, in my backpack. But that was only accessible when I reached a ledge or an anchor. In between, while I was working hard, I often needed a little boost to my sugar and energy level. That's what pockets were for.

"Then put it in your back pocket."

"Those are filled with food, too."

He looked me over as if he was evaluating a side of beef. Then he smiled. "No chalk bag?"

"I don't use chalk."

Many climbers have a small bag filled with chalk that hangs off the back of their harness, in the middle, that they dip their hands into to help dry them if they sweat. Mine had been bathed in chalk dust from blackboards for all of my decades of teaching. The tips often cracked and split open, making climbing or playing the piano very painful, and occasionally impossible.

"Don't go away!" he said as he disappeared quickly. Go away? That's what I wished they'd all do.

Friends of mine from Sacramento had come to see the start of my big climb. Other onlookers had gathered. Alex had last-minute advice. The first pitch was the crux, or the hardest section, of the climb, the part that gave the route its difficulty rating. The first pitch. Of course. Where everyone was standing around watching. I listened closely as Alex described where we would head inside, behind a huge flake of rock where a massive chockstone was wedged. We had to climb behind that chockstone. In the dark chimney.

During all that commotion, the man with the microphone had come back. He had put the transmitter in a chalk bag and was attaching it to my harness.

"I don't want to wear a chalk-bag—"

"You won't even know it's there," he said again as he clipped it on, then disappeared.

"Okay, Mom," Alex said, "put me on belay."

I did, and it began.

· · · · · · · · · ·

IF THE FIRST PITCH was the crux, I reasoned, the rest should be no problem. I'd gone up the first chimney pitch with relative ease. Now, I wasn't sure where we were on the route, but we were cruising up Royal Arches faster than I'd expected.

Traveling up my first Yosemite big wall!

After that delicious realization, the slogging began. The hard work. The thinking. The failing.

One pitch demanded crack climbing. Granite often has vertical cracks, or fissures, that are often the only climbable feature on a rock face. The goal is to insert fingers or hands in the crack, as far as possible, then close them or wiggle them to make them wider so that they can support body weight. Hanging the entire weight of my body on a knuckle, or several, never seemed like a good idea to the piano player in me. If I fell on that hold, my piano days could be over. That was unacceptable.

While hanging on a knuckle or two, the climber is also supposed to insert toes, or as much of the front of the foot as possible, in that same crack. Twist it, wedge it in, then step up on it while moving hands farther upward. If you can stand the pain. Step. Grimace. Reach. Until the end of the crack.

Flexibility is essential for that move to work. But bunions stuck out on both my feet, which made that maneuver amazingly painful. And my toes were neither mobile nor flexible. Two different accidents as a kid had seen to that. Neither big toe bent at all. If I inserted them in the crack, and then fell, or changed my angle, they would just snap. In my head I could *hear* the snap.

After much wrangling to see if I could find any other way to climb that section, I finally had to admit defeat. I pressed hard against both edges of the crack with my hands, tried to just work my feet up the face, and Alex helped by pulling on the rope. Completely unprofessional. Totally bad form. But necessary.

I hated doing it. But I didn't want to hold everyone up while I hung there trying to figure out another way to get past that section.

I had won the chimney, failed the crack. Aced some of the in-between pitches. Now I stood on a lumpy, bulging rock face that had absolutely no holds on it, only odd little curved divots here and there. Too smooth to hold, but big enough to plant one's foot, lean in, and step up. . . . At least, some of them were.

Leaning in did no good on the tiny ones. No handholds where I could get some purchase and pull myself up. Nothing.

I tried left, tried right, tried going down a bit and around the large bulge. I tried everything I could. And there I hung. Stymied. Furious! Some of that seldom-heard rock language came pouring out of me. There had to be a way. This route was only 5.7. And then, Jimmy Chin, the renowned extreme-sports photographer, and another photographer, came sauntering past and saved me.

He didn't know he saved me. He just walked past. Just casually walked on by, no rope—or at least it looked like that to me—and lots of video equipment. They both had cameras or other equipment hanging from their bodies—shoulders, harness, everywhere.

Which made me even more furious.

It was so easy that they were just *walking* up the damn thing. Carrying heavy, awkward stuff!

I watched his feet closely. If he could walk it, I could, too.

I tried to memorize all the little divots where he placed his feet, and once they'd gone by, I began placing mine in exactly the same spots. Now that I knew it was doable, and how and where, I could do it.

And I did.

. . . .

GRANDFATHER CLOCKS. THAT'S WHAT I think of when I hear the word "pendulum." A pendulum swings, slowly, back and forth. It is grace and deliberate purpose.

I was quite the opposite.

I had never seen a pendulum on a climb before, so I had no idea what to expect. I reached a big ledge, following Alex, but it wasn't the belay ledge. It was midway on the pitch. Alex was about twenty feet to the left and about fifteen or twenty feet higher than the ledge where I stood. He was still belaying me, but between the two of us there was nothing. A sheer, empty rock face. Unclimbable, not just for me, but for most climbers. Alex, of course, had scampered across it. For the rest of us, some thoughtful soul had put up a pendulum rope.

The pendulum rope hung down to the ledge from directly above, maybe twenty or thirty feet up. There were knots at intervals up the length of it, so it could be gripped. That seemed unnecessary, I thought. Why not just hold the rope? I would soon find out.

When I was ready, I held the rope with both hands. I scooted as far right as I could, paused for a deep breath, and ran left as fast as my feet would go. I should have swung far enough over to join Alex. But instead, I found myself back on the ledge.

"What the—?" was my intelligent reaction.

Again. Push right, pause, run left. Again, I found myself stuck on the ledge. At the extreme left end of it, maybe, but still on the stupid ledge. At the left edge of the smooth rock face, where Alex waited, the rock stuck up to form a huge lip. At each attempt, I reached as far as I could to grab it, to hold me there. It was always out of reach, and I would be pulled back.

What was going on?

Because the pendulum rope was fixed directly above the ledge, it insisted on pulling me back there. No matter how hard I pushed. Over and over, I ran right, then left, and stopped, completely shocked at how much sheer, physical work this was. I shook out my arms and hands, worn out from the pulling. I dragged in a breath as deep as I could manage while panting from the exertion. It was getting embarrassing. Was this where my big wall climb would end?

Photographers were all over the place, it seemed. A young climber was poised high above me, somehow, watching. I had only vague impressions of what was going on around me, only the damn rope had my complete attention. I began to doubt whether I was strong enough to pull this off.

Normally, when I climb, brute force is a last resort. I usually rely on technique rather than muscle to get me over rough spots. With skinny arms like mine, I've learned not to depend on strength. This, though, was a purely brute-strength move.

So I'd have to dig deep and find some. I was getting angry. That's usually what it took.

Damn it, I just have to get angry enough! I kept thinking. Just angry enough. I ran as far right as I could, pulling hard against the damn rope. If it was hanging there to help me move left, why the hell did it keep pulling me right, back to where I started?

I fought it, and fought equally hard to suck in a deep, deep breath, which I knew I'd need all of to get to the lip at the far edge of the rock face. Then I exhaled a bit and sent my legs whirling around as fast as they could go, like in the cartoons when the character's legs turn into rotors. I was a rotor, rolling, spinning across the rock to my son.

My eyes were fixed on that edge, where he was waiting. The jagged rim looked bigger, closer. I leaned left, leaned until it felt like I was falling over. Leaned more, pulled against the damn rope with one arm, leaned against the rock with the other. My feet slid over the marble-like rock. I leaned more, absolutely sure I was falling. Alex's voice, other voices, cheered.

My fingers closed around the edge! I squeezed them closed harder, willing all of my remaining strength into that grip. I let go of the rope.

I'd done it!

I pulled myself deep into the corner under the ledge where Alex sat and scrambled up to join him. Then we continued climbing.

· · · · · · · · · ·

THE END. WE MADE it. The top of Royal Arches! But a climb isn't a success until you're back down on the ground. As usual on our huge climbs together, I wouldn't have any time on top to savor the fruits of my efforts. The sun wouldn't wait for that. It was already beginning to dip behind the towering walls of the Valley.

We were going to simul-rap, Alex announced. I glanced quickly around our perch fifteen pitches above the Valley floor, where I'd just arrived, breathless. I've never been a fan of rappelling in the dark; I like to see where I'm putting my feet. And if the temperature dropped any lower than where it was now, I'd need my wind jacket on the way down. I rolled down my sleeves, which I'd rolled up while I was working hard on the last few pitches.

Alex and I had simul-rapped on several climbs together, each of us on a strand of rope, lowering ourselves at the same time, almost next to each other, using one another for balance. It requires a sense of equilibrium, and solid control of the lowering device. I was getting better at it, but I still occasionally yanked him off his footing when I braked too suddenly.

He was infinitely patient, though, and each time I learned a little more. I wondered what I'd learn this time.

After a few pitches, we had to admit that the sun had actually, really set, so we stopped to pull our jackets and headlamps out of the pack Alex wore.

"Mom, don't you have a jacket?"

"Yes, the red one—"

As soon as the words left my mouth, the awful truth hit me: my jacket lay on the ground, next to the spot where the photographer had hijacked me in midpreparation, with his stupid mike and transmitter. I hadn't had time to think about retrieving the jacket, or to hand it to Alex to stuff in his backpack.

Waylaid by a damn mike that I didn't even want! Now, no jacket, and worse, even more dangerous: my headlamp was in my jacket pocket.

My thermostat is set lower than most, and I am often cold, even when others aren't. Death by exposure while high up on a climb wasn't unheard of. Even if it didn't kill me, I knew from experience that it's hard to control things when you're shivering hard enough to shatter.

"*Merde!*"

But even worse than shivering all the way down was shivering all the way down *in the dark*. Not being able to see where I was planting my feet as I bounced around. Not being able to see the ledges. The running water. Cracks. Crevices. Overhangs . . .

"*Merde!*"

Alex couldn't get his headlamp to stay attached to my helmet, so he had to wear it. As we headed down our first pitch like that, the tiny circle of light bobbed around wildly, sometimes around my feet, sometimes not. I tried to follow it, tried to see where he had planted his feet against the wall and do the same. As much as he could, he aimed the light upward to allow me some visibility. It wasn't nearly enough, but it was all I had.

So I limped down my first big wall climb, chilled, semi-blinded. Thrilled!

Royal Arches was no longer a dream. I hadn't climbed it well, but I *had* climbed it. I'd toughed it out, fought my way up the crack section that I thought I couldn't do. Followed Jimmy Chin up the blank section I'd watched him on. I was learning. That was the best part about climbing:

each time I worked my way up another route, I learned more, about rock, about physics, and especially about myself. As we rappelled, I ran some of the scenarios from this climb through my memory and could see where I would do it better next time.

I could take Royal Arches off my list now. Another impossible climb, rendered possible by having the best guide in the world, and following him. Another dream accomplished.

As I navigated the last crux pitch of my first big wall climb in the dark and stepped back onto the Valley floor, I knew it wouldn't be enough. The whole day, my mind had been drawn west, just a few miles, to the bigger wall a few minutes down the road. Today was a warm-up. As hard as it had been for me—almost impossible in spots— I knew that this wall was small in comparison with the real one.

The *one*. The wall that climbers from all over the world pitted themselves against, broke records on, made history on.

El Capitan.

I couldn't explain why it drew me. Maybe it was all the hours I'd listened to my son describing his adventures on it. Maybe the allure, the fantasy of it had something to do with that Thanksgiving dinner when Alex, only twenty or so, called from two thousand feet up El Cap as we all sat down to turkey and fixings. Watching everyone's faces as the phone was passed around the table and they each shouted, "You're where?!" was enough to fuel stories for years. The immense, ineffable beauty of the wall had something to do with it, too. As did my fondness for challenges.

All of the above. Royal Arches was my training, my crucible. I knew there was a world of difference between this and El Cap. The naked eye made that clear. But, still, I'd done a big wall. If I could do one big wall, then . . .

thirty-four

"WHY EL CAP?"

"What's your motivation?"

These were the questions a couple of my climbing friends asked me. The first time I heard the question, it surprised the hell out of me. I'd always assumed that all climbers wanted to climb El Cap. Doesn't every pianist dream of playing in Carnegie Hall? Don't all baseball players dream of the World Series?

When I was teaching languages in my twenties, a teaching colleague told me that most Americans never master a foreign language because they didn't have a real, personal reason to learn one. I didn't understand. I still don't. A reason? Besides the challenge of it? The fun? The accomplishment? Besides the amazing fulfillment of being able to talk with millions of people you couldn't talk with before? Those all seemed like personal reasons to me.

Why go up El Cap? I never knew I needed more reason than the wanting, the dreaming. The challenge. There are rocks all over the world; for a climber, of any age, challenges abound. This is one of the most outstanding ones on the planet. To me, that was reason enough.

The first time Charlie and I drove into Yosemite, back when I was new to California, and I looked up and saw climbers hanging on the sheer wall of El Cap, I was captivated. *How must it feel to be up there? To be one of those specks hanging on the wall? What do they see from up there? How do they feel?* I wondered . . . but I knew that I'd never have answers to those questions. Back then, I wasn't a climber or an adventurer.

Even after I started climbing, I still wondered. How can a climber look up at the immensity of the wall and not want to climb it, not want to know what it feels like to be up there? How the world looks from the top? What the top itself looks like? Climbers go to places most people will never see and are granted vistas that thrill the soul. Climbing is the only way to see them.

Instead of questioning whether I *should* climb El Cap, the only question in my mind was: *Could* I? At my age? At my skill level? At sixty-six, I would be by far the oldest woman to attempt it. I'd retired from forty-four years of teaching several years ago. I was definitely not the usual type of climber you find on El Cap.

Climbing it was never a decision, more like a feeling that struck me back when I first saw it, and just never really disappeared completely. It lay dormant for years, ignored for decades, completely out of the question. I never told anyone. It wasn't the kind of thing that came up in conversation in my old life. Not among my teacher friends, certainly, nor my family or city friends. They didn't climb and would never understand. And then I became a climber and woke it up again. As my skills improved and I gained experience in many parts of the world, it would occur to me now and then, tickle my brain with *what ifs* and *maybes*. I always shut it down, but more and more gently each time.

If there was any chance of my climbing El Cap, it had to be with Alex. I knew it would be terrifying, and I wanted to go up with my son, whom I'd trusted with my life over and over, and who had skills that no one else on the planet seemed to have. He could handle anything up there. But he knew how I climbed. I never expected him to agree to such a crazy idea.

But after Royal Arches, it no longer seemed so crazy, at least to me.

thirty-five

JUGGING. JUMARS. THE EAST LEDGES. The Heart lines. The Nose. NIAD (Nose in a Day). The world of El Capitan has its own lexicon, a whole vocabulary of acronyms and place names and technical jargon. It was a language I didn't speak yet. But I was quickly becoming immersed in it, as I liked to do in foreign countries. Total immersion was my favorite way to learn a new language. It began the very first time I mentioned my dream to Alex.

"Alex, do you think there's any chance you could lead me up El Cap someday?"

"Sure. But you have to learn how to jug."

He had reduced it to a very simple quid pro quo. If I learned to use jumars—to jug—and acquired all the other skills that go with it—Alex would lead me up El Cap.

• • • • • • • • •

A JUMAR IS A device that attaches to the rope, with a large grip, or handle. Its teeth grab the rope, allowing the jumar to be pushed up, but not down. From each handle hangs a nylon strap, like a soft ladder, or alternately, a strap that attaches firmly to your foot. Two jumars are attached to the rope, one for each hand/foot combination, and each jumar also attaches to your harness, so you can sit back and hang if you need to rest or adjust anything. The movement is slide-up/step-up right, slide-up/step-up left, over and over. Jugging is like climbing a ladder that moves up with you.

Except that you're on a rope, not a hard ladder. The natural tendency is for the foot to thrust out sideways instead of down, which throws the body backward. You wind up hanging horizontally, rather than gliding vertically upward. Core control is the answer, but I didn't have any. Being able to lock off your bent arm was essential, but I couldn't. It would take time to develop all those skills. Time, and lots of muscles that I seldom used. And training.

At the climbing gym, a friend and I set up to try it. I had borrowed the gear from another climber, and watched the videos; I knew how to attach it all, knew the moves. We got permission to attach my rope to a top anchor—attaching it correctly took a few tries. Adjusting for the right length in the straps took more tries. And then more. I put on my leather gloves, checked all the gear again, and stepped up. And began to spin. I reached out with one foot to touch the wall near me, which only made me spin in the other direction. Tried again. Got accustomed to spinning slowly in space as I tried to push the gear up the rope.

Such hard physical work! Such coordination! So much to learn! It was a million times harder than it looked. Halfway up the rope, which only hung about thirty-five feet from the top anchor, I was exhausted. By the end of that first session, my forearms hurt, my triceps burned, one finger was beaten raw from jamming against all the metal gear I was pushing up, and my lower left leg was covered in massive, ugly bruises from the metal buckles on the leg strap. To make progress, I knew I'd need to set up a schedule. It began immediately, in February, since I hoped to do the climb for my birthday in September. That was my tradition with Alex.

Jugging requires the ability to set up a rope from a high enough place (and, ideally, leave it there). City parks frown on doing that off bridges or other structures. So my practice options were few, and I used them fully. I found climber friends who let me set up a rope in a tree at their house, and twice a week at least I would jug at the gym. An increasing number of laps each time. I would need to make serious progress if I was going to climb a three-thousand-foot wall.

. . . .

A THREE-THOUSAND-FOOT WALL. MY mind knows that there's no difference between hanging on a rope at fifty feet up, or a hundred feet, or a thousand. Or three thousand. Falling off any of those would be deadly. My head knows that. Doesn't help at all.

I went to Yosemite to join Alex on a glorious spring-like day in early March. He was going to take me up some real ropes to help me train for our climb. He also wanted to see whether I knew how to jug. So far, I had only jugged on one outdoor rope on real rock, at Mount Potosi, outside Las Vegas. It had taken me several tries to make it all the way up the ninety-foot rope. Not because it was ninety feet, but because that ninety-foot rope hung out over a valley whose floor was about a thousand feet lower.

Yep, my head knows the difference. Doesn't help one bit.

So Alex would help me get acclimated, help me wrap my mind around being so high on jumars, by taking me up the fixed ropes that are the lower part of the descent from El Cap. No matter which route a climber takes up El Cap, getting down requires walking—clambering, scrambling, climbing—down the East Ledges for a while, then rappelling down a series of six ropes, and then hiking for over an hour down to the ground.

We hiked up for over an hour, over a stream, tree trunks, other debris—ordinary words, like *hike* or *walk*, take on new meaning when following climbers. Then for a few minutes we scrambled over rocks, using hands and feet. Eventually, we reached a rope hanging down from about a hundred feet or so overhead.

"Okay, Mom, you know what to do?"

I nodded and stepped up to attach all my gear to the rope. Alex would either wait for me to finish the pitch and then follow me up, or he'd free-solo alongside me. If he attached himself to the rope at the same time as me, it would jerk the rope, pull it taut, pull me away from the rock, and probably make it harder for me to move upward. So for a while, at the beginning, he just let me jug. But waiting for me to finish each rope was too time-consuming for an El Cap speed-record holder, so he just climbed up behind me with a Micro Traxion, a tiny backup device with teeth that slide up the rope, attached to his harness by an extralong sling. If he fell, it would jerk my rope, and me—but we both knew he wasn't going to fall.

The second rope hung down to the top anchor of the first, and so on up to the fourth. I transitioned from one to the next as fast as I could—a bumbling first-timer. At the fourth, and last, ledge, we stopped for a few minutes. It was big enough to recline on, to eat, drink, replace some of our spent energy. And gawk at the vistas of Half Dome, Sentinel, and the south sides of the granite walls. The huge trees below us looked like tiny broccoli florets.

"Okay, Mom, so, you're okay getting back down, right?"

What? By myself?! "Alone?"

"I want to go up and do some rapping on El Cap."

You couldn't have told me that before we started? Given me time to get used to the idea?! I would have paid more attention to the route!

Other climbers were probably meeting Alex up there, waiting for him now. This is the descent. Made to ease the process of coming back down. I'd just come up it. Surely I could find my way down.

"Well, I guess . . . " I hated to sound so . . . afraid. Tentative. I wanted to sound like a climber. One who knew where to go and how to get there. To my ears, though, my wavering voice sounded like anything but.

It didn't stop Alex, though. He knew where he was going. Up. But he did wait until I was on the rope again, and checked all my gear one last time.

"Okay, Mom, I'll see you back at the house. You remember where we stashed the bikes?" We'd both come here several miles by bike from his friend's house in the Village and left the bikes locked together under a tree, at a safe distance from the trailhead. It had been a complicated morning.

"I think so." I nodded, thinking furiously about all the steps necessary before I'd be "back at the house." I'd just have to figure it out as I went.

He was gone before I got more than ten or fifteen feet down, still about one thousand feet up from the Valley floor. I rapped about halfway down the top rope and stopped at a small overhang. I glanced around. Half Dome to the right—I'd climbed that with Alex. Sentinel behind me—my son had free-soloed that. Manure Pile Buttress just below me—I'd climbed that several times with my friends from Sacramento and a few times with my son. Several of my articles about those climbs had been published in magazines in various parts of the world. It had taken years, but I had created a history with all the features I now saw around me.

So much had changed since my husband had abandoned me up on one of these hikes. I was at home here now. Not as much as my son, of course, but at home nonetheless. I told myself that, again and again, as

I rappelled down all the ropes, navigated the hike through the woods, found the bikes, and headed back to the house.

. . . .

EL CAP IS A MYTH. It's a story we tell about superhuman feats and impossible exposure and vistas to thrill the soul. Its face hangs on walls around the world, on calendars or large prints or postcards or photos in bars and restaurants and sports stores, in dorm rooms and basements and cubicles. It looms over Yosemite Valley, a reminder of what we might be capable of, if we let ourselves dream.

After I'd jugged the East Ledges ropes, I knew I had to go to El Cap, touch it, make friends with it—as much as one could make friends with a behemoth. In my head, it was still that myth, a legend. I needed to make it real so I wouldn't fear it quite so much.

I had never been close to El Cap, so Alex suggested that I stop by the Heart lines. A heart-shaped formation on the face of El Cap, about a third of the way up, the Heart is visible from the road or meadow, where tourists stand or sit or wander, awed by the majesty of El Capitan.

A series of six ropes connect the bottom of the Heart down to the ground, like the ropes on the descent ledges. These ropes allow climbers to jug up to some of the harder routes that begin at the Heart, and to haul up all the gear they'll need for their multiday ascent without exhausting themselves. Sort of an easy head start off the ground.

Or, as in my case, just to practice jumaring up, then rappelling back down.

As I bushwhacked through the woods between the road and the rock face, trying to follow Alex's off-handed directions, the doubts began to pile up. I didn't belong out here. The only people I passed were young men, in their prime of strength and daring, about to tackle the beast above them. They all carried packs the size of small refrigerators. I carried a small day pack that held only my jumars and some water. My pockets held a few packets of energy gels—running fuel that I could easily tear into and eat while climbing.

They were all young. I was old. They all climbed in pairs or groups. I was alone. They all knew where they were going. I had to ask everyone

I passed. But my son had recommended that I do this. When it came to climbing, he knew what he was talking about. So I kept walking, kept asking, kept ignoring the discrepancies, and finally found the fixed ropes that hang down from the Heart.

The Heart lines are popular with climbers who attempt El Cap, so I had to wait my turn. As the two young men before me and I sat or moved about, flexed or stretched, the two of them occasionally chatting about some piece of gear or other, the full force of the monster above me bore down on my psyche. The granite seemed to sway and swoop upward, like a playground slide shimmering in the sun. From the road, it had appeared gray. But sitting at its feet, under its spell, I could see huge swaths of creamy gold, melding into cascades of white and black and darker gold and ochre. It was a rich palette of earth colors, a visual feast that only added to the turmoil in my head, the overwhelming feeling of intimidation.

The sun had just hit this side of the rock, around the corner from the Dawn Wall—the hardest climb in the world. The climbers Tommy Caldwell and Kevin Jorgensen had recently completed it, to accolades worldwide. As with my son's accomplishments, I knew the words, but I doubted that I would ever grasp their true significance. I was a novice, and I wouldn't be pitting my skills against the real rock, just against the demons in my own head—and my lungs, and my arms—as I jugged up El Cap. I was going to have to dig deeper than I'd ever imagined possible.

Today, though, I was on my own. As I waited my turn, I tried to quiet my mind, still unconvinced that I belonged out here, alone. But I would follow Alex's advice and at least try. The young men in front of me didn't speak to me; I probably reminded them of Mom. I kept silent, too, not wanting to distract them as they got ready. I thought about my headlamp, lying useless at the bottom of Royal Arches. I would never do that to anyone.

An overwhelming riot of impressions beat at my brain. Waves of earth colors pulsed under the unrelenting sun. Swifts and swallows flitted about the rocks, and an occasional scolding raven. Gravel crunched underfoot as I stretched every muscle I knew how to stretch. My gaze was repeatedly drawn to the monstrous walls on the other side of the Valley. But the noise in my head overwhelmed all the other sensations.

I watched the first kid attach his jumars to the rope. One-two-three-done. Wow. I had a long way to go to get that fast and comfortable. And then he was gone, jugging smoothly and quickly. His partner, clearly the junior member of that twosome, had lots of questions for him before he left the ground. Some of his questions surprised me. It seemed that if he was preparing to climb El Cap, he should have already known most of what he was asking. I did.

The second kid took longer to attach than I probably would. That filled me with hope! Silly, no doubt, but I was ecstatic to discover that I might not be the slowest, most uninformed, most uncomfortable climber out here.

And then it was my turn. No more wavering, questioning, doubting. It was time.

But I couldn't attach my jumars to the rope until the second kid had attached to the next rope. I didn't want to pull him off or make his job any harder. So I waited. And waited. The first set of bolts, where he was transitioning to the next rope, was probably close to two hundred feet up, so high that I couldn't see what he was doing. It was clearly something very energetic, and the rope moved back and forth as he climbed, bending, stretching across to grab something—the second rope?—then some more animated moving around. Whatever he was doing, it took almost fifteen minutes before he started up the next rope and left mine free.

Another bit of hope. Yesterday, with Alex on the East Ledges, I had transitioned from rope to rope in just a few moments. Clumsily, maybe, not as fast as he would have liked, not professionally or confidently, but way faster than this guy.

I thrust my right jumar up the rope, raising my right foot at the same time. Then the left, to join the right. The dynamic rope stretched and stretched . . . and finally my feet left the ground.

I was on El Cap. On my own.

The first rope went smoothly. My mind was on one thing only: fluidly operating the jumars. I tried to will them to glide steadily upward, sometimes tipping them slightly to one side or other to accomplish that. My unbending toes felt the painful pressure of being forced straight into the rock. I might need stronger, more reinforced approach shoes for the real day, or maybe steel-toed shoes that I could switch to at the beginning, after the hike. Something that would protect and support the front of each foot.

"Having fun?"

Merde! I spun around to the sound of a male voice to my right. I'd been so focused I hadn't noticed the huge flake attached to the rock face next to me. On top of it, about eighty feet or so off the deck, a climber reclined as he belayed his partner up.

"Sorry," he said, smiling. "Didn't mean to scare you."

I chuckled. "Didn't expect anybody up here."

We chatted for a few moments. He was from Arkansas, or Alabama, some A-place whose name I almost caught. My mind was too busy to really listen. Half Dome had gotten lower. The trees below were smaller.

I was on El Cap!

I was moving smoothly upward, I was in control, I knew what I was doing.

I was jugging on El Cap!

Still, it felt surprisingly good to have a distraction, and we chatted for a while before I continued up. It was a tiny bit of ordinary amid a world of monstrously huge and foreign. We chatted like neighbors at the back fence, rather than like two people in the most outrageous, non-human-friendly place imaginable.

I was jugging on El Cap. I knew I'd have to get over this ridiculous starstruck attitude if I was going to actually do this climb. But just for this morning, I allowed myself to bask in the thrill.

thirty-six

I SAT DOWN WITH a thud at the rest area picnic table, my hand over my mouth. My daughter's text stared up at me, screaming. Shouting. Demanding.

"Alex soloed el cap! Phew!!"

Tears, then a shudder or two. I shook my head in disbelief, slowly, like in a dream. It was only eleven o'clock in the morning. June 3, 2017. *I just hiked with him in Yosemite yesterday afternoon.*

Not even lunchtime yet, and Alex had free-soloed the massive granite wall that most climbers took several days to climb, with ropes. Without a rope, it was unthinkable.

El Cap. I knew he'd always wanted to free-solo it. But he'd *always* wanted to—and anyone looking up could see it was impossible. And I knew he was training hard. But he *always* trained hard. He was in Yosemite. He *lived* there in the spring and the fall, every year. Everything was as it always was.

And yet.

He never told me in advance about his free-solos, big or small. I'd always appreciated that—a simple choice that helped keep me sane, and his own mind clear. He'd probably done hundreds of little solos. And I knew that some, equally notable as his several massive ones, had gone relatively unnoticed by the media, or anyone. But this one . . . This feat defied the imagination of even the most accomplished professional climbers. I would find out later that one of his friends, one of the best on the wall, had left the Valley rather than watch.

"Alex soloed el cap!"

How could I get back in the car and keep driving up to Portland, where Stasia was waiting for my friends and me? How could I do anything right now? I thought again of Bill Bryson's summing up of those emotions: "You don't hike the Appalachian Trail and then go home and cut the grass." If hiking—walking!—had that extreme effect on the psyche, where would Bryson have put this? I wouldn't be cutting the grass for a long, long time.

I knew if I removed my hand from over my mouth, I would make some sound that I really didn't want to share with anyone. The friends who were making this six-hundred-mile drive with me understood, and left me alone. They were parents, too.

This was one of those moments:

Where were you when the Twin Towers fell?

Where were you when they landed on the moon?

Where were you when Alex free-soloed El Cap?

. . . .

"ALEX HONNOLD CLIMBS YOSEMITE'S El Capitan Without a Rope"— *National Geographic*

"Alex Honnold is First to Scale Yosemite's El Capitan without a Rope"—*CNN*

"Alex Honnold's Perfect Climb"—*The New Yorker*

"Triumph of Tenacity"—*Newsday*

"An 'Incomprehensible' Climb in Yosemite"—*New York Times*

Incomprehensible is perhaps the best word for my son's accomplishment on El Cap. Who could possibly wrap their mind around such a thing?

I should probably have seen it coming. The signs were always there.

As I write this, my daughter is stealth-camping, alone with her bike, among the ponderosas that line the Deschutes River in eastern Oregon. Hundreds of miles from her home in Portland. In a few months, she plans to climb the highest peak in Mexico, El Pico de Orizaba, eighteen thousand feet high.

As I write this, my son has just been dropped off by plane to camp on a glacier in a gorge in Alaska, from which he and two other professional climbers will ski up to climb a four-thousand-foot wall. After that, he's off to Antarctica to do the same.

Last week I hiked up to Pyramid Peak, 9,964 feet, in Desolation Wilderness near Lake Tahoe. Before that, I'd hiked Mount Whitney.

I should have seen it coming. And yet.

. . . .

A FEW YEARS PRIOR to Alex's free-solo of El Cap, I was leading a 5.10a in the Berkeley climbing gym with him, just to get back into the swing of things, as it were. I hadn't climbed for over three weeks, life being what it often is, and this route offered jugs, or huge, deep handholds, all the way. Felt great, like home.

Both hands comfortably deep in bucket-sized holds, right foot firmly planted on another jug, I leaned left, pulled up some rope. But instead of clipping cleanly, I suddenly found myself airborne.

"What the—"

I was furious! Everything had been so solid—until I was flying through the air.

When I fall climbing, I always assume it's my own fault. I started climbing when I was fifty-eight. Things are pretty much set by that age. You know you're responsible for everything you do. The fall took my breath away, just for a moment.

I got back on and climbed up to where it had happened, shaking a bit from the surprise. I know everyone falls. If you don't, you're not trying hard enough. But a 10a? And it felt so solid!

I found the same comforting, huge jugs for my hands, placed my right foot firmly, more carefully, on the bigger jug, leaned left.

"*Merde!*"

This time, as I felt air beneath my foot, I saw that the jug I'd put all my weight on had spun upside down. And in that millisecond, nanosecond, that scintilla of a second, all the questions people have asked me about my son gripped me by the heart and squeezed the remaining breath out of me. In that microinstant, my little 10a was El Capitan. And I had just plunged to my death—through no fault of my own.

I'd been solid. I'd done everything right. *I was solid.* And then I was dead.

But I wasn't. As I saw the hold spin and realized I was flying off, the slo-mo frame flashed past my widened eyes: foothold breaks, son plunges (through no fault of his own) three thousand feet to his death—and my disengaged brain screamed "No!" and squeezed my fingers shut in a non-death grip that wrenched both shoulders but kept me on the wall.

"How can you stand it?"

It wasn't me I saw flying through the air. And the wall wasn't forty feet high, but thousands. This scenario has played a million times in my head. My body knows what to do—what he would do. So my hands took over, held on as if both our lives depended on it.

The lines blur when I climb with Alex. He and I are one, a unit, as we were for nine months so long ago. He probably won't see it that way for decades, but such is youth.

I should have just taken the fall. But in my head, where climbing really happens, falling was not an option. Not on a big wall.

Imagination can be a terrible thing. Without it, I'd be leading far harder climbs, but I never would have dreamed up the adventures I've had, with and without Alex. Without imagination, my friend who fell off his free-solo climb this summer would still be around to laugh and climb with me, but we never would have met. Without it, my son wouldn't be on the cover of *National Geographic* . . . and would he be really alive, the way he is now? Or would he be biding time, like so many of us? Dying takes many forms. So does living. The hard part is recognizing them.

thirty-seven

FOR MANY YEARS, ALEX told me stories about his Yosemite season as he breezed through my house on his way there or back or somewhere else. Spring and fall, the best climbers from all over the world can be found in Yosemite, testing themselves, honing their skills, getting together and accomplishing feats other climbers only dream about. If you drive through the Valley, you can see the tiny dots, hanging so high up you need a telescopic lens or binoculars.

I never imagined that I would have my own Yosemite season one day.

It began simply, tentatively, sometime during the summer I started to realize my dream of climbing El Cap. While hiking out to the wall for some jugging practice, I happened to meet a climber I recognized from magazines and videos. A friend of my son's. He was with another climber, who invited me to come along on a tiny adventure, where I met other climbers . . . and the momentum built. And grew. And soon I was out there with them, on El Cap and in other parts of Yosemite, hanging on bolts, swinging on ropes, learning more of the skills I'd need to go up El Cap with my son. They knew what I needed to learn and were happy to teach me.

With Diana, I mustered the courage to ascend to the Mammoth Ledges, one pitch higher than the Heart, far more exposed and harder to reach. Ryan taught me how to lower myself out across the rock face, when the rope I needed to attach my jumars to was hanging way to the left or right of the ledge I stood on. With every one of them, I enlarged my skill set and layered on a bit more of the courage I would need. My stomach knotted as I watched their insouciance, as they bounced around on ledges I could barely see. They terrified me with their confidence.

They were all young. In their prime. I was so far from my prime that I didn't even want to think about the comparisons. My knees got weak at the disconnect between their life and mine—or what I had previously thought of as mine. As the sun glided across the Valley, highlighting one slab of wall after another, I considered another option: this could be my life, too.

These people all loved what I love. They sought what I sought. But they hadn't spent years, decades, trying to protect very small people and keep them safe. That changed one's mind-set.

And they didn't do it as fast as my son. With Alex, I'd go up and down in one day, on a monster wall that takes other climbers three or four days. They sleep on ledges or on portaledges that they lug up in huge haul bags and assemble up there. They make coffee up there, and hang out, and take pictures and enjoy the view. But Alex is the speed king of Yosemite, and he doesn't haul gear behind him. That was tedious, hard work and took lots of time. Alex's MO was simple: Climb fast and get it over with. Then go home and rest.

Maybe the only difference in our climbing styles was that when they jugged they clipped in with one daisy or sling, and I'd always clip in with two. They jumared without backup, and I'd always have my little Micro Traxion, its teeth firmly gripping my rope. My safety. My life.

We'll all get to the same place.

thirty-eight

THE JOURNEY OF A lifetime began in the dark. Alex and I both wanted to start our climb early enough that we wouldn't have to navigate the East Ledges in the dark on the way down to the rappel ropes. It wouldn't turn out that way, but that was my fault.

The part of El Cap that we'd be climbing is twenty pitches, several pitches longer than Royal Arches. From the videos I'd seen, they all looked like harder, longer, more complex pitches than the ones I'd done there. It was, after all, El Capitan.

That myth thing kept messing with my head.

The three of us—Alex, his friend Sam, and I—scrambled up the rocky approach in the dark before dawn, a long, steep slog of about an hour and a half. I kept the wall next to my right shoulder as I stumbled upward, following the tiny circle of my headlamp. At least I knew I had the lamp this time. I felt my way over big blocks and small blocks, over talus—accumulated broken rock debris—and tree trunks, and then up a series of piled rocks so steep there were hand-ropes to grab and pull on. I glanced up. The sun hadn't reached the Valley yet, so only a hulking black shadow hung over us, slightly darker than the graying sky. The darkness comforted in a weird, intimate way. I couldn't see anything, couldn't see the monster wall looming over me—only the clarity of my own heart and how much I wanted this.

I had never thought of it in those terms. I wanted this. Of course—but I'd always thought about it in a very matter-of-fact way, over all those months of practicing, of jugging, of driving to Yosemite and back, of teaching some of my friends from Sacramento to jug. Just another goal. Just another climb.

But it wasn't. As I hauled myself up the last hand-rope, using my jumar instead of my hands for security, I was unable to see the wall or anything around me, yet I was also seeing clearly for the very first time. I'd done all the research, watched all the videos of other climbers on the route we were going to climb, called—so appropriately—Lurking Fear (we were climbing it on Halloween day). I knew about the big rocky ledge near the top, and which pitch had the traverse where I'd have to lower myself almost horizontally across the wall to reach the next rope. My new friends had taught me to do all that.

My fiction-writer mind had pictured this scene so many times! I knew exactly how everything would go, who would be there to send me off, how it would feel. I'd been a writer all my life. Fiction was my world. Living for years with someone who never spoke had made me quite adept at imagining verbal scenes. By extension, any time I had been about to meet someone in a social setting, especially if my husband was going to also be there, my imagination would tell me what would be said by whom, who would do what, and what it would all mean. In reality, none of it ever happened the way my writer's imagination had dictated. Fiction was always better.

The voices I thought I heard as we finally approached the base of the climb were so familiar, so right for the scene, because I'd heard them there so many times in my writer's head. I knew who would show up, what they would say, how our conversation would go, and the emotions it would evoke in my head, in my heart, in my life.

But this was nonfiction. Real life. A real big wall. Although I knew three of my friends wanted to be at the base of the climb as we launched, we were climbing on a weekday, when most people had to work. The friend who'd hoped to video our start wasn't able to come from Sacramento. This was nothing like the way I'd imagined the beginning of our climb, so many times. But then again, nothing had been as I'd imagined it for the last five months. As we roped up, I suspected that this whole long day would be very different from the rosy scene in my head. My imagination was far too timid for this outrageous new world of mine.

But if they *had* come to see us off, though…! I wiped away a few tears for all the new friends who populated my life, the ones who would have been here if they'd been able to. They couldn't know, any of them, the years I'd spent friendless and bewildered, or how long I'd hated Yosemite, when all my memories of it were stained by abandonment. Silence. Emptiness. My real life now was such a rich mosaic of people, of extraordinary challenges, like this one, of colors. The old life was fading into a pale sepia version that I had trouble recalling.

Shadows faded into light while we pulled out all our gear and began to get ready to climb. I dumped my jumars onto a smooth, flat rock and began attaching the two nylon daisy chains to my harness. Then I slid each foot into the leg straps, pulled them tight, and checked that the straps that linked them to the jumars were the right length. Heavy leather fingerless gloves would keep my hands from getting burned from friction when the weighted rope slid through them, and would help keep callouses from forming as I handled the jumars all day. My knees were always bruised and bloodied after a hard day on the rock, so I'd vacillated for weeks about whether to wear kneepads. But I'd never used them on a climb before, and on this day, when habit mattered, I didn't want to start anything new, so I'd left the new red kneepads a friend had lent me in the car. I stood, straightened, and checked everything again.

Alex and Sam tied in to both ends of one rope; Sam would belay Alex up. He and Alex had climbed together before, and both of them seemed completely comfortable as they got ready. Their laughter sounded like little kids in the school recess yard. It wasn't just banter, though; they talked strategy for the climb, how they would do this or that. I just listened and concentrated on preparing everything correctly as I tried to catch my breath from the hike.

Normally, when a pair of climbers attempts El Cap, they swap roles, alternately leading and jugging. A leads and B jugs up behind him, cleaning the gear A has placed. Then B leads and A jugs up and cleans. They leapfrog all the way up the wall this way.

That's why there were three of us today. I wouldn't clean—I wasn't strong enough. I would jug the whole wall, using only the second rope Alex was planning to drag up. Sam would jug up behind Alex and clean all the gear Alex had placed.

Alex attached the second rope to the back of his harness. Once he stopped at a set of bolts and made an anchor, he would attach that rope to it. Only then could I clamp my jumars onto the second rope and begin jugging, while Sam jugged on the first rope, cleaning the gear. Sam and I would often be going in quite different directions, with my rope hanging straight down, while his wound its way up whichever route Alex had taken. Sometimes it would move horizontally across the rock face or go under a roof, attached to gear that dealt with whatever topography the rock offered. When we topped out, Sam would have pulled out all the gear and given it back to Alex to use again for leading the next pitch. There would be no trace of us left on the rock.

No trace. Like when he'd free-soloed it.

There are probably pitches on El Cap that I could climb. But it's easier and far less time-consuming to just stay in one mode, rather than switching all my gear and shoes from jugging to climbing and back. And I had the best guide, the best leader in the world, willing and able to lead Mom up the whole wall.

I watched Alex glide over the rock. Some rock language came tumbling out of my mouth, mumbled, whispered. Clearly, what he'd done was impossible. This was a smooth, flat granite wall. A mirror. To us. To me. What I was about to do was nothing in comparison.

A very intimidating nothing.

· · · · · · · · · ·

I STEPPED UP CLOSE to the wall. Sam had let me know he'd gone high enough so that my rope wouldn't affect his, in case they came close together. I attached my jumars. I attached my Micro Traxion, just in case. In my mind, I could see Alex's eyes rolling, hear his derisive tone: "In case of what? You have two jumars." He's young. I know there's always an "in case" waiting. Lurking. Sometimes it happens, sometimes it spares us.

The straps around my feet were snug. Both daisy chains attached my harness to the jumars, and they were the right length to allow me to sit back in my harness if I needed to. I took a few gulps of water, then clipped the bottle back onto my harness. Then I checked everything again.

I slid the jumars up the rope and stepped up, but the rope had so much stretch in it that my own weight dragged it back down. I had to do that several times before my feet left the ground. Then training took over. For a few minutes, I was a machine. Push. Step. Change sides. Push my toes against the wall to help. Push. Step. Check that the rope is feeding through the Micro Traxion backup. I didn't want to have to stop to deal with it later if there was a problem. Push. Step. At the beginning, when I'd started training for this, my triceps ached, burned. Now I didn't feel them.

At the first transition, I thought about the young man in front of me when I'd first jugged the Heart lines. I'd waited for him to move to the next rope for more than ten minutes. Even I could tell how slow he was— me, a rank beginner. Maybe he was an excellent climber, but he was definitely new at jugging. Newer than me.

Now I was waiting again, but not for the same reasons. I couldn't start until Alex finished the next pitch, made an anchor, and put the rope up. So I had to wait, my harness attached to a hanging belay, which is nothing but two or three permanent bolts in the wall. No ledge, nothing to put your feet on but the vertical wall. I chatted with Sam, who was hanging from the same two bolts as he belayed Alex, but I didn't really hear anything he said.

I'm one of those tiny dots that people watch from El Cap Meadow with binoculars.

Sam started upward, climbing and cleaning the gear Alex had placed.

A tiny sound, maybe a moan, or a shout. I glanced around. It must have been me. I was alone. On the first belay station of El Cap.

Holy shit!! my mind screamed. *I'm on El Cap!*

I'd known I would be, when I started learning how to jumar months ago. I knew I'd train hard, and I'd get here eventually. I hadn't doubted that for a moment. The reality, though, left me shaking and breathless. El Capitan! The myth! And I was climbing it with a legend among climbers. My son.

"White rope's fixed!" Alex shouted, letting me know that my rope was ready. My moment was over. Time to get back to business. I attached my jumars and started up the second pitch. Gotta go. Lots to do.

I blasted up the first few pitches, surprising myself more than Alex. I jugged faster than I'd ever done in any practice. The unrelenting sun, the vast sea of rock, my own tenuous state of nerves as I approached each belay station—none of it slowed me down as I'd expected it to.

When I climb with Alex, I never know where we are in the route. I'm not good at counting pitches. So I'd counted nine when Alex announced that we were on pitch twelve. Yes! We were going far faster than I'd expected. I knew it wouldn't stay that way, but for that moment, it felt wonderful.

As he started leading the next pitch, I looked up. My mouth gaped open. He was climbing a very distinct crack that started right above me and went up, and up, and up, cutting straight through an empty face of pure, clean granite. It looked like an artist's illustration of perspective. Its black line went straight up, narrower and narrower, until it petered out of view, lost against the cerulean sky.

Endless crack. Endless challenge. Like life. An endless, decades-long challenge had brought me to this point. Someday, I'd like to be able to climb things like that . . . not like Alex, of course, but just . . . better. Much better. For now, my job—and it was plenty—was just to jumar up to him, stop, and wait. I could do that.

We were at one of the two traverse pitches—where our route went sideways. As Sam and I hung off the belay point, Alex wandered farther and farther to the right, not getting much higher than the two of us for quite a distance.

He was brilliantly silhouetted against the sun as it slowly progressed around the Nose, the sharply angled front of El Cap, and onto our side of the wall. Behind him, the lines of the granite walls swooped down to the Valley floor, where a carpet of towering conifers stood, reaching upward toward us, minuscule in the distance and misty gray-green in the early light.

I looked down, beyond him, to the trees. Nothing. No queasies, no fear. No dizzies. Just amazement at the endless beauty, marred only by the brown trees here and there that had succumbed to the combination of beetles and years-long drought. All that practice on the Heart lines and descent ropes had made the incredible, mind-numbing exposure, if not comfortable, certainly less terrifying.

When the sun reached our side of El Cap, its stark rays highlighted the streaks of earth colors that ran through the rock. But where there were shadows—under flakes that stood out from the rock face, or in corners—the contrast was startling, from brilliant gold or ochre or snowy white to intense black. It was a palette to make an artist cry.

Okay, so tears are understandable up here. They weren't for me, though, so I swiped them away.

Before I'd started climbing, I had only my imagination to tell me what Alex was up to when he went climbing. And what a vivid, frightening story my imagination told me! That can be far, far worse than the actual scenario, but can feel just as real. It's the source of that question, the one everyone asks me: How can I stand it? How can I watch the videos of what my son has done? How do I stay sane knowing what he does for a living?

Learning to climb, being up here, with him, was the antidote. Some of the fears dissipated in the face of knowledge, when I saw firsthand what he was up to, what he faced, what his world was like. Not all of them disappeared. I'm still his mother. But climbing has been the best armor against that specter.

Until I began this odyssey, this adventure, months ago, El Cap was an unimaginable, frightening monster. Little by little, I'd grown accustomed to it, made friends with it, come to feel more comfortable in its presence. As a climber must, to climb it.

So: tears, but not exactly for me. I was beginning to understand what free-soloing this wall had required. That my son met those requirements is both frightening and comforting. Skill, of course—but there are many climbers physically capable of climbing what he'd free-soloed. Mental control—maybe the biggest requirement, and probably the one that made Alex unique. Keeping his head together, blocking out the circumstances. Equally as necessary as the climbing skill, but far less easily mastered. And a level of stamina not easily reached.

"How could anyone . . . ?" people often start, as they gaze up at El Cap. And they're right. Not just anyone, though. Clearly Alex is different, in ways the rest of us will never comprehend.

The tears were for the culmination of months of training and hard, hard work. For the chance to be here, a step closer to understanding his feat. When I looked down at the tiny trees so far below us, my mom imagination kicked in, every time. A very different outcome is so easily understood, here. I could imagine the headlines. He could so easily have ended as a statistic, instead of becoming a legend.

And, especially, some tears for the awe of motherhood. Parenting—like life in general—is a crapshoot. We can't know how it'll turn out, so we just plod along, doing the best we can with what we're given. We all learn that, if we're lucky. So while we can strive for something in life, we should. The bigger the challenge, the greater the reward. My son knows things that have taken me a lifetime to begin to embrace.

Stasia does, too. When she digs deep inside herself to pedal just a few more miles, to reach a river or a campground or a town, to get out of bear country, or to keep to her thousand-mile schedule, or to run just a few more miles, she's accessing the same aquifer of stamina and tenacity that feeds her brother's feats.

Who had learned more from whom? I'd often wondered that over the years as my children continued to surprise me. Her scintillating, contagious smile and his unique take on life provided the only answer I'd probably ever have to that question. We were a winning team—and like any successful team, all the members learned from each other.

I hoped we always would.

. . . .

AS I WAITED MY turn at a belay station, waited to attach my jumars and start climbing, I looked up. Alex was moving slowly left, under a small roof. His fingers were against the granite, hooked up under the small space between the roof flake and the wall. He kept sliding them a few inches to the left as his feet followed, then a few more, a tedious, slow crawl. I'd done that kind of move before, on a smaller scale, and knew how hard it was. It required enormous arm strength. I instinctively shook out my arms and hands, glad I wouldn't have to actually climb that.

Someday, though, it would be so gratifying to know I was strong enough to execute a move like that.

"Watch me!" Alex shouted down to Sam, climber-speak for "I'm on something really precarious and might fall, so be ready to pull the rope taut!"

When Alex and I climb together, it's so simple for him that I'd never heard him use that phrase. This, though, was the real deal. Both Sam and I watched him really closely.

Suddenly the implication of what I was watching hit me: Alex was moving left. *Way* left. Away from above me. I was no longer looking up at him, but rather, sideways and up. Like from the bottom of a pendulum.

"Oh, *merde!*" Some more rock language came spilling out as I thought back to my first attempt at a pendulum, on Royal Arches. I wasn't going to escape this day unscathed.

Sam looked at me with his eyebrows raised, but said nothing. Maybe he didn't like pendulums either. Then he smiled.

"It's not as hard as it looks. Not like climbing on the rope." What he was doing. "All you have to do is lower yourself out as you start. Then it's straight up."

He nodded toward the roof Alex just navigated. "I have the hard job." He had to clean all of Alex's gear, which was all over the wall now, right and left and all along the underside of that roof. I looked down. We were at least a thousand feet off the ground. Probably a lot more; I have no head for that. The thought of swinging on the rope activated a tiny little corner of nausea waiting in my stomach. Lurking, I think. Lurking Fear.

I managed a short laugh. "I know."

I didn't blink. If I did, the tears would have started pouring down my face. Instead, I looked up, my moist eyes wide and attentive, and watched Alex, hoping Sam wouldn't see my terror. I thought about asking him to let me tie into a bight, or short section, of his rope just for the first few moments of the swing, so I'd be under control from both sides. If I did something stupid and swung out of control, or started to spin, he could stop me. But that would be cheating, the chicken way out. I had to lower myself out, not depend on him. This whole day was my idea. They were doing this, both of them, going through all this work, all day, for me. I had to play by their rules.

With my jumars attached to my white jugging rope, I would also pull a long bight of the same rope, which was tied to my harness, and clip it through a 'biner at the bolts where Sam and I were hanging. Then, slowly, as I inched to the left with my feet, I would feed out that bight as I pushed the jumars up the rope, simultaneously moving up and left. Hard, physical work that tested my balance and nerve.

Suck it up, I told myself. *You're not gonna swing.* That wasn't a given, not by a long shot. But I fervently hoped it was true.

I looked over my knots, tightened my gloves, checked my foot straps, my daisies, my backup device, the locks on my locking 'biners, then checked it all again. Sam went over how I'd attached my rope to the bolt where we were both hanging. Good to go.

I began to feed out rope and lower myself sideways and slightly downward. With each arm's length of rope, I fought my own weight as I pushed my jumars up the jugging rope. Each feed of rope got me a few feet closer to hanging straight below Alex. Once he was more or less straight above me, I would push the jumars up as high as I could reach, and release the restraining rope. This was the first time I'd ever tried this maneuver. The theory was quite different from the actual heavy, scary fact.

But it worked, more or less the way I'd imagined it, just harder. Before too long, I was straight beneath Alex, back in familiar territory. I released the long bight of rope, checked all my gear again, and continued jugging up to my son.

. . . .

"WOULD YOU LIKE SOME TEA?"

Two young men smiled broadly as I popped over the ledge to join Alex, who was standing next to them flaking his rope. The older one held up a Jetboil full of boiling water, for tea, apparently. The cave they sat in was deep enough for them and all their sleeping gear. Across the front they'd strung strands of rope, back and forth several times, from which they'd hung helmets, bandannas, shoes, several ropes of different colors, pounds and pounds of metal gear, and their massive haul bag that held all that stuff when they were climbing up the wall. It was a strange, colorful mosaic behind which they sat eating their supper.

Teatime? In a big, comfortable cave? On El Cap?

"I'd love to," I said, "if I weren't pressed for time." I nodded toward my son. "As soon as he gets to the top, Sam and I have to start moving. And the top doesn't look so far away—I can see trees."

"Yeah, probably only about two, three hundred feet left."

Three hundred feet! We were going to make it! I didn't have much left in me, and each time I looked up, that worried me a bit more. Three hundred feet sounded doable. About one-tenth of the total feet we'd climb today. Hard, but manageable.

"Almost there." Sam flashed me a broad, open smile as he reached us.

The three of us did all the necessary rope maneuvers while Erik and Curt introduced themselves—Sam gave Alex back the gear so he could keep leading, and put him on belay. I removed my jumars from the second rope so Alex could carry it up and attach it for me to use again. Soon we were done and Alex was off, Sam's hands moving rhythmically as he belayed Alex up from the ledge where Erik and Curt were camping for their last night on the wall.

"Nice bivy," I said to them. "First time on El Cap?"

They both nodded. "You're Alex's mom?" Curt, the younger one, asked me.

"That's me. Does your mom know you're up here?"

"Yeah, she was a good sport about it."

"Does she climb?"

"No!" he said, with an emphatic head shake. "She's a nurse."

"Two of my climbing friends are nurses."

"Really?!" His eyes widened at the possibility of sharing this very important side of his life with his mother.

Sam was too busy watching his climber and belaying to join in our chat. But he did tell me the name of the cave and ledge where Erik and Curt had made their home for the night: Thanksgiving Ledge.

"It's still light," I said to Erik, "how come you didn't just finish it?"

"It's a few more pitches. A couple hundred feet, maybe more, and we're hauling lots of gear. More fun to sleep here and finish in the morning. Our last night on the wall."

"Okay, he's done," Sam said, watching Alex as he pulled the rope out of his belay device.

It took me a few tries to clamp my jumars onto the rope; I could barely squeeze my hands closed anymore. I thrust the first jumar upward, but my reach had gotten shorter. My biceps trembled. Triceps complained bitterly. I hoped I could ignore them just a little bit longer. I added my Micro Traxion, checked my foot straps and my daisy chains, and headed slowly, deliberately up to finish my climb of the wall that had filled my dreams for so long.

. . . .

MORE OVERHANGING BLOCKS. I looked up, breathing hard. Hurting.

I wasn't going to make it. My entire body was screaming that message, loud and clear. But there was no alternative—I *had* to make it, we were committed. The only way off this wall was up. But at the same time, every part of my body was telling me, in no uncertain terms, that I was done. I didn't have anything left.

"Don't hold the rope, Mom!" Alex shouted down for the second time.

"*Merde!*" I muttered under my breath. I knew he meant well. He was trying to get me up these last few sections of lumpy, blocky, overhanging rocks as efficiently as he knew how. And I knew that holding the rope while jugging was bad form. But I also knew it was the only way I was going to be able to follow him up there. Besides, I wasn't really *holding* it: I was wrapping my whole arm around it to keep myself vertical. To make up for the core muscles that had abandoned me several pitches ago. Left elbow around the rope, right hand pulling or pushing the jumar up the rope. Switch sides. Do it again. Back and forth. Over and over. And over.

Alex probably couldn't even imagine such weakness.

My fingers were cramping. My forearms hurt so much I could hardly close my hands around the jumars. My shoulders and toes alternated between sharp, stinging stabs and dull aches. From the pain in my shin, I knew that it would be covered in purple blotches. I didn't mind the pain. But it was making me weaker, slower. Which made me angry. While I'd been jugging up El Cap, the sun had traveled the whole Valley and was settling behind the wall to the left of us. It would be dark soon. My nightmare scenario.

I had already done that part of our descent in the dark, when one of the friends I'd taught to ascend ropes had been so slow during a climb that nightfall caught us while we were rappelling down the East Ledges ropes. So I knew I could handle it. But we were far from the point where we'd begin our rappel down the East Ledges. We were still going *up*. As the sun went down.

"*Merde!*"

"Last pitch!" Alex shouted back toward me. His encouraging tone was exactly what I needed. Despite the physical misery, with one eye on the disappearing sun, I pushed the jumar up for the millionth time. Last pitch—I might actually make it.

But where was the top? The summit? Alex didn't seem to be climbing anymore, just scrambling, jumping. I, however, was struggling over blocks and overhanging rocks and cracks and working just as hard as I'd been all day. I looked up, squinting against the last weak rays of sun. More rocks. More walls. No flat land. No summit. Nothing I would call a top.

It was getting hard to see where I was putting my feet. Everything was uniformly gray. Granite gray. Dark gray. About to be black. I pushed myself just a little faster.

On my computer, I'd read or watched everything everywhere that described the top of El Cap. This bore no resemblance to any of it. We clearly weren't there yet.

"One more rope, Mom!" Alex shouted back down to me through thick darkness. The sun had only just set, but I couldn't see where his voice was coming from. One more rope? The end of the rope I'd been jugging on was tied to my harness. We'd only brought two. Where was Sam?

"Use the hand-rope." His instructions came floating through the vast dark as I approached what I'd thought was more wall. It was wall, sort of, but not *the* wall. This was a citadel of low, lumpy rock blockades— several, I soon discovered—that guard the summit from invaders. Like us.

I probably had read something about the unprotectable scrambling at the top. But my memory, my mind, my whole body was intently focused on making it up just a few more feet, a few more inches, then a few more, and a few more . . . After all that endless jugging, suddenly I was climbing, using hands and feet. But I couldn't see where I was putting them, and the approach shoes I'd worn all the way up gave me little purchase on the rounded rocks. I had a headlamp in my backpack, but didn't want to take the time to stop, take off my pack, rummage around to find it, zip it up again, and put it all back on while somehow still hanging on to the hand-rope. It all sounded like way too much work. The "one more rope" he'd warned me about was a series of hand-ropes fixed there to help climbers over these last daunting sprints. But having climbed the whole wall, all two thousand feet of it, in under one day, I had very little sprinting left in me.

Now I knew why most people take four days on this route.

So I kept feeling for handholds and footholds, following Alex's voice— that beautiful, deep, encouraging voice that had gotten me through my very first road race, so many years ago. It was a beacon I could focus on right then, rather than on my situation.

"Over here, Mom. Come straight toward me." Out of the dark. Simple, clear, oh so welcome.

"Nice, Mom." He'll never know how important those little words of encouragement were! I knew I wasn't doing a nice job of this climb, by his standards. By anyone's standards, even my own. On this last daunting series of rock walls I had slowed to a crawl, and my fingers weren't responding, so it took me forever to clip or unclip the rope.

When I got to the last bolt on the last rock wall, I struggled to release the rope he'd clipped in as a directional guide in the dark. My hands and fingers wouldn't do what I wanted them to do. Expletives didn't help. Anger didn't even do it this time. I was furious—at myself, for being weak. For not knowing these rocks were up here. For not being a better climber who could sprint over them, like most climbers no doubt did. Mostly for being so damned weak.

"Alex, I can't get this out!"

As I wailed the words upward, I knew they were the wrong words.

"What do you mean, you can't?"

I knew what he meant by can't. He probably never felt this desperate, though. But then my anger, my flailing, my yanking on it popped the rope out of the 'biner.

"Nothing. It's fine." And I kept following his voice.

For almost thirteen hours, we'd been moving as fast as we could go, almost nonstop—or rather, as fast as *I* could go; they would have been back at the car already. I'd eaten only half a sandwich, and even if I had been able to reach the second half in my backpack, I couldn't eat while jugging. My tank was on empty. Fortunately, I'd clipped a water bottle to my harness, so at least that need was met. Only one other was: Thanksgiving Ledge stretched across the whole west side of El Cap, with large rocks strewn here and there, creating large, private nooks. The perfect toilet stop.

But it would be many more hours before any other needs could be met. A climb isn't over until you're back on the ground.

The ground! In my head, I ran through all the steps before we'd see ground again. First, we had to hike across the whole rounded top of El Cap, up to the center—we were at the extreme west end of the wall—then back down to the east side descent. More than a mile of rough terrain, in the dark, across the almost-flat summit booby-trapped with boulders, patches of slick glacial polish, stubby trees, thorny shrubs, all manner of traps waiting to spring on my fatigue-wracked body. The worst trap, though, was in my head. Knowing we were only a few steps away from the edge of a three-thousand-foot drop, obscured by the velvety black around us, would make my steps even more cautious, more thoughtful, more wary. Then, after we reached the east side of the summit, we would hike the descent ledges, a grueling, dangerous several-hour-long scramble. That would leave us at the top of the six fixed ropes we'd have to rappel down. And the last of those would leave us at the top of the hour-and-a-half hike down through rocky stream beds and woods, to the parking lot where we'd left my car.

It was hard to even imagine a car.

My mind was insanely focused, had been for thirteen hours. Every move, hand or foot, required concentration. To make a mistake, up here, could mean death. I was still trying to process, to comprehend where we were and what we were doing. Or trying to do.

The hand-ropes did, finally, end. Alex was sitting on a small boulder under a stunted tree in the dark, waiting for me, pointing his headlamp down so I could navigate the terrain up to him. I vaguely remember hugging him, briefly, or maybe we just slapped a high-five—extreme fatigue does odd things to one's memory, and other faculties. When I reached him, I took off my pack, pulled out the rest of my sandwich, donned my headlamp. We immediately started walking. Fast.

We were walking now on a more or less horizontal surface. The top? This wasn't the summiting my fiction-writing head had crafted so many times over the last few months. That one took place in daylight, with friends that met me on top to share champagne and accompany us down the long, long descent, talking all the way about our day, our adventure. That one involved lots of high-fives and cheers and camaraderie. Exultation. Very little fear.

This one involved following Alex for more than a mile across the rugged terrain of the top, as fast as I could manage, while grabbing bites of the sandwich I'd stashed in my pocket. Then the ledges. The ropes. The forest. We had a long way to go. I'd celebrate later.

Following the circles of our headlamps, we picked our way across slabs of slippery rock, over or around boulders, through thickets of manzanita and other prickly bushes, over more slab, more boulders, around an occasional gnarled conifer twisted and bent against the ferocious wind. There was no wind tonight, for which I was grateful. The sliver of a moon cast just enough light to make the slabs a bit lighter than the dark valley beyond.

"Just keep heading down, Mom," Alex repeated each time I aimed my headlamp across the slabs and wondered aloud which way to go. Down? Down was three thousand feet straight to the Valley floor. We had hiked up a thousand feet that morning to get to the start of Lurking Fear, at the west end. Here, at the center of El Cap, the wall was a thousand feet higher than the climb we had done. Down was to be avoided. At least that kind of down.

Thorny bushes grabbed at me, probably poking holes in my favorite down jacket. I stepped on what I thought was a rock, but it snapped in two and almost sent me sprawling into those nasty shrubs. Glacial polish, like glass, coated the next section of slabs and made each step treacherous, as if I were walking on ice. My whole being just wanted to sit down and stop moving. Instead, I picked my way oh-so-cautiously, fully expecting each step to send me sailing over the side. Down.

Once in a while, a word of encouragement came back to me through the night: "Don't worry, Mom, we're about fifty meters up from the edge here."

That helped. Down just got farther away.

Or: "See the bivy, Mom?"

Climbers had moved boulders and large rocks around (how did they have the energy, once they got up here?) to form protective walls so they could bivouac out of the fierce wind that often battered this exposed summit. Each little campsite of faintly moonlit white granite looked like the snow forts we used to make as kids, back in New York, to throw snowballs from. The image made me stop and smile. But up here, today, there was no snow, no wind—I'd left my light jacket open all day, and even now, with no sun, the cool, calm air felt good as we hiked.

And hiked. And hiked.

Sam had gone down earlier, faster, since there was nothing left for him to do. No more belaying, no more helping me lower out to the rope. Nothing but walking, hiking, and rappelling—at a pace that I didn't want to inflict on anybody else.

My son hadn't tired of reminding me of that: "Mom, I can't even *make* myself go that slow!"

Weakness annoyed both of us. But I had no choice. My pace got slower and slower. On the wall, during the climb, I had only focused on the rope in front of me. I only executed. Now, faint moonlight and extreme fatigue created a strange, unending world. Time was suspended. There was no such thing as time. I never thought about hours or minutes, or how long it was taking us, had taken us, would take us. Nothing else existed, only my son and me, floating in this dark world of rock three thousand feet above the invisible Valley floor. We had all the time in the world—although I was forcing my poor body to move as fast as I could manage, faster than I would otherwise have deemed safe.

Fatigue and fear had ceded their place. Magic had taken over. Maybe I was hallucinating.

My ragged breathing punctuated the complete natural stillness, and all the nylon I wore rustled with a sibilant rhythm. Intermittent comments provided the only other sound. Alex knew I needed diversion, and he provided it. An occasional climbing tale floated through the dark as we clambered through shrubbery and over rocks and around trees, of previous climbs, of people who worked up here with him, of adventures. I could picture those adventures now, having now been on one of my own.

Interspersed with his stories, he tossed in some comments about our unbearably slow (to him) progress. I ignored those. Nothing I could do about it anyway. In that erratic fashion, we chatted our way down for several hours, stopping every now and then for me to figure out how to approach a section of rock I found tricky, slippery, dangerous, or just impossible.

"Look, Mom!"

Alex stopped, pointing east across the abyss we'd been skirting for hours. The flat, two-thousand-foot-tall face of Half Dome dominated that whole end of the Valley in daylight; now it was only a hulking shadow, rendered a bit lighter than the black valley below by the weak sliver of a moon. Against its almost-black backdrop, two tiny lights shone, near the top.

"I've never seen lights on Half Dome before!"

We stopped and watched. The upper light moved slightly. Climbers.

"Hey, that's Jimmy!"

When we'd left for our climb at five o'clock this morning, Jimmy Chin had also been leaving the same parking area for his climb of Half Dome. Although my son never speaks in exclamation points, I could hear them now. His excitement flowed into me—both Alex and I had shared a new experience today, up on his favorite wall. In some tiny way, this day was a first for him, too.

As we got closer to the ledge where we would begin rappelling, Alex had to spot me even more carefully—he went down a section of rock first, turned back up toward me, and guided me down, verbally. A foothold here. A handhold there. A tiny ledge to walk across. Using only words, he helped me navigate the steep terrain. That section of rock had been so difficult when I'd worked my way up it with friends that they'd let me tie into a short rope for protection. Here, today, in the dark, exhausted, I did it all myself.

And then we stopped on the platform-like ledge at the top of the rappel ropes.

Although we were still a thousand feet or so up on the side of El Cap, in my mind our climb was over. I'd done these ropes many times, up and down, alone or with friends. I'd crossed paths with famous climbers on these ropes, and some not-so-famous, new friends. I knew where the knots were, which pitch had a small roof to watch out for, where to duck under the tree bough. These six pitches were my friends.

I was home!

The six ropes all ran together in my mind; I just executed, did in automaton-style what I had done so many times before. Anchor myself to the bolts. Attach my Grigri. Attach my backup. Check everything. Lean back, weight it, and test it all. Check it again (because it's me; Alex skips some of those steps). Then check it again because I know I'm exhausted and that's when climbers start to make stupid mistakes. Remove my anchor from the bolt and descend as fast as I can.

By the fifth rappel or so, the steps had diminished. Fewer backups. Fewer gear checks. Then, suddenly, finally—flat ground! But we were still about an hour or so higher than the Valley floor. Exhilaration had to wait. First we had to hike down through the woods, over the stream beds, through more woods, and out to the parking lot.

The forest was as still as the summit had been. No faint moonlight here, only the small bug-filled circles from our headlamps that cast eerie, supernatural-looking shadows that bounced along as we passed. No wind. No sounds but my ragged breathing, small branches snapping, our footfalls, occasional rustling as we slipped on leaves. It was an insensate dreamworld made real only by our constant movement through it.

My mind was maintaining a constant vigilance, in that dreamworld, to keep me from thinking about what I had just done. It couldn't allow that in yet. It was deliberately emptied, void of any thought beyond those vague physical impressions. And faint reminders of pain; my body had stopped complaining, but I could still feel all the things that I knew would hurt later.

It was a given now. I'd gone up El Cap. And down. I'd think about it tomorrow. Not now. Tomorrow.

Oh, wait. It was tomorrow. We'd been on the go since yesterday. Nineteen hours, car to car. That's how climbers measure their times, I've heard. Car to car.

It was over. Almost two o'clock in the morning. I would call my daughter later. After I'd stopped moving. After I'd slept.

The journey of my lifetime ended, then, just around the corner and down the road from where it had begun. But was it the journey of my lifetime? Each time I've summited with Alex, I've said, "I'll never top this!"

I have to learn to stop thinking that. It's never been true.

This time it might be, though.

This time, it just might be.

At least until the next one.

acknowledgments

MY WHOLEHEARTED THANKS go to my guide on this fascinating journey from idea to book, my agent Jennifer Chen Tran. Thank you for believing in me and my story. Writing is a lonely process; thanks for being on my team, for clarifying, for encouraging. For always being there. I look forward to our next journey together.

I'D ALSO LIKE TO THANK:

- The whole infinitely patient team at Mountaineers Books, always willing to instruct, repeat, teach, and just generally go that extra mile, technological and otherwise;
- Kirsten Colton, Laura Lancaster, and Mary Metz for helping me wrest the clearest version out of my muddled words;
- The friends who generously lent me their gear, their knowledge, and their time to help me work on my skills for El Capitan—Ryan, Bob, Mike, Mike and Michael, Kelly, Jonathan and Shaghig, Ron and Lori, Nicole, David: I couldn't have done it without you;
- My friends who kindly offered their insights—Mark, Brian, Michelle, Christina, Brian and Niki, Naz, Joe, Frank, Katie, Cheryl, Matt and Jannette, Alex and Stasia; it would be a vastly different book without your help.
- Cheryl and Jan, without whose encouragement, suggestions, and unflagging support my story might never have been told.

MY SPECIAL GRATITUDE AND APPRECIATION to Alex Honnold and Samuel Crossley. If you hadn't willingly offered your skill and your encouragement, and spent an entire grueling day and night helping me up the wall, El Cap would probably still be a just a vague, unattainable dream.

I can never thank you enough.

about the author

DIERDRE WOLOWNICK GREW UP in New York City and has lived and worked in many parts of the world, teaching five languages on three continents. Now a retired college professor, she travels often in order to do research, to climb, or just to keep up her language skills.

Inspired by her daughter, Stasia, Dierdre began long-distance running at the age of fifty-five, and she has since completed several marathons, as well as numerous half-marathons and other races. At fifty-eight, she took up rock climbing with her son, Alex, and at the age of sixty-six, she became the oldest woman to climb El Capitan, the iconic 3,200-foot granite wall in Yosemite National Park.

Dierdre's award-winning writing has appeared in magazines, newspapers, and books worldwide, and she created a publishing company that sells internationally. A musician and artist all her life, Dierdre founded the West Sacramento Community Orchestra, which she conducted for four years. She has played in many local and regional orchestras, as well as performed solo or in a duet on flute and piano. She is also a talented visual artist. Learn more at dierdrew.us and on Instagram @dierdrewolownick.

A portion of Dierdre's royalties are being donated to The Honnold Foundation. Learn more about the foundation's work to promote the use of solar energy at www.honnoldfoundation.org.

recreation · lifestyle · conservation

MOUNTAINEERS BOOKS is a leading publisher of mountaineering literature and guides—including our flagship title, *Mountaineering: The Freedom of the Hills*—as well as adventure narratives, natural history, and general outdoor recreation. Through our two imprints, Skipstone and Braided River, we also publish titles on sustainability and conservation. We are committed to supporting the environmental and educational goals of our organization by providing expert information on human-powered adventure, sustainable practices at home and on the trail, and preservation of wilderness.

The Mountaineers, founded in 1906, is a 501(c)(3) nonprofit outdoor recreation and conservation organization whose mission is to enrich lives and communities by helping people "explore, conserve, learn about, and enjoy the lands and waters of the Pacific Northwest and beyond." One of the largest such organizations in the United States, it sponsors classes and year-round outdoor activities throughout the Pacific Northwest, including climbing, hiking, backcountry skiing, snowshoeing, camping, kayaking, sailing, and more. The Mountaineers also supports its mission through its publishing division, Mountaineers Books, and promotes environmental education and citizen engagement. For more information, visit The Mountaineers Program Center, 7700 Sand Point Way NE, Seattle, WA 98115-3996; phone 206-521-6001; www.mountaineers.org; or email info@mountaineers.org.

Our publications are made possible through the generosity of donors and through sales of more than 800 titles on outdoor recreation, sustainable lifestyle, and conservation. To donate, purchase books, or learn more, visit us online:

MOUNTAINEERS BOOKS

1001 SW Klickitat Way, Suite 201 • Seattle, WA 98134

800-553-4453 • mbooks@mountaineersbooks.org • www.mountaineersbooks.org

An independent nonprofit publisher since 1960